STERLING

PERFORMANCES

Diverse and dynamic Guilds members boast an unbroken history of accomplishment and service to the people of Orange County. Guilds members were at the forefront of the effort to build The Center and have provided leadership and support at every step in The Center's development.

All proceeds realized from the sale of *Sterling Performances* help ensure that The Center can continue to provide free education and outreach programs as well as maintain The Center's complex facilities. The Guilds share in the vital role of enabling The Center to present the world's great artists in a joyous succession of performances.

Published by The Guilds of the Orange County Performing Arts Center, Costa Mesa, California
Printed in the United States of America by R. R. Donnelley & Sons Company

First printing • March 1994 • 20,000 copies

ISBN No. 0-9638430-0-1
Copyright © 1994
The Guilds of the Orange County Performing Arts Center
Library of Congress Catalog Card Number 93-073 418

STERLING PERFORMANCES
Includes index,
      1. Cookery American, California — Orange County Life Style
      2. Orange County Performing Arts Center 3. Entertaining
      I. The Guilds of The Center, Publisher; II. Jane Biel, Editor;
      III. E. L. Smith, Designer; IV. Jan Collier, Computer Compositor;
      V. Marilyn Langsdorf, Writer; VI. Gail Forney, Recipe Coordinator

Additional copies of **STERLING PERFORMANCES** may be obtained from your favorite retailer or by contacting The Guilds of The Center:

STERLING PERFORMANCES
Orange County Performing Arts Center
600 Town Center Drive
Costa Mesa, CA 92626

Information and phone orders: 714-556-2122, Ext. 558

STERLING PERFORMANCES

The Zest of Orange County

A Cookbook by The Guilds of the Orange County Performing Arts Center

STERLING PERFORMANCES PATRONS

CONNOISSEUR

ROBERT MONDAVI WINE & FOOD CENTER
THE TIMES ORANGE COUNTY
THE ORANGE COUNTY REGISTER
THE OAKS
STEELCASE - TUSTIN
THE GUILDS OF THE CENTER

GOURMET

SOUTH COAST PLAZA
WILLIAMS-SONOMA

PLATINUM CIRCLE

PAT AND ALAN RYPINSKI
CLARK AND CYNTHIA VITULLI

GOLD CIRCLE

GALLERI ORREFORS KOSTA BODA
MRS. HAROLD SEGERSTROM, JR.

STERLING CIRCLE

Mrs. Nancy L. Baldwin
Boehm Porcelain Gallery
Mrs. Robert L. Forrest
Barbara C. Hoyt
Marilyn Langsdorf

Marilyn W. McIntyre
Tom and Marilyn Nielsen
Lori and Michael Stephanson
Jean Weiss
Betty Hutton Williams

CRYSTAL CIRCLE

Carrie Allen
Ms. Jacqueline Beattie
Brea Mall
Jane and Bill Biel
Mary and Ken Bryant
Carolyn Churm
Joy Curry
Dolores de Kruif
Eldorado Bank
Harry and Shari Esayian
Ed and Jean Evans
Gelson's Market, Newport Beach
Johanne Gibson
Ginny and Ledge Hale
Jean Hamann
David A. and Dione Hayes
Mrs. William Jackson

Kitchen Spaces, Costa Mesa
Madame Helena Modjeska Chapter
Mr. and Mrs. Frederick L. Piterak
Mr. and Mrs. Gary L. Prickett
Mary and Carl Raymond
Patricia Rowley Robertson
Mr. and Mrs. Robert E. Short
Mary Jean Simpkins
Babs Jacobs Soros
Georgia Hull Spooner
Richard and Carol Thompson
Mrs. Valaree Wahler
Carol L. Wilken
Villeroy & Boch
The Westin, South Coast Plaza
Lucy Zahran & Company

FRIENDS OF STERLING PERFORMANCES

Applause Chapter
Arthur Fiedler Chapter
Arturo Toscanini Chapter
Victoria & Michael Avey-Gertner
Sally B. Barden
Betty Barr
Chris Beaver
Betty Belden-Palmer
Barbara J. Benson
Jo Ellen Benson
Beverly Sills Chapter
Corinne P. Black
Mr. & Mrs. Ronald E. Blanchard
Mr. & Mrs. Robert Boragno
Nancy Bowman
Nancy Bushnell
Camelot Chapter
Melida Canfield
Jennifer Carlson
Carmen Chapter
Trudy Chatham
Chopin Chapter
Harold Anson Clayton Family
Connie Coble
Jan Collier
Con Brio Chapter
Laura Condrey
Con Gusto Chapter
Con Tempo Chapter
Lynn Davies Cook
Mr. & Mrs. James S. Cooley
Gloria A. Cormier
Brenda Corwin
Crescendo Chapter
Sharon C. Dahl
James & Carol Davies
Debussy Chapter
Nona J. Demetre
Marion H. Devick
Susan Dolbee
Gisela Doniguian

Betty Donnell
Martha Fluor
Gail Forney
Mr. & Mrs. A. R. Friedel
Mary O. Fryer
Marilyn Galt
George Gershwin Chapter
Hali Morrisa Gewelber
Mrs. Donald Goodwin
Ellie Gordon
Jim & Joanne Grant
Dr. & Mrs. Ted P. Griffin
Nancy Scharf Hansmann
Jean R. Haugeland
Shirley Hoesterey
Bonnie Holmes
Mrs. Marion Honsacker
Linda Adler Hughes
Mrs. Reuben Paul Hughes
Regina M. Hunsaker
Suzanne G. Hurlbut
Diane B. Janssen
Mr. & Mrs. William Kellams
Joy Kemble
Diana Kendall
Mrs. Marilyn Kent
Robert & Barbara Kleist
Carolyn Knight
Warren & Joey Knudson
Mary Kunz
K. Kwon
Dr. & Mrs. Lyle Larsen
La Traviata Chapter
Mrs. Robert H. Lind
Linda Martin
William D. & June M. McIntyre
Margaret Merritt-Parsons
Ruth M. Miller
Sandi Mitchell
Juanita Moore
Mozart Chapter

Dorothy Needelman
Susanne Newby
Virginia Perryman
Fiona Petersen
Mrs. William E. Pettengill
Nancy Plows
Trudy Polkinghorn
Mr. & Mrs. Ronald G. Radelet
Eleanor & Stanley Raffel
Sharlene B. Rauch
Linda Reagan
Sharon Rediess
Joan B. Rehnborg
Richard Rodgers Chapter
Corinne Rostoker
Janet & Larry Sanders
Marty Schmid
Floss Schumacher
Dr. & Mrs. Charles H. Sears
Micky Shannon
Annette Sherwood
Barbara D Siegel
Jeanne Siegel
Jean M. Spearman
Stage Door Chapter
Barbara J. Steinberg
Mrs. Ralph James Stokes
Susan M. Strader
Mrs. Ann E. Summers
The Magic Flute Chapter
The Masked Ball Chapter
Mrs. John R. Thomas
Marion R. Thompson
Kathy Urban
Barbara Vogel
Marilyn von KleinSmid-Randolph
Harriette and Lon Watson
Sue Weber
Cynthia Weitz
Bonne L. Wheeler

* * *

Georg Jensen, South Coast Plaza
Scribner's Bookstore, South Coast Plaza, Crystal Court
Orange County News

Dear Reader,

The Guilds of The Center present **Sterling Performances,** *a cookbook for the benefit of the Orange County Performing Arts Center. Each recipe, donated by members and friends, was tested and tasted for careful selection of the best of the best. Wine suggestions to complement the recipes were recommended by Robert Mondavi Wine and Food Center, Costa Mesa.*

The story of The Center is highlighted and we have provided a glimpse of the zest of Orange County, our special county in Southern California, where the sunshine, beaches, theme parks, shopping malls, sporting events, gardens, museums, churches, universities, historic sites, art and music centers mingle to create our lifestyle.

We dedicate **Sterling Performances** *to the supporters of the Orange County Performing Arts Center, who generate the sparkle in our lives.*

We welcome everyone to enjoy our special cookbook.

Jane Biel, Editor
The Sterling Performances Cookbook Committee

The Guilds of The Center

STEERING COMMITTEE

Chairman and Editor
  Jane Biel

Art Director and Designer
  E. L. Smith

Recipe Chairman
  Gail Forney

Writer
  Marilyn Langsdorf

Computor Compositor, Page Formats
  Jan Collier

Food and Life-style Photography
  Chester Maharaj, Irvine

Index Chairman
  Patricia Rowley Robertson

Food and Prop Styling
  Denise Stillman, Laguna Niguel

Business Chairman
  Carol Thompson

Treasurer
  Marty Schmid

MARKETING, UNDERWRITING AND SPECIAL EVENTS COMMITTEE

Marlene Short, Fiona Petersen, Jane Biel, Cynthia Weitz, Shari Esayian, Jan Powell,
Carol Thompson, Kathy Rolfes, Bonne Wheeler, Mary Jo Hitchner, Pat Wescombe,
Lyla Rogers, Bev Adams, Cheryl Moore, Barbara Moreland

CHAPTER RECIPE CHAIRMEN

Appetizers   Marlene Short
Breads and Brunch   Jackie Hubbard
Salads and Salad Dressings   Haroldene Wiens
Soups   Sheila Mann, Susan Tomasello
Vegetables, Grains, Pasta   Betty Braun
Meat   Teddy Wells
Poultry   Jackie Terrell
Seafood   Diana Conner
Desserts   Jan Martens

ADDITIONAL RESEARCH AND DEVELOPMENT

Claire Burt, Secretary; Johanne Gibson, Susie Hurlbut, Faith Cherney

Please see additional contributors on page 272.

Published by The Guilds of the Orange County Performing Arts Center

INTRODUCTION

There must be magic in that hint of orange blossoms in the air. Or is it the year-round sunshine and fresh sea breezes that give every aspect of life in Orange County a certain sparkle?

Since the time of the Spanish conquistadors, visitors have been drawn to this region by its stunning natural beauties. Rugged cliffs, here and there draped with brilliant strands of magenta bougainvillea, tower over white sand beaches. Lush green acres of gently rolling farmland spill down to a shining blue sea. A rainbow of brightly colored sails reflects off the sparkling waters of spotless marinas lined with one of the largest collections of pleasure boats in the world.

But good looks aren't everything, and Orange County has always had something more: an energy, a verve, a feeling that all things are possible. It's as if there is a signpost at the county line saying "Dreamers Welcome Here." The examples are legendary. Walt Disney arrived with high hopes and blueprints for a new kind of family amusement park. Walter and Cordelia Knott began with a roadside berry stand and saw their tiny business grow into a 135-acre theme park. Visionary developers transformed acres of quiet agricultural land into up-scale model communities built around man-made lakes and parks. In the past forty years, a once sleepy area of orange groves and working ranches has been catapulted to national prominence as a center of high technology, business, education, and the arts.

Yet with all this newness and development, some things have remained the same. There is a vitality, a sense of fun, and an easy sophistication about Orange County. We celebrate this spirit of zestful living in *Sterling Performances*. It comes as no surprise that the cuisine most enjoyed dockside at Lido Isle or poolside in Tustin is fresh, original, easy to prepare, and beautifully presented. Our hope is that this collection of recipes will capture the spirit of Orange County for you and add a special sparkle to your next family gathering or company dinner.

THE CENTER

It is opening night. The balmy evening air is electric with excitement. Backstage, costumes are adjusted, make-up applied, lines gone over. As a stream of cars pulls up to the elegant Carriage Circle, theatergoers in evening dress emerge into the sparkling lights, a moving pageant of black and white and radiant color. In a few moments, the curtain will rise on *Les Misérables* or *Swan Lake* or *La Traviata* and the magic of live performance will cast its spell once again.

Since the first opening night in 1986, some of the most remarkable talents of our time have sung or sauntered, postured or pirouetted across the footlights of the Orange County Performing Arts Center. World-renowned ballet companies such as The Kirov and Royal Ballets; hit Broadway musicals such as *Crazy for You, Cabaret,* and *The Phantom of the Opera*; and top artists in jazz and popular music such as Ella Fitzgerald, Tony Bennett, and Liza Minnelli have enthralled audiences. In the world of classical music and opera, who can forget performances by Isaac Stern, Itzhak Perlman, or by Plácido Domingo and Dame Gwyneth Jones in *The Girl of the Golden West?*

As thrilling as it is to present such stellar international talents, The Center is also proud to be the performance home for five highly respected Southern California groups—Pacific Symphony Orchestra, Opera Pacific, Orange County Philharmonic Society, Master Chorale of Orange County, and Pacific Chorale. One of The Center's founding objectives was to nurture the arts in its own backyard, and the growth and accomplishments of these groups point toward the attainment of this goal.

**Created by Richard Lippold, the vast metal sculpture "The Fire Bird"
that appears to fly through The Center's Grand Portal
symbolizes the eternal spirit of the arts.**

OUTREACH PROGRAMS
FOR THE SOUTHERN CALIFORNIA COMMUNITY

How do we bring art into the lives of every man, woman, and child in Orange County? The founders of the Orange County Performing Arts Center dreamed of a magnificent facility, distinguished programming—and more. They dreamed of giving access to everyone visiting and living in Orange County.

The Center brings performances into the lives of many thousands of people. "From The Center" brings music, dance, puppetry, and theater into public schools, along with specially designed study materials and activity suggestions for use after the performances. Tickets are available for those who normally could not attend performances. Founders Plus, a Center volunteer organization, distributes tickets to the economically and physically disadvantaged through more than 200 community nonprofit groups such as shelters for battered women and abused children.

"Stage One" programs bring together students and distinguished touring companies, such as American Ballet Theatre and The New York City Opera, for lecture and demonstration programs at The Center. Younger children and their families experience the joy of live performances and hands-on workshops through the vastly popular county-wide event, "Imagination Celebration."

The Center personalizes the performance experience. At sites throughout the county and backstage at The Center, "Informally Yours" gives audience members a behind-the-scene look at performances. Visiting artists perform and then personalize by sharing comments about their lives and careers as they welcome interaction with the audience.

The Center also helps support the distinguished educational programs of Orange County Philharmonic Society, Pacific Symphony Orchestra and Opera Pacific by waiving rental fees for children's programs and providing space for South Coast Repertory's Young Conservatory Players.

The Center reaches out to at-risk individuals and brings them into the arts experience: "Summer at The Center" offers musical theater training that encourages the development of self-confidence.

Has this impressive list of outreach programs shown the visibility and availability of the arts in Orange County and beyond? Profoundly, and may it continue to grow.

RECIPES
TABLE OF CONTENTS

THE STORY OF THE CENTER AND THE GUILDS

It all started with a bean field. Perhaps no story so captures the spirit of Orange County as the one that begins with straight rows of lima beans and ends, a handful of years later, with a $72.8 million performing arts center.

The journey from farmland to *My Fair Lady* began when a visionary group of volunteers saw the need for a cultural center for this rapidly growing county and set out to build one.

In 1978, The Guilds of The Center, the earliest and largest of today's six Center support groups, started the grassroots effort that would raise $600,000 in donations while The Center was still just a gleam in their eyes. When a Guilds Board member spotted a tidy bean field, conveniently located near freeways and at a central point in the county, The Center seemed meant to be. The Segerstrom family's energizing gift of prime land and a generous grant to spur the fundraising effort gave the project a crucial boost. The rest, as they say, is history.

Volunteer involvement in The Center did not end when the curtain went up on the first season in 1986. Today Guild chapters for women, couples, mixed singles, professionals, and juniors support The Center through an exciting variety of educational and fundraising events throughout the year. Besides planning and executing a smorgasbord of county-wide events on behalf of The Center, the chapters in the nine area Guilds have contributed millions of dollars to The Center since 1978.

Today the Orange County Performing Arts Center stands as vibrant testimony to the can-do spirit of this community. Brought to life by volunteer energy and vision, it is the only performing arts facility of its size and scope ever built and maintained solely through the financial support of individuals who believe in the importance of the arts in our world. Bravo!

Segerstrom Hall: Ask any performer. A theater is only as good as its sound. Recognizing this fact, The Center founders hired an international team of experts to carefully integrate The Center's acoustics and build an acoustical model one-tenth the size of the proprosed hall. In the model, the sound engineers even placed an audience of fully dressed doll "patrons" to take into account the way the audience absorbs and reflects sound. As a result of highly sensitive sound tests, every surface—floor, wall, panel, curtain—in Segerstrom Hall is a deliberate part of the building's remarkable acoustical design, making for sound that is truly superb.

THE MAGIC OF BALLET

As the lights go down, a hush falls over the audience. The conductor appears, acknowledges the audience, and turning, signals the first downbeat of the overture. The curtain slowly rises, revealing an ensemble of 100 dancers who begin to move with incredible grace, precision, and beauty. The audience hardly breathes as the magic unfolds.

The best-loved ballet companies and foremost dancers in the world have danced their way into the hearts of audiences at the Orange County Performing Arts Center. The list of touring companies that have performed here is a balletomane's dream come true: The Kirov Ballet, The Joffrey Ballet, American Ballet Theatre, The Royal Danish Ballet, New York City Ballet, The National Ballet of Canada, The White Oak Dance Project, and many more. The most respected dancers of our time, from Rudolf Nureyev to Mikhail Baryshnikov, from Sylvie Guillem to Julio Bocca, have illuminated the stage of Segerstrom Hall.

Now regarded as the West Coast's leading presenter of national and international ballet troupes, The Center proudly presents both timeless classics and fresh explorations of ballet's new frontiers.

Russia's fabled Kirov Ballet
performed the American premiere of its historic *Nutcracker* at The Center
in December 1992. The sold-out engagement celebrated the 100th anniversary of
Tchaikovsky's holiday masterpiece, originally created for The Kirov.

OPERA AT THE CENTER

It's truly a black-tie occasion when The Center hosts opera, the grandest art of all with its high theater, expansive music, lavish sets, ornate costumes, and full orchestra. In opera, some of the most beautiful music ever written showcases both the power and delicacy of the world's great voices. Perhaps because of its epic scale, opera touches the heart and moves an audience like no other performing art can.

The New York City Opera and The Los Angeles Music Center Opera have visited The Center, and Opera Pacific was born here in 1986 when The Center opened. Now the twelfth largest opera company in the United States, Opera Pacific annually presents major works from the operatic repertoire in Segerstrom Hall, fully staged with distinguished guest artists.

With the works of Mozart, Puccini, Verdi, Massine, Wagner, Britten, and Bernstein, the talents of such performers as Plácido Domingo, Dame Gwyneth Jones, Luciano Pavarotti, and Dame Joan Sutherland, and the staging of such electrifying productions as *The Girl of the Golden West,* grand opera has truly come of age in Orange County.

**Some of the most memorable evenings on the stage in Segerstrom Hall
have been when opera—that exquisite blend of music, dance, and drama—was
in the spotlight. In 1990, Orange County's Opera Pacific staged Puccini's *Turandot.*
The opulent production, boasting more than 100 singers and extras, was
a box-office and critical success.**

The cultural scene in Orange County is rich and diverse. There are outstanding art museums in Fullerton, Laguna Beach, Irvine, and Newport Beach; the Bowers Museum of Cultural Art in Santa Ana features the arts of Native America, Mexico, Central America, and historical Orange County and California. The Richard Nixon Library and birthplace landmark is in Yorba Linda. For theater, a cultural success is the South Coast Repertory Theatre, adjacent to the Orange County Performing Arts Center, which began in 1964 in an old marine swap shop in Newport Beach. It is now a nationally recognized professional resident theater.

APPETIZERS

Cooking is an art form in California, as seen in these delectable appetizers pictured at a showing at the Irvine Museum. Founded in 1992, the Museum is dedicated to the preservation and display of California art of the Impressionist Period (1890-1930).

SCALLOP AND SHRIMP REMOULADE

This is an ideal appetizer or first course served on butter lettuce.

1/4 cup Dijon mustard
1/2 teaspoon pepper
1/4 cup champagne vinegar
1/2 cup olive oil
2 teaspoons sugar
1 tablespoon chopped fresh dill
1/4 cup finely chopped shallots
1/4 cup chopped fresh parsley

1 pound cooked bay scallops
1 1/2 pounds medium shrimp,
   cooked and cleaned
Fresh greens or spinach,
   washed and dried
Minced parsley or dill for garnish
Capers for garnish

In a food processor or blender, gently combine all ingredients except seafood, greens, and garnishes. Adjust seasonings to taste. Pour mixture over seafood and chill for 1 to 3 hours, gently tossing occasionally to make sure seafood is well marinated.

Line chilled bowl with greens or spinach leaves. Top with marinated seafood and sauce. Sprinkle with parsley and capers. Serve with cocktail forks or toothpicks.

Preparation Time: 30 minutes
Marinating Time: 1 to 3 hours
Servings: 8 to 12

SHRIMP AND BEET COCKTAIL

This first course appetizer is lovely served in a silver goblet.

1 1/2 cups sour cream
1/2 cup mayonnaise
1 teaspoon salt
1 tablespoon horseradish
1 16-ounce can julienne-cut beets,
   drained reserving 1/4 cup liquid

6 lettuce leaves
24 jumbo shrimp, cooked,
   cleaned, with tails left on and chilled

Combine sour cream, mayonnaise, salt, horseradish, and reserved liquid. Fold beets into sauce. To make individual servings, line dish or goblet with lettuce; place 4 shrimp around rim. Put dollop of beet mixture in center. Serve with cocktail or fish forks.

Preparation Time: 15 minutes
Servings: 6

Robert Mondavi Brut Reserve Sparkling Wine

CHILI-MAYONNAISE SAUCE FOR CRAB OR SHRIMP

A good sauce to serve with a fish entree, too!

3/4 cup mayonnaise
1 hard cooked egg, chopped
3 tablespoons diced sweet pickle
1 tablespoon chili powder

2 tablespoons diced
    pimento-stuffed green olives
1 tablespoon grated onion

In a bowl, combine mayonnaise, egg, pickle, olives, chili powder, and onion; mix well. Refrigerate at least 2 hours before serving.

Preparation Time: 15 minutes
Chilling Time: 2 hours
Yield: 1 cup

DIJON-HORSERADISH SAUCE FOR CRAB

A zesty sauce

1/3 cup mayonnaise
1/4 cup Dijon style mustard
3 tablespoons vegetable oil
2 tablespoons cider vinegar
1 1/2 tablespoons drained
    prepared horseradish

1 tablespoon paprika
1/2 cup minced celery
6 green onions, minced
1/3 cup minced parsley
Salt and pepper, to taste
Hot pepper sauce, to taste

In a bowl, combine mayonnaise, mustard, oil, vinegar, horseradish, and paprika; blend well. Add celery, onions, parsley, salt, pepper and hot pepper sauce; stir to combine. Cover and refrigerate up to 3 days.

Preparation Time: 20 minutes
Chilling Time: 2 hours
Yield: 1 1/3 cup

SPICED PECANS

3 tablespoons unsalted butter, melted
1/2 teaspoon cinnamon
3 tablespoons Worcestershire sauce
1/4 teaspoon cayenne pepper

2 teaspoons salt
3 to 4 drops hot sauce
4 cups whole pecans

Preheat oven 350 degrees. In a large bowl, combine melted butter with all the seasonings. Add the pecans and toss well. Spread nuts on a large ungreased baking sheet and bake for 10 minutes. Remove to stir and toss nuts once more. Return to the oven for 5 to 10 minutes, until pecans have dried slightly. Let cool and store in an airtight container. Pecans can be frozen.

Preparation Time: 10 minutes
Cooking Time: 20 minutes
Yield: 4 cups

CINNAMON-SUGAR NUTS

1/2 cup sugar
2 teapoons cinnamon
1/2 teaspoon salt

1 egg white
3 cups whole pecans, almonds,
    walnuts, or any combination

Preheat oven to 350 degrees. Combine sugar, cinnamon, and salt. Whisk egg white until frothy and add the nuts. Toss until well coated. Add dry ingredients and stir well. Spread nuts on a cookie sheet lined with foil, in a single layer. Bake for 20 minutes. Cool and store in an airtight container. These snacks can be frozen.

Preparation Time: 10 minutes
Baking Time: 20 minutes
Yield: 3 cups

MODJESKA COCKTAIL MEATBALLS

1 1/2 pounds lean ground beef
1/4 cup rolled oats
2 eggs
1/4 cup milk
1/2 teaspoon ginger

1/2 teaspoon salt
1/2 teaspoon onion salt
2 medium mushrooms, chopped
Horseradish sauce, recipe follows
Parsley, for garnish

Preheat oven to 350 degrees. Combine all ingredients, except horseradish sauce and parsley, and form into 1-inch meatballs. Place on a cookie sheet and bake for 12 minutes. Prepare horseradish sauce; add meatballs to the sauce and heat until hot throughout. Serve meatballs with the sauce in a chafing dish. Garnish with parsley.

Note: Meatballs may be frozen; just thaw before adding to the sauce.

Preparation Time: 30 minutes
Baking Time: 12 minutes
Servings: 12 to 14

HORSERADISH SAUCE

2 cups sour cream
1/4 cup prepared horseradish
1 teaspoon salt
1/4 teaspoon pepper

In a medium saucepan, combine all ingredients; heat gently on stove. Do not boil.

Preparation Time: 5 minutes
Yield: 2 1/4 cups sauce

ALPINE COCKTAIL MEATBALLS

1 pound bulk turkey, or pork sausage
1/4 cup minced onion
1 pound sauerkraut, rinsed, drained, and chopped
1 3-ounce package cream cheese
3/4 cup plus 2 tablespoons fine bread crumbs, divided

1 teaspoon prepared mustard
1/4 teaspoon garlic salt
1/8 teaspoon pepper
1/4 cup flour
2 eggs, beaten
1/4 cup milk
Vegetable oil

Crumble sausage and brown with onion; drain well. Combine sausage mixture, sauerkraut, cream cheese, 2 tablespoons bread crumbs, mustard, garlic salt, and pepper. Refrigerate until cool. Preheat oven to 400 degrees. Shape into walnut-sized balls and coat with flour. Whip eggs and milk together. Dip each meatball into egg mixture; roll in bread crumbs. On a lightly oiled cookie sheet, bake for 10 minutes or until browned. Drain. Serve with toothpicks.

Preparation Time: 30 minutes
Baking Time: 10 minutes
Servings: 30

ORIENTAL CHICKEN DRUMETTES

1/2 cup light soy sauce
1/4 cup dry sherry
1 cup plus 2 tablespoons hoisin sauce
3/4 cup plum sauce
6 whole green onions, finely chopped

6 large cloves garlic, minced
1/3 cup cider vinegar
1/4 cup honey
4 pounds chicken drumettes

Combine soy sauce, sherry, hoisin sauce, plum sauce, green onion, garlic, vinegar, and honey. Stir well. Pour sauce over drumettes, turning to coat. Cover and refrigerate 8 hours or overnight. Preheat oven to 375 degrees. Line 2 shallow baking pans with foil and spray with nonstick spray. Drain the drumettes, reserving marinade. Place in a single layer in the pans. Bake, uncovered, for 1 hour. After the first 30 minutes, drain off all liquid, turn chicken over and baste with reserved marinade. Serve either hot or cold. If serving cold, refrigerate 1 hour on baking sheet.

Note: This marinade may be used on pork ribs or thinly sliced beef threaded onto presoaked bamboo sticks and quickly grilled.

Preparation Time: 15 minutes
Marinating Time: 8 or more hours
Baking time: 1 hour
Servings: 12

LIVER PATE CONCERTO

2 small celery stalks, with leaves
3/4 tablespoon whole peppercorns
1 teaspoon salt
6 cups water
1 pound chicken livers
1/8 teaspoon cayenne pepper
1 cup unsalted butter, softened

2 teaspoons dry mustard
1/2 teaspoon grated nutmeg
1/4 teaspoon ground cloves
1/2 cup coarsely chopped yellow onion
1 garlic clove, minced
1/4 cup apple brandy, or similar brandy
1/2 cup dry currants

Combine celery, peppercorns, salt, and water in a large saucepan; bring to a boil. Reduce heat and simmer for 10 minutes. Add chicken livers and cook 10 more minutes. Drain and discard celery. In a food processor, combine cooked ingredients with remaining ingredients, except for currants. Process until smooth. Carefully add the currants with a few short pulses. Currants should remain whole.

Place pate in a 3 or 4-cup crock or serving tureen. Refrigerate 4 or more hours to allow flavors to blend. Serve at room temperature with water biscuits, unsalted crackers, or apple slices. Garnish with chopped parsley or an herb sprig.

Preparation Time: 25 minutes
Cooking Time: 20 minutes
Servings: 12

SALMON ALLA TUSTIN

6 ounces fresh salmon, poached
  and chilled
1 1/2 tablespoons capers
5 green onions, whites only,
  chopped

1 tablespoon mayonnaise
1 tablespoon Dijon mustard
2 teaspoons lemon juice

In a mixing bowl, flake salmon with a fork and fold in remaining ingredients. Without over mixing, gently stir just to blend. Serve with baguettes or crackers.

Preparation Time: 15 minutes
Servings: 8

ZUCCHINI ROUNDS

1 pound zucchini, cut into
　1/4-inch rounds
4 tablespoons minced green onion
4 tablespoons minced fresh parsley
2 tablespoons minced fresh basil

2 cloves garlic, minced
2 tablespoons grated Parmesan cheese
1/2 cup real mayonnaise
1 cup bread crumbs
3 tablespoons butter, melted

Preheat oven to 375 degrees. Place zucchini on greased baking sheet. Blend onions, parsley, basil, garlic, Parmesan cheese, and mayonnaise in a small bowl. Spread mixture on each round. Mix bread crumbs with melted butter and top each slice with 1 teaspoonful of crumbs. Bake until golden brown. With a spatula, transfer to a serving tray and pass while still hot.

Preparation Time: 30 minutes
Cooking Time: 5 minutes
Servings: 20

MARINATED BROCCOLI

1 pound broccoli florets, sliced
　in 2-inch lengths
1 cup vinegar of your choice
1/2 cup olive oil
1 cup vegetable oil
1 tablespoon dill weed

1 tablespoon sugar
1 teaspoon salt
1 teaspoon pepper
1 clove garlic, crushed
1/2 teaspoon crushed red pepper flakes

Combine all ingredients except broccoli in a container with a tight lid and shake well. Pour dressing over broccoli and refrigerate, marinating for 24 hours. Drain before serving. Serve with toothpicks.

Note: This broccoli makes a flavorful addition to a tossed salad.

Preparation Time: 15 minutes
Chilling Time: 24 hours
Servings: 8

ROYAL CROWN MUSHROOMS

This easy appetizer is always popular.

1 pound lean bacon
1 8-ounce package cream cheese,
  softened
1 tablespoon chopped chives

25 to 30 mushrooms, cleaned,
  stems removed
Parmesan cheese

Preheat oven to 350 degrees. Fry bacon until crisp; drain and crumble. Combine bacon, cream cheese, and chives. Fill dry mushroom cavities with cheese mixture. Sprinkle with Parmesan cheese. Place on ungreased baking pan. Bake for 5 minutes; broil for 3 minutes. Watch closely to avoid overcooking.

Preparation Time: 15 minutes
Baking Time: 8 minutes
Serves: 10 to 12

CAJUN BAGUETTES

Arrange a basketful of these crisp and zesty toasts and watch them disappear.

3 French bread baguettes
1 cup extra virgin olive oil
2 teaspoons cayenne pepper
1 teaspoon salt
1 1/2 teaspoons sugar

1/2 teaspoon finely ground black pepper
1 teaspoon paprika
1 1/2 teaspoons garlic powder
1 1/2 teaspoons onion powder

Preheat oven to 200 degrees. Using a serrated bread knife, cut baguettes into rounds about 1/4-inch thick. Lay slices in a single layer on ungreased cookie sheets.

In a bowl, whisk together remaining ingredients until blended, continuing to whisk often so seasonings do not settle to bottom of bowl. Using a pastry brush, lightly coat one side of each round with the topping. Dry in oven until very crisp, about 1 hour. Texture should be similar to Melba toast. Remove from baking sheets and cool on wire racks. When cool, store in airtight containers up to 2 days or freeze up to 2 months. Serve with your favorite spreads.

Preparation Time: 15 minutes
Baking Time: 1 hour
Servings: 15 to 18

CHEESE PINWHEELS

These pinwheels are colorful appetizers for holiday parties.

1 17 1/4-ounce package
   puff pastry, 2 sheets
2 3-ounce packages cream
   cheese, softened

2 tablespoons minced green onions
1/4 teaspoon chili powder
1/8 teaspoon garlic powder
32 small pimento-stuffed olives

Thaw folded pastry sheets for 20 minutes. Meanwhile, blend cream cheese with onion, chili powder, and garlic powder. Set aside.

Preheat oven to 400 degrees. Unfold pastry sheets on cutting board. Roll each sheet to a 10 x 10-inch square and cut into sixteen 2 1/2-inch squares. Place squares on ungreased cookie sheet. From each corner of each square, cut towards the center; being careful not to cut completely to the center. Pick up the tip of each corner, one at a time, and press into the center of the square to form a pinwheel. Arrange on ungreased cookie sheets. Repeat these steps with remaining pastry.

Place one teaspoon of cheese mixture in the center of each pinwheel; top with an olive. Bake for 10 to 15 minutes, or until golden brown. Remove, cool, and store carefully in airtight containers.

Note: Cheese rosettes can be piped in the center of cooked pinwheels and garnished for a special display. Chopped black olives, onion slices, or bay shrimp can also be used for centers.

Preparation Time: 1 hour
Baking Time: 10 to 15 minutes
Yield: 32 appetizers

TORTILLA WHEELS

1 8-ounce package cream cheese, softened
1 1/2 tablespoons fresh lemon juice; divided
Garlic salt, to taste
1 cup finely shredded Monterey Jack cheese

1 2 1/4-ounce can diced green chilies
3 tablespoons thinly sliced green onions
1 tablespoon chopped black olives
1 teaspoon chopped cilantro
Cilantro sprigs, for garnish
4 8-inch flour tortillas

In a small bowl, mash cream cheese; add 1 tablespoon lemon juice and garlic salt, blending well. Add shredded cheese, chilies, onions, olives, and cilantro. Mix remaining 1/2 tablespoon lemon juice with 1/2 tablespoon water. Lightly moisten both sides of tortillas with lemon-water. Divide the cheese mixture evenly among the 4 tortillas and spread within 1/2 inch of edges. Roll up and wrap tortillas individually in plastic wrap. Chill long enough to allow cheese to set up. To serve, slice rolls crosswise with a serrated knife into 1-inch slices.

Note: This recipe can easily be doubled or tripled. Mashed avocado, roasted sunflower seeds, or fried crumbled bacon make tasty additions.

Preparation Time: 1 hour, 25 minutes
Yield: 24 wheels

MUSHROOMS AND OLIVES IN FILO

1/3 cup chopped onion
2 tablespoons butter
3 cups chopped mushrooms, about 1 pound
1/4 teaspoon black pepper

1/8 teaspoon garlic powder
1/4 cup black olives, chopped
1/4 cup sour cream
1 1-pound package filo pastry
1 cup butter, melted

In a large skillet, saute onions in butter until tender. Stir in mushrooms and spices; saute for a few seconds. Remove from heat and add olives and sour cream. Preheat oven to 350 degrees. Following package directions, place two sheets of filo pastry on cutting board; using pastry brush, brush with melted butter. Cut lengthwise into 2-inch wide strips. Place 1 heaping teaspoon filling at end of strip. Fold over one corner to opposite side, to form a triangle. Continue folding, keeping triangle shape. Brush triangles with melted butter. Place on ungreased cookie sheet. Repeat with remaining filo and filling. Bake approximately 20 minutes.

Preparation Time: 60 to 90 minutes
Baking Time: 20 to 40 minutes
Yield: 64 appetizers

HOT CRAB WEDGES

Wonderful wedges!

6 ounces Cheddar cheese, shredded
1 tablespoon butter
1 1/2 cups crabmeat
1 8-ounce container soft cream
 cheese with onions and chives
1/2 teaspoon dill weed

6 pimento-stuffed olives, diced
1 3-ounce jar chopped mushrooms,
 drained
1/2 cup mayonnaise
1 package English muffins, split

Preheat oven to 350 degrees. Combine all ingredients except muffins; spread mixture on muffins. Place on baking sheet. Bake for 12 to 15 minutes, or until bubbly. Cool slightly and cut each muffin into 6 wedges. Serve warm.

Preparation Time: 15 minutes
Baking Time: 12 to 15 minutes
Serves: 12

SAN CLEMENTE CRAB QUICHE

A lot of appetizers with little effort for the cook!

1/2 cup flour
1 teaspoon baking powder
10 eggs, lightly beaten
1/4 pound butter, melted and cooled
2 cups small curd cottage cheese
1 pound Monterey Jack
 cheese, shredded

2 4-ounce cans diced green chilies
1 pound fresh crab, cooked and flaked
Dash of hot pepper sauce or
 cayenne, optional
1/4 cup grated Parmesan cheese

Preheat oven to 350 degrees. Grease a 13 x 9-inch baking dish. Combine flour and baking powder; blend in eggs and butter. Add remaining ingredients, except Parmesan cheese.

Pour the mixture into baking dish; sprinkle with Parmesan cheese. Bake 45 minutes, or until set. Cut into small, square serving pieces.

Preparation Time: 15 minutes
Baking Time: 45 minutes
Yield: 48 appetizers

CRACKER BREAD WITH SMOKED SALMON SPREAD

1 large Armenian cracker bread (Lahvosh)
1 8-ounce package cream cheese, softened
1/4 cup mayonnaise or plain yogurt
1 1/2 tablespoons fresh lemon juice
1/4 cup chopped green onions

2 tablespoons fresh dill leaves
1/2 to 3/4 pound thinly
   sliced smoked salmon
2 tablespoons capers

Soften cracker bread by holding it under a soft spray of water until moistened. Turn cracker over and moisten other side. Cover with clean damp towels and let sit for at least 1 hour, or until soft and pliable. Check it periodically, sprinkling any dry spots.

Meanwhile, combine cream cheese, mayonnaise or yogurt, lemon juice, onion, and dill. Thin with more juice, if necessary, for spreadability. When crackers are softened, coat with spread except for one edge, which will fill in as the cracker is rolled. Top with slices of smoked salmon and sprinkle with capers. Roll up tightly; cover with damp towel until ready to use. At serving time, slice cracker crosswise with serrated knife to desired thickness, 1 to 2 inches.

Note: These appetizers can be prepared ahead, secured tightly in plastic wrap, and refrigerated overnight.

Preparation Time: 1 hour 20 minutes
Yield: 20 to 25 appetizers

ARTICHOKE AND OLIVE PIZZA

1 cup tomato sauce or pizza sauce
1 6-ounce jar marinated artichoke hearts,
   drained and chopped
1 2 1/4-ounce can chopped black olives

1 large boboli shell
1/4 teaspoon dried thyme, crushed
1 cup shredded Gruyere cheese

Preheat oven to 400 degrees. Spread tomato sauce over boboli shell; top with artichoke hearts and olives. Sprinkle with thyme and cheese. Place on a cookie sheet and bake for 15 minutes. Cut into bite-sized pieces with a pizza cutter and serve hot.

Note: Served in large wedges, this pizza becomes dinner for four. Just add a tossed green salad.

Preparation Time: 15 minutes
Baking Time: 15 minutes
Servings: 10 to 12

VEGGIE PIZZA

A popular snack that is a hit for any occasion!

1 8-ounce can refrigerated crescent rolls,
    or 2 cans for thicker crust
2 8-ounce packages cream
    cheese, softened
2/3 cup real mayonnaise

1 tablespoon dill weed
1 teaspoon minced onion
2 cups or more vegetable topping, see note
Mild Cheddar cheese, optional

Preheat oven to 375 degrees. In a greased 15 x 10-inch cookie sheet, press crescent roll dough to fit into bottom. Pinch perforation together. Bake for 10 minutes; cool. Beat cream cheese with mayonnaise until smooth; blend in dill weed and onion. Spread on crust and sprinkle mixed vegetables evenly over top; press in lightly. Cut into 2-inch squares or triangles.

Note: Topping ingredients may be grated, minced, chopped, sliced, or diced—any combination to give pizza color and flavor. Some choices are radishes, carrots, black or green olives, tomatoes, parsley, broccoli, snow peas, bean sprouts, sunflower seeds, green onions, artichokes, peas, corn, and peppers of all colors and flavors. Many other cheeses may be substituted for the Cheddar cheese. Have fun! Create!

Preparation Time: 30 minutes
Baking Time: 10 minutes
Servings: 15 to 20

REFRESHING PARTY FINGER FOOD

The appetizer section photograph shows these colorful appetizers.

Asparagus, even sized, tender cooked
Smoked salmon, in 3-inch strips
Cream cheese, room temperature
Bread cut in diamond shape and
    toasted
Ham slices, cut to fit toast

Turkey slices, cut to fit toast
Real mayonnaise
White bread, thinly sliced
Seedless cucumber
Garnishes

Wrap asparagus with smoked salmon strips and line on serving dish, seam-side down. Spread toast with cream cheese and cover with turkey and ham slices. Cut bread into rounds the circumference of the cucumber slices; spread with mayonnaise and top with slices of cucumber. Each appetizer can be garnished with piped cream cheese rosettes and herb sprigs or bits of peppers or olives.

TARTLET AND BARQUETTE SHELLS

Boat-shaped pastry shells, called barquettes, and tarts of many shapes and sizes are filled with simple warm or cold concoctions. Try our fillings or a finely-diced chicken, seafood, or vegetable salad fillings.

3/4 cup unsalted butter
2 cups sifted flour

Pinch of salt
1/3 cup ice water

Cut butter in small pieces in the bowl of a food processor and add the flour and salt. Process until mixture resembles coarse meal. Add water by droplets, mixing until the dough holds together. It should not be wet or sticky. Wrap dough and chill 30 minutes. Prepare tartlets, using twice as many pans as the shells you plan to make. Spray inside half the pans with vegetable oil.

Roll half the pastry on a floured board to 1/8-inch thick, turning to prevent sticking. Cut pastry slightly larger than the pans and press into prepared pans. Cut off excess pastry. Press unbuttered pan into pastry-lined pan to act as a weight during baking. Chill at least 30 minutes.

Preheat oven to 375 degrees. Sandwich tartlets between cooksheets, the top one will give additional weight and prevent puffing of pastry. Bake 10 minutes until edges begin to color; remove top sheet and liner pans; continue to bake 5 minutes. Remove shells from pans and cool on racks.

Note: Shells can be frozen and crisped.

Preparation Time: 1 hour 30 minutes
Yield: 30 to 40 small tartlets

PETITE CRUSTADES

Crustades are fun to make. Fill them with a spread or filling of your choice.

3 loaves sliced white bread
1 cup melted butter or margarine
Spread or filling of choice, recipes follow

Preheat oven to 350 degrees. Flatten bread slices with rolling pin. Using pastry brush, brush with melted butter. Cut out circles with 2 3/4-inch cookie cutter. Press into mini-muffin tins. Bake for 8 to 10 minutes, or until golden brown.

Note: Save time by making crustade shells ahead; they can be frozen for a week or longer.

Preparation Time: 25 minutes
Baking Time: 10 minutes
Yield: 48 crustades

FETA CHEESE SPREAD

This recipe is meant to fill crustades, but it is wonderful to serve as a spread with crackers, too.

1 8-ounce package cream cheese, cubed
6 green onions, minced
1/4 cup frozen, chopped spinach,
  cooked, and squeezed dry
1/2 cup Monterey Jack cheese,
  finely shredded

1/2 cup crumbled Feta cheese
1/2 cup grated Parmesan cheese
Petite Crustades, see recipe
Pimento stuffed olive slices

Combine cream cheese and green onions in a non-metal bowl. Heat in microwave until cheese is creamy and onions are softened, about 1 minute. Add spinach and cheeses. Heat again until hot, about 1 or 2 minutes. This spread may be thinned with a little milk if it seems too thick.

At serving time, preheat oven to 350 degrees. Spoon cheese mixture into crustade cups and bake in oven for 5 to 6 minutes. Garnish the centers of each appetizer with an olive slice.

Preparation Time: 20 minutes
Baking Time: 5 or 6 minutes
Yield: 2 1/2 cups

MUSHROOM APPETIZER FILLING

4 green onions, finely chopped
1 large garlic clove, minced
1/4 cup butter
1/2 pound fresh mushrooms,
   finely chopped
2 tablespoons flour
1 cup cream

1/4 cup minced fresh parsley
1 teaspoon lemon juice
Salt, to taste
1/8 teaspoon cayenne pepper
Petite Crustades, see recipe
3 tablespoons freshly grated
   Parmesan cheese

In a skillet, saute onions and garlic in butter for 1 minute. Add mushrooms and simmer uncovered until liquid evaporates, about 10 minutes. Add flour and stir to combine. Add cream and bring to a boil, stirring constantly until mixture is thick, about 2 minutes. Remove from heat, add parsley, lemon juice, salt, and cayenne pepper. Cover and refrigerate until ready to serve. Preheat oven to 350 degrees. Fill baked crustades with mushroom mixture; sprinkle with Parmesan cheese and place on ungreased baking sheet. Bake for 10 minutes or until heated through. Serve immediately.

Note: Crustades or tarts can be filled ahead and frozen; thaw before baking.

Preparation Time: 25 minutes
Cooking Time: 10 minutes
Servings: 2 dozen

SAUSAGE-LEEK APPETIZER FILLING

2 12-ounce packages pork sausage,
   flavor of choice
3 leeks, white part only,
   cleaned and sliced in 1-inch pieces

3/4 cup chicken broth
1/4 cup cream
Petite Crustades or appetizer tarts,
   see recipe

Preheat oven to 350 degrees. Crumble sausage into a large skillet and cook until well done; drain thoroughly. Combine the leeks and chicken broth in a saucepan. Bring to a boil, reduce heat, and simmer 5 minutes. In a food processor, combine the cooked sausage, leeks, broth, and cream; process until sausage is finely chopped with an on/off pulsing motion. Do not overprocess. Refrigerate or freeze until ready to serve. Fill crustades or tarts with mixture. Place crustades on baking sheet; bake 15 minutes or until heated through. Serve immediately.

Preparation Time: 25 minutes
Baking Time: 15 minutes
Yield: 2 1/2 cups

GUACAMOLE SUPREME

2 large avocados, peeled and seeded
1 tablespoon lemon juice
1 large tomato, peeled, seeded,
 and coarsely chopped
3 to 4 green onions, thinly sliced

1 4-ounce can diced ortega
 chilies, drained
1/2 teaspoon cumin powder
Salt and pepper, to taste

In a small bowl coarsely mash the avocados. Add the lemon juice, tomato, onions, chilies, cumin, salt and pepper; stir to combine. Serve immediately or refrigerate, covered, for several hours.

Note: For a spicier taste, add a seeded and minced jalapeno pepper.

Preparation Time: 15 minutes
Yield: 2 cups

STRINGED PEA PODS

1/2 pound fresh sugar peas, even sizes
Boiling water
Ice water

2 to 3 ounces string cheese,
 room temperature

Trim ends of peas, pulling strings away from both sides. Add peas to boiling water in a 12-inch skillet; cook, uncovered until bright green, about 30 seconds. Drain peas and immerse immediately in ice water to end cooking. Drain well and blot dry. Cover and chill 1 hour. Separate cheese into strings slender enough to tie easily. Loosely tie around center of each pea pod.

Note: Snow peas can be used easily without cooking. For extra special holiday variation, a strip of pimento or red pepper can be tucked in for a colorful presentation.

Preparation Time: 20 minutes
Chilling Time: 1 hour
Servings: 20

RADISH CHEESE SPREAD

1 8-ounce package cream cheese,
  at room temperature
1/2 cup butter, softened
3 tablespoons capers, drained
2 teaspoons caraway seeds

2 green onions, finely chopped
Beer or milk, enough to soften
1 bunch radishes, stemmed, cleaned,
  and chopped

Combine cream cheese, butter, capers, caraway seeds, onion, and beer with electric mixer or food processor. Stir radishes into cheese mixture. Place mixture in a small serving bowl and garnish with parsley. Serve chilled or at room temperature surrounded with crackers.

Note: For another presentation, the cheese mixture may be formed into a ball and rolled in additional chopped radishes; serve on a tray circled with crackers.

Preparation Time: 15 minutes
Servings: 12

TERRINE CHEESE SPREAD

This appetizer takes center stage when guests arrive at a party.

2 8-ounce packages light cream cheese,
  softened
1 1-ounce package dry ranch
  dressing mix
1 6-ounce jar marinated artichoke
  hearts, drained and chopped

1 2 1/4-ounce can chopped black olives
1/4 cup chopped fresh parsley
1/2 cup bottled roasted red peppers,
  drained and chopped
Butter lettuce, or edible leaves,
  of choice

Blend cheese and dressing mix. In a separate bowl, combine artichoke hearts, black olives, parsley and peppers. Line a small bowl or mold with plastic wrap. Fill with 5 alternate layers of cheese and vegetables, beginning and ending with cheese layers. Cover and chill 4 hours or overnight.

At serving time, invert onto serving platter lined with butter lettuce or edible leaves. Serve with crackers or French bread slices.

Preparation Time: 25 minutes
Chilling Time: 4 hours, or overnight
Servings: 10 to 12

HOLIDAY CHEESE LOG

An easy-to-prepare-ahead log that is delicious and attractive

1/2 cup dried apricots
1 cup water
1 pound Monterey Jack cheese
1 8-ounce package cream cheese,
  softened
1/3 cup sherry
1 teaspoon poppy seeds

1/2 teaspoon seasoned salt
1/3 cup golden raisins
1/3 cup chopped dates
2 tablespoons chopped red
  candied cherries
1 tablespoon chopped walnuts

Soak apricots in one cup of water for 2 hours. Blend cheeses in a food processor and remove mixture to a large mixing bowl. Add sherry, poppy seeds, and seasoned salt. Drain and chop the apricots; add to cheeses along with raisins and dates. Stir well to distribute through the cheeses. Turn onto a sheet of waxed paper and shape into a 9-inch log or several smaller logs. Wrap securely; chill until firm.

Combine chopped cherries and walnuts and roll the log in the mixture to give a light confetti appearance. Rewrap the log and store in the refrigerator. To serve, place the log on a tray surrounded with crackers.

Preparation Time: 1 hour
Chilling Time: 4 hours
Yield: 1 9-inch log, or several smaller logs

MATTERHORN TORTA

This delectable layered cheese spread blends cheeses, pesto, and sun-dried tomatoes. It can be made several days ahead.

2 8-ounce packages cream cheese, softened
5 ounces mild goat cheese
2 cloves garlic, minced
4 teaspoons minced fresh oregano or 1 1/4 teaspoons dry oregano
Ground pepper, to taste

1/4 cup prepared pesto, drained
1/2 cup sun-dried tomatoes, packed in oil, drained
Slivered toasted almonds, for garnish, optional
Herb sprigs, for garnish
Crackers or baguette rounds

Line a 1-quart bowl or mold with clear plastic wrap. In a food processor bowl or large mixer bowl, add cheeses, garlic, oregano, and pepper. Process or beat until smooth.

Spread 1/3 of cheese mixture in the bottom of a bowl or mold. Spread pesto evenly over cheese. Add another 1/3 of cheese mixture. Drain and chop tomatoes and arrange on cheese layer. Add remaining cheese layer. Cover with plastic wrap and press gently to pack the cheese. Chill 2 hours or longer.

Uncover cheese and invert on a serving plate. Garnish torta with thin cutouts from tomato, almonds, and herbs to create flower shapes with stems and leaves. Serve on tray surrounded by crackers or thinly sliced baguettes rounds.

Preparation Time: 25 minutes
Chilling Time: 2 hours, or longer
Servings: 12 to 16

GOURMET GLAZED CHEESE

Thrill your guests with this show-stopping appetizer!

2 cups dry white wine, or regular chicken broth
1 envelope unflavored gelatin
Wheel of Brie, or 3 8-inch rounds , see note
Edible decorations, see note

Combine wine or broth and gelatin in a 2 quart pan; set aside for 5 minutes. Stir over medium heat until gelatin is dissolved and clear. Place pan in a large bowl filled with ice water. Stir mixture slowly, to avoid forming bubbles, until it looks syrupy and thickened. If mixture becomes too firm, reheat to soften, and repeat steps to achieve syrupy texture.

Meanwhile, arrange the cold cheese on a wire rack in a shallow pan. Place decorations atop the cheese in attractive pattern. Remove decorations for a few minutes and coat top and sides of cheese with a layer of the gelatin aspic. After a few minutes, when gelatin is tacky, replace the decorations as planned and spoon on a layer of gelatin. Refrigerate, uncovered, for about 15 minutes.

Continue to spoon more gelatin glaze over top and sides of cheese in 15 minute intervals until all surfaces of decorations and cheese are completely coated. Refrigerate after each application. When glazing process is completed, cover cheese with inverted bowl, being careful not to touch the surface. Refrigerate until ready to serve, up to 36 hours.

Note: Have fun creating a masterpiece with the following suggestions for edible decorations: Use small blossoms or petals of flowers, leaves, and herb sprigs. Consider nasturtiums, violets, pansies, lemon blossoms and chive flowers, as well as tarragon, parsley, basil, watercress, chives, dill, cilantro, and sage. Rinse decorations and blot dry with paper towels. Store in plastic bags in the refrigerator until ready to adorn the cheese.

Camembert, Monterey Jack, Cheddar, or Gourmandise cheese may be substituted for the Brie. Any remaining glaze stores in refrigerator for several weeks.

Preparation Time: 1 to 1 1/2 hours
Yield: Your choice, depending on size of cheese

SUN-DRIED TOMATO AND ROASTED GARLIC TORTA

Thank you to Sarah Scott, Chef at Robert Mondavi Wine and Food Center, for this flavorful torta recipe.

3 heads garlic, tops removed
1 teaspoon olive oil
1/2 teaspoon dried rosemary
1 bay leaf
1 pound unsalted butter,
room temperature
1 pound cream cheese,
room temperature

2 teaspoons chopped, fresh thyme
2 teaspoons chopped, fresh parsley
2 teaspoons chopped, fresh chives
1 cup softened sun-dried tomatoes
Sprigs of fresh herbs, for garnish
Baguettes, sliced

Preheat oven to 350 degrees. In a small baking dish, combine garlic with olive oil, rosemary, and a bay leaf; cover and bake for 1 hour. Uncover and continue to bake until garlic cloves push up out of the heads and are very soft, about 1 hour. When heads are cooled, turn upside down; squeeze out the softened garlic paste into a bowl and set aside.

In a mixer, combine butter and cream cheese and beat until creamy. Set aside. In a food processor, combine the fresh herbs. Pulse with on/off motion to chop, then add the sun-dried tomatoes and continue to pulse. Last, add the garlic paste and pulse to combine. Set mixture aside.

Line a small loaf pan or bowl with dampened cheesecloth or plastic wrap. Spoon in 1/3 of the cheese mixture, spreading evenly over the bottom; spoon on 1/2 of the tomato-garlic mixture, spreading evenly over the cheese layer. Continue building layers, ending with a layer of cheese.

Fold the plastic wrap or cheesecloth over the top to cover and tap the torta on the countertop a few times to settle the contents. Place in the refrigerator for at least 1 hour, or overnight.

Unmold by inverting onto a plate, peel off the covering and garnish with fresh herbs. Serve with sliced baguettes.

Preparation Time: 30 minutes
Baking Time: 1 hour
Chilling Time: 1 hour or longer
Servings: 15 to 20

Robert Mondavi Pinot Noir

PESTO PARTY SLICES

1 8-ounce baguette of French
  or sourdough bread
7 ounces pesto sauce, commercial
  or homemade

6 to 7 Roma tomatoes,
  skinned and sliced
3 ounces grated Romano or
  Parmesan cheese

Preheat oven to 350 degrees. Slice baguette into rounds and place slices on cookie sheet; bake 5 minutes. Spread a thin layer of pesto sauce on each slice, top with a slice of tomato, and sprinkle with cheese. Bake for 10 minutes. Serve slices on a party tray while they are hot.

Preparation Time: 20 minutes
Servings: 8 to 10

SWISS PARTY RYES

1 loaf party rye bread
Mayonnaise, or choice of spread
2 small white onions, thinly sliced

1 1/2 pounds Swiss cheese, thinly sliced
Paprika, for garnish

Preheat oven to 350 degrees. Spread each slice of bread with mayonnaise. Cut onion and cheese to fit the bread. Place onion, then cheese on the bread. Dust with paprika. Freeze for later use or place appetizers on cookie sheet and bake 10 minutes.

Preparation Time: 25 minutes
Servings: 10 to 12

COCKTAIL REUBENS

36 slices of cocktail rye bread
Mustard of your choice
1/2 pound thinly sliced corned beef
1/2 pound thinly sliced Swiss cheese

1 8-ounce can sauerkraut,
  drained and squeezed very dry
1/4 to 1/2 pound butter or margarine

Spread half of the bread slices with mustard to taste. Cut corned beef and cheese in pieces to fit bread. Place 2 slices of each on top of the bread with mustard. Add a teaspoon of sauerkraut and top with remaining bread slice. In a large saute pan, melt 4 tablespoons butter. Grill sandwiches, several at a time, until both sides are golden brown; add butter as needed to finish grilling all sandwiches. Serve immediately. If you prefer, cut sandwiches in half.

Preparation Time: 1 hour
Servings: 18 sandwiches

WARM CHEESE SALSA DIP

1 medium white onion, chopped
2 tablespoons butter or margarine
1 medium tomato, peeled,
   seeded, and chopped

Garlic salt, to taste
1 4-ounce can diced green chilies
2 8-ounce packages cream cheese, cubed
Tortilla chips or crackers

In a one quart microwavable dish, saute the chopped onion in butter. Add tomato, garlic salt, green chilies, and cream cheese. Serve with tortilla chips or crackers.

Preparation Time: 20 to 30 minutes
Servings: 10 to 12

SUNDOWNER CRAB DIP

1 7-ounce can crab meat or shrimp
1 8-ounce can water chestnuts,
   drained and chopped
1 tablespoon chopped green onion

2 teaspoons soy sauce
1/4 cup mayonnaise
1/2 cup sour cream
Dash seasoned salt

Combine all ingredients and chill for 1 hour. Serve with sturdy chips or crackers.

Preparation Time: 10 minutes
Chilling Time: 1 hour
Servings: 8 to 10

CURRY DIP

3 green onions, chopped
1 cup mayonnaise
3 tablespoons ketchup
1 tablespoon curry powder

1 tablespoon Worcestershire sauce
1/2 teaspoon hot pepper sauce
Crudites, of your choice

In a small bowl, combine all ingredients except vegetables. Cover and refrigerate at least 24 hours to blend the flavors. Serve with crisp, fresh crudites.

Note: Possible choices of crudites: green onions, sugar peas, jicama, asparagus, zucchini spears, carrot and celery sticks, fresh mushroom slices, broccoli and cauliflower florets, and cherry tomatoes.

Preparation Time: 10 minutes
Chilling Time: 24 hours
Yield: 1 1/4 cup

ARTICHOKE DIP

This recipe was submitted by many Guild members. We decided such a popular recipe should be included in our book!

1 8-ounce can water-packed artichoke hearts, drained and chopped
4 ounces grated Parmesan cheese
1 8-ounce package cream cheese, softened
1 cup mayonnaise

Preheat oven to 350 degrees. Combine ingredients and place in oven-proof serving dish topped with extra Parmesan cheese. Bake for 20 minutes. Serve with crackers or unsalted tortilla chips.

Note: Freezes well. Chopped Ortega chilies can be added to the recipe.

Preparation Time: 10 minutes
Baking Time: 20 minutes
Servings: 10 to 20

SWEET ONION DIP

No one can guess the contents of this dip.

2 cups chopped sweet onion
2 cups shredded Swiss cheese
2 cups real mayonnaise

Preheat oven to 375 degrees. Combine ingredients; spread in quiche or pie dish. Bake for 30 minutes or until golden brown on top. Let stand for 15 minutes and serve with your favorite crackers.

Note: Premium onions such as Vidalia, Walla Walla, or Maui are recommended for their mild flavor.

Preparation Time: 10 minutes
Baking Time: 30 minutes
Yield: 6 cups

FIESTA CORN WALNUT DIP

A guaranteed hit!

2 8-ounce packages cream cheese
1/4 cup lime juice
1 tablespoon cumin
1 teaspoon each: salt, pepper,
   cayenne pepper
1 8-ounce can whole kernel corn,
   drained

1 cup chopped walnuts
1 4-ounce can diced green chilies,
   drained
3 green onions, chopped

Whip cream cheese until fluffy. Beat in lime juice. Stir in all remaining ingredients; refrigerate at least 8 hours. Serve with chips.

Note: This dip can be made several days ahead.

Preparation Time: 15 minutes
Chilling Time: 8 hours
Servings: 16 to 20

CRANBERRY CHUTNEY SPREAD

This colorful sweet and sour condiment makes a festive holiday gift!

1 16-ounce can whole cranberry sauce
1/2 cup wine vinegar
1/2 cup golden raisins or currants
1 tablespoon Worcestershire sauce
1 cup sugar

2 tablespoons molasses
1 8-ounce package cream
   cheese, softened
Chopped walnuts, optional

In a saucepan, combine cranberry sauce, vinegar, raisins, Worcestershire sauce, sugar, and molasses and simmer for 30 minutes Cool before storing in refrigerator. Spoon over cream cheese and top with chopped walnuts or pecans. Serve surrounded with crackers on a decorative tray.

Preparation Time: 5 minutes
Cooking Time: 30 minutes
Servings: 10

IMAGINATION CELEBRATION

How can we create pint-sized lovers of Beethoven, Baryshnikov, and Broadway? Surround them with music. Expose them to fine art, dance, and theater. Invite them to the Imagination Celebration.

Orange County's week-long festival of creativity draws 150,000 children and their families to a breathtaking array of arts activities. Where else can a child design and then fly his own kite, take part in a workshop on Caribbean rhythms, and then board a fully-rigged sailing ship to act in a play about rounding Cape Horn?

At shopping malls and parks, at art museums and at The Center, 30 area arts organizations unite to give youngsters a taste of the thrill of live performance and of excellence in artistic expression. The emphasis is upon "hands on" participation, and put their hands on, they do: on paint brushes and slabs of wet clay, on glue bottles, musical instruments, and computer synthesizers. Young singers, dancers, and musicians fill stages, large and small, and Orange County fairly bubbles with the joyous energy of creating.

First staged in 1986 with technical and financial assistance from the John F. Kennedy Center for the Performing Arts in Washington, D. C., the Imagination Celebration is now presented by The Center and the Orange County Department of Education. In an era of decreasing school budgets for the arts, the Imagination Celebration is a magical week when the sky's the limit for creative expression in all its rich variety, and children, the artists of our future, are the stars.

**Young people dream, create, and experience the arts in all their variety
at the Imagination Celebration.
This photograph was underwritten by
CYNTHIA AND CLARK VITULLI**

All that sunshine draws Orange Countians outdoors. Many head to neighborhood parks to jog, walk, or push a child on a swing. Tennis players can always find a match; golfers claim that this is paradise. Horse-lovers explore the hilly inland canyons and miles of equestrian trails on horseback. Artists are sure to find a scenic spot to place an easel or plant a tripod in this area of stunning natural beauty.

BREAD AND BRUNCH

Could there be a more welcoming sight than a delicious breakfast in a sunny kitchen?
The North Orange County morning photograph was underwritten by
THE TIMES ORANGE COUNTY

ZESTY LIME MUFFINS

Good with or without frosting

2 cups flour
1 2/3 cups sugar, divided
3 teaspoons baking powder
1/4 cup milk

2 eggs, beaten
1/4 cup oil
1 teaspoon fresh lime zest
1/4 cup plus 1/3 cup fresh lime juice, divided

Preheat oven to 400 degrees. In a large bowl, combine flour, 1 cup of sugar, and baking powder. In another bowl, combine the milk, eggs, oil, zest, and 1/4 cup lime juice; add to the flour mixture. Lightly mix with a fork just until moistened; do not overmix. Divide the batter among 12 greased or paper-lined muffin cups. Bake for 20 minutes, or until lightly browned. Cool about 2 minutes. Dip top of each muffin in remaining lime juice and then in remaining 2/3 cup sugar. Serve warm.

Preparation Time: 7 to 10 minutes
Baking Time: 20 minutes
Yield: 12 medium muffins

BANANA MINI-CHIP MUFFINS

1 egg, beaten
2 ripe bananas, mashed
1/2 cup oil
1/3 cup buttermilk
1 teaspoon vanilla
1 tablespoon grated orange peel

2 cups all-purpose flour
1/2 cup sugar
1 tablespoon baking powder
1 teaspoon cinnamon
1 teaspoon salt
2/3 cup mini-chocolate chips

Preheat oven to 400 degrees. Beat egg in large bowl. Add bananas, oil, buttermilk, vanilla, and grated orange peel. Stir together flour, sugar, baking powder, cinnamon, and salt. Stir banana mixture and dry ingredients together until just moistened. Add mini-chips and stir to distribute the chips. Fill greased mini-muffin cups about 3/4 full. Bake 12 to 18 minutes, or until golden brown. Remove from pan and serve warm.

Note: Regular-size muffins will require a longer baking time.

Preparation Time: 15 minutes
Baking Time: 12 to 18 minutes
Servings: 24 to 30 mini-muffins, or 12 regular muffins

COFFEE PRALINE MUFFINS

1 3/4 cups flour
1/3 cup brown sugar
3 teaspoons baking powder
1/2 cup plus 2 tablespoons finely
   chopped pecans
3/4 cup milk

1/4 cup instant coffee granules
1 egg, beaten
2 teaspoons vanilla
1/2 cup margarine, melted
1 tablespoon sugar

Preheat oven to 375 degrees. In a large bowl, combine flour, brown sugar, baking powder, and 1/2 cup of the pecans. In a small bowl whisk milk and instant coffee together until coffee is dissolved. Add the egg and vanilla to coffee-milk mixture. Stir egg mixture and melted margarine into the dry ingredients. Hand mix the batter just until dry ingredients are moistened. Pour batter into greased muffin tins, about 2/3 full; sprinkle tops with sugar and remaining nuts. Bake for 18 to 20 minutes.

Preparation Time: 10 minutes
Baking Time: 18 to 20 minutes
Yield: 12 medium muffins, or 24 mini muffins

ORANGE COUNTY MUFFINS

2/3 cup plus 2 tablespoons sugar, divided
1/3 cup plus 2 tablespoons margarine,
   divided
2 eggs
2 1/2 cups plus 2 tablespoons cake flour
2 teaspoons baking powder

1/2 teaspoon baking soda
1/2 teaspoon salt
Peel of 1 orange, orange part only
Juice of 1 orange
2/3 cup milk
1/2 teaspoon cinnamon

Preheat oven to 350 degrees. Spray 18 muffin tins with non-stick cooking spray and set aside. In a large bowl, cream together 2/3 cup sugar and 1/3 cup margarine. Add eggs and beat until light yellow in color. Sift together 2 cups plus 2 tablespoons flour, baking powder, baking soda, and salt. In a food processor, pulse orange peel with 1/2 cup of the flour mixture; pulse 8 to 10 times until peel is finely grated. Add to creamed mixture along with remainder of flour mixture, blending until smooth. Add juice and milk and mix well. Spoon batter into prepared muffin cups. To make topping, combine remaining 2 tablespoons margarine, 2 tablespoons sugar, 1/2 cup flour, and cinnamon. Sprinkle a heaping teaspoon of topping over each muffin. Bake for 25 minutes, or until light brown.

Preparation Time: 25 minutes
Baking Time: 25 minutes
Yield: 18 muffins

BREAKFAST IN A MUFFIN

These appetizing muffins are full of nutritious ingredients: apricots, orange, and bran. Serve them for your family: they are special enough to serve for a party brunch.

1 cup raisins
1/2 cup chopped dried apricots
2 cups boiling water
1/2 cup butter, softened
1 egg
1 cup sour cream
1 whole orange, peeled, seeded,
    and finely chopped

1 cup sugar
1 cup natural bran
1 cup all purpose flour
1 cup whole wheat flour
2 teaspoons baking powder
1 teaspoon baking soda
1/2 teaspoon salt

Pour boiling water over raisins and apricots and allow to sit for 30 minutes to plump up and soften; drain. Preheat oven to 375 degrees. In a large bowl, combine softened butter, egg, sour cream, orange, sugar, and bran. Combine the white flour, wheat flour, baking powder, soda, and salt in a medium bowl. Add plumped raisins and apricots and mix well. Stir the flour-fruit mixture into the butter mixture and blend only until moist. Spoon the batter into greased or paper-lined muffin tins. Fill each cup almost to the top. Bake for 20 minutes, until firm and brown.

Preparation Time: 35 to 45 minutes
Baking Time: 20 minutes
Servings: 16 to 18 regular-size muffins

CROWN VALLEY RHUBARB MUFFINS

1 cup diced rhubarb, about 1 stalk
1 1/3 cups flour
1 cup brown sugar, divided
1/2 teaspoon baking soda
1/4 teaspoon salt
1/2 cup sour cream

1/4 cup vegetable oil
1 egg
1/3 cup rolled oats
2 teaspoons melted butter
1/2 teaspoon cinnamon

Preheat oven to 350 degrees. In a mixing bowl, combine rhubarb, flour, 2/3 cup brown sugar, baking soda, and salt. In a small bowl, blend sour cream, oil, and egg; add to rhubarb mixture, stirring until all ingredients are just moistened. Spoon into 12 greased muffin cups. Combine remaining 1/3 cup brown sugar, rolled oats, melted butter, and cinnamon. Sprinkle oat mixture on the muffins as a topping. Bake 25 to 30 minutes.

Preparation Time: 15 minutes
Baking Time: 25 to 30 minutes
Yield: 12 muffins

HEALTHY CRUNCH MUFFINS

A healthy take-along breakfast treat for a walk on the beach

1 cup plus 2 tablespoons quick
   cooking rolled oats
1 cup buttermilk
1 1/2 teaspoons vanilla
1 cup flour
1/2 teaspoon baking soda
1 tablespoon baking powder
1 teaspoon salt

1/2 teaspoon cinnamon
1/2 teaspoon nutmeg
1/3 cup diced walnuts
1 medium tart apple, diced
1 large egg, beaten
1 cup firmly packed brown sugar
1/4 cup margarine, melted
Cinnamon-sugar, for topping

Preheat oven to 350 degrees. Combine oats, buttermilk, and vanilla in a bowl. In a larger bowl, combine flour, baking soda, baking powder, salt, cinnamon, and nutmeg. Combine oat mixture with flour mixture; add walnuts, apple, egg, brown sugar, and margarine. Stir just to moisten all ingredients. Grease 18 muffin cups and spoon batter into cups. Sprinkle with cinnamon-sugar. Bake for 18 minutes. Remove from pan and cool on rack before serving.

Preparation Time: 30 minutes
Baking Time: 18 minutes
Yield: 18 muffins

APPLE-NUT-CINNAMON MUFFINS

1 3/4 cups raisin bran cereal
1 1/4 cups flour
3/4 cup plus 1 1/2 tablespoons sugar,
   divided
1 1/4 teaspoons baking soda
1/4 teaspoon salt
3/4 cup buttermilk

1/4 cup oil
1 large egg
1/2 cup peeled, finely chopped apples
1/2 cup chopped walnuts
2 tablespoons unsalted butter, melted
1/2 teaspoon cinnamon

Preheat oven to 400 degrees. Grease 12 muffin tins and set aside. In a large bowl, mix together the cereal, flour, 3/4 cup sugar, baking soda, and salt. Set aside. In a small bowl, whisk together the buttermilk, oil, and egg; add to cereal mixture. Let batter stand for 15 minutes. Meanwhile, in another bowl, combine the apples, walnuts, butter, 1 1/2 tablespoons sugar, and cinnamon. Spoon 2 tablespoons of batter into each muffin tin. Spoon some of the apple-nut mixture over the batter, then add more batter over the apple-nut filling. Bake for 23 minutes.

Preparation Time: 45 minutes to 1 hour
Servings: 12

ALMOND KRINGLE

Sensational for a holiday buffet—even better the second day

2 cups flour, divided
1 cup butter, divided
2 tablespoons ice water
1 cup water
3 eggs

1 teaspoon almond extract, divided
1 cup powdered sugar
1 tablespoon milk
3/4 cup chopped almonds

Preheat oven to 350 degrees. Combine 1 cup flour, 1/2 cup butter, and ice water; divide in half. Use lightly floured hands to make two 12 x 3-inch strips on a lightly greased cookie sheet. Set aside.

Combine 1/2 cup butter and 1 cup water together in saucepan and bring to a boil. Remove from heat and add 1 cup flour and the eggs, beating well. Stir in 1/2 teaspoon almond extract. Spread mixture onto the strips on the cookie sheet. Bake for 50 to 60 minutes. To make frosting, combine powdered sugar, 1/2 teaspoon almond extract, and milk. Spread icing on top of warm kringle and sprinkle the top with chopped almonds. Set aside to cool. To serve, cut in slices.

Note: Kringle can be made a day ahead; store in an airtight container.

Preparation Time: 20 to 30 minutes
Baking Time: 50 to 60 minutes
Yield: Two 12 x 3-inch kringles

CRAN-ORANGE COFFEE CAKE

A tangy blend of orange and cranberry flavors make this a holiday standout

2 eggs, beaten
1 1/3 cups sugar
1/2 cup butter, melted
1 cup flour, sifted

1/2 cup chopped nuts
2 cups whole raw cranberries
2 tablespoons orange juice
2 tablespoons orange zest

Preheat oven to 325 degrees. In a large bowl, combine all ingredients and pour into a 10-inch, greased pie pan or quiche dish. Bake for 50 to 60 minutes. Best served warm.

Preparation Time: 20 minutes
Baking Time: 50 to 60 minutes
Serves: 8 to 10

EASY BUTTERMILK COFFEE CAKE

2 cups all purpose flour
2 cups brown sugar
1/3 teaspoon salt
1/2 cup vegetable oil
1 egg, beaten
1 teaspoon baking powder

1 teaspoon baking soda
1 1/4 cups buttermilk
2 teaspoons cinnamon, divided
1 cup chopped pecans or walnuts,
    divided

Preheat oven to 350 degrees. Grease and flour a 13 x 9-inch baking pan. In a large bowl, combine flour, brown sugar, salt, and oil, mixing well. Set aside 3/4 cup of this mixture in a small bowl for the topping. Add the egg, baking powder, baking soda, buttermilk, and 1 teaspoon cinnamon. Mix well. Stir in 1/2 cup chopped nuts. Pour batter into the prepared baking dish. Combine the remaining teaspoon of cinnamon and 1/2 cup nuts with the reserved topping mix; sprinkle over the batter. Bake for 40 minutes. Serve warm or at room temperature.

Preparation Time: 25 minutes
Baking Time: 40 minutes
Servings: Approximately 12

DOCKSIDE SOUR CREAM COFFEE CAKE

1 cup butter
2 cups sugar
2 eggs
1 cup sour cream
1 teaspoon vanilla
2 cups sifted cake flour

1 teaspoon baking powder
1/4 teaspoon salt
4 teaspoons brown sugar
1 teaspoon cinnamon
1 cup chopped pecans or walnuts

Preheat oven to 350 degrees. Grease and flour an angel food cake pan. In a large bowl, cream butter and sugar with an electric mixer; beat in eggs; blending well. Fold in sour cream and vanilla. Add the flour, baking powder, and salt, mixing well. Spoon half the batter into the prepared pan.

In a small bowl, combine brown sugar, cinnamon, and nuts. Sprinkle half of this mixure over the batter in the cake pan. Pour remaining batter in the pan and sprinkle remaining nut mixture on top. Bake for one hour. Cool, completely, before cutting. It will taste even better if made 24 hours ahead.

Preparation Time: 15 to 20 minutes
Baking Time: 1 hour
Servings: 8 to 10

DO-AHEAD FRENCH TOAST

A delectable French toast, conveniently made the night before, for your favorite houseguests.

1/4 cup butter, softened
12 3/4-inch slices French bread
6 eggs, gently beaten
2 tablespoons sugar
1 tablespoon maple syrup

1 teaspoon vanilla
1/2 teaspoon salt
Cinnamon, to taste
Additional maple syrup for topping
1 cup chopped walnuts

Butter bottom and sides of a 13 x 9-inch baking pan and arrange bread slices in it. Combine beaten eggs, sugar, 1 tablespoon maple syrup, vanilla, and salt. Mix and pour over French bread and turn pieces to coat. Sprinkle with cinnamon. Cover pan and refrigerate overnight. In the morning, preheat oven to 400 degrees. Bake bread for 10 minutes; turn bread and bake an additional 10 minutes.

Note: Heat maple syrup and 1 cup chopped walnuts to serve with the French toast.

Preparation Time: 10 to 15 minutes
Standing Time: Overnight
Baking Time: 20 minutes
Servings: 6

TRABUCO TOAST

A quick recipe for family dinners or a luncheon

1 8-ounce package refrigerated
 crescent rolls
Creamy Caesar salad dressing, of choice

1 cup herb-seasoned croutons, crushed
1/4 cup grated Parmesan cheese

Preheat oven 375 degrees. Unroll and separate refrigerated rolls. Form into four rectangles, pinching perforations to seal. Brush each rectangle generously with salad dressing and cut crosswise and lengthwise to form 4 smaller rectangles. With a wide spatula, lift each rectangle and invert onto crushed croutons, pressing gently. Place, crumb side up, on greased cookie sheet. Sprinkle with Parmesan cheese. Bake 12 to 14 minutes until golden brown.

Preparation Time: 10 minutes
Baking Time: 12 to 14 minues
Yield: 16 toasts

SPRINGTIME STRAWBERRY BREAD

1/2 cup butter or margarine, softened
1 cup sugar
1/2 teaspoon almond extract
2 eggs, separated
2 cups all-purpose flour
1 teaspoon baking powder

1 teaspoon baking soda
1 teaspoon salt
1 cup strawberries, crushed,
    or 1 10-ounce box frozen strawberries
Strawberry butter, recipe follows

Preheat oven 350 degrees. Cream together softened butter, sugar, and almond extract with an electric mixer. Beat in egg yolks, one at a time. Sift together flour, baking powder, baking soda, and salt. Add the dry ingredients alternately with the mashed strawberries into the butter-egg mixture. Beat the egg whites until stiff, but not dry. Fold into the creamed mixture.

Grease and flour a 9 x 5-inch loaf pan. Turn batter into prepared pan and bake for 50 to 60 minutes. Cool 15 minutes in the pan and then invert onto a rack. Serve warm with butter, jam, or strawberry butter.

Note: The bread makes delicious toast on the second day. It freezes well.

Preparation Time: 20 minutes
Baking Time: 50 to 60 minutes
Yield: 1 loaf

STRAWBERRY BUTTER

1/2 cup butter, room temperature
1/2 cup strawberries, crushed
1 1/2 tablespoons powdered sugar

In a small bowl, combine all ingredients. Put in mold; cover and chill.

Preparation Time: 5 minutes
Yield: 1 cup

BALBOA BANANA BREAD

Quick, easy, and so scrumptious you'll want to double the recipe. The first loaf will disappear right out of the oven.

2 cups flour
1 cup sugar
1 teaspoon baking powder
1/2 teaspoon baking soda

2 ripe bananas, mashed
1/2 cup milk
1/4 cup butter or margarine, softened
1 egg, beaten

Preheat oven to 350 degrees. Combine dry ingredients. Combine bananas, milk, softened butter, and egg; add to dry ingredients, stirring until well mixed. Pour into a greased and floured 9 x 5-inch loaf pan. Bake for 1 hour. Cool for 15 minutes.

Note: Make banana muffins; just spoon batter in paper-lined muffin cups and shorten the baking time to 25 minutes.

Preparation Time: 10 minutes
Baking Time: 1 hour
Yield: 1 loaf

POPPY SEED QUICK BREAD

2 cups sugar
1 1/2 cups vegetable oil
3 eggs
1 teaspoon vanilla flavoring
3 cups all-purpose flour
1 1/2 teaspoons baking soda
1 teaspoon salt

1 12-ounce can evaporated milk
1/2 to 3/4 cup poppy seeds
1 cup chopped walnuts
1 cup powdered sugar
1/4 teaspoon almond or vanilla extract
1/4 cup milk

Preheat oven to 350 degrees. Measure sugar into large mixing bowl. Beat oil into sugar. Add eggs and vanilla and continue to beat until well blended. In a medium bowl, sift flour, baking soda, and salt together. Stir sifted dry ingredients, alternating with canned milk, into sugar mixture until well blended. Stir in poppy seeds and nuts. Pour into 2 greased 9 x 5-inch loaf pans and bake for 1 hour, or until a toothpick inserted near the center comes out clean. Cool in pan on rack for 10 minutes. Remove from pan. For glaze, combine powdered sugar, almond or vanilla extract, and milk. Pour on top of warm bread. Serve at room temperature.

Preparation Time: 15 minutes
Baking Time: 1 hour
Yield: 2 loaves

PERSIMMON-DATE-NUT BREAD

1/2 cup white bread cubes
1/2 cup half-and-half
1 1/4 cup flour
1 cup sugar
1 1/2 teaspoons soda
1/2 teaspoon salt
1 1/2 teaspoons baking powder

1 cup persimmon pulp,
   about 2 medium persimmons
1/2 cup chopped dates
1 cup chopped walnuts
1 teaspoon vanilla
1 1/2 teaspoons butter, melted

Preheat oven to 350 degrees. Soak bread cubes in half-and-half. Sift together the flour, sugar, soda, salt, and baking powder. Add persimmon pulp, dates, walnuts, vanilla, and melted butter to the sifted flour mixture and blend well. Add the soaked bread and combine well. Put in greased 1-pound loaf pan and bake 1 1/2 hours. Serve warm or at room temperature.

Preparation Time: 10 minutes
Baking Time: 1 1/2 hours
Yield: 1 loaf

PINEAPPLE BREAD

1 cup butter, softened
1 cup orange juice, divided
3 eggs
1 1/2 cups firmly packed brown sugar
1 cup graham cracker crumbs
2 cups sifted all-purpose flour

1 teaspoon baking powder
1 teaspoon baking soda
1 8 1/2-ounce can crushed pineapple,
   including juice
2/3 cup apricot preserves, divided
1/2 cup slivered almonds

Preheat oven to 350 degrees. Grease and flour two 9 x 5-inch loaf pans. Combine butter, 1/2 cup orange juice, and eggs in the large bowl of electric mixer. Add sugar, graham cracker crumbs, flour, baking powder, baking soda, pineapple, and 2 tablespoons of the apricot preserves. Beat at medium speed 2 minutes. Pour the mixture into loaf pans and bake for 50 minutes, or until the center springs back when lightly touched. Cool in pan for 15 minutes.

Meanwhile, heat remaining 1/2 cup orange juice and remaining apricot preserves in a small saucepan until preserves are melted and bubbly. Remove bread from pan; poke holes in surface of bread and pour hot glaze over the warm bread. Sprinkle with almonds. Cool completely before slicing.

Preparation Time: 20 minutes
Baking Time: 50 minutes
Yield: 2 loaves

OATMEAL-GRANOLA BREAD

Even beginner bread-makers are assured success with this easy, hearty bread.

1 1/3 cups boiling water	1 1/4-ounce package dry yeast
3/4 cup rolled oats	3/4 teaspoon salt
1/4 cup granola	1 tablespoon vegetable oil
1 3/4 cups white all-purpose	1/4 cup molasses
or bread flour	3/4 cup whole wheat flour

In a medium-size bowl, pour boiling water over the rolled oats; stir and let stand until lukewarm, approximately 20 minutes. Place granola in a food processor and process approximately eight pulses. Add lukewarm rolled oats, white flour, and yeast to the granola in the food processor and process briefly until combined, about 20 seconds. Transfer the mixture to a medium-sized bowl, uncovered, and place in a warm, draft-free location until doubled in bulk, approximately 1 1/2 hours.

Punch down dough and return to processor; add salt, cooking oil, molasses, and wheat flour. Process until mixed, about 20 seconds. You may have to add a small amount of additional white flour, up to 1/4 cup, to make a smooth, pliable dough. Continue processing just until dough starts to clean the inside of the work bowl, then let the machine run for 1 1/2 minutes to knead the dough. Form into a loaf shape and place in a greased 9 x 5-inch loaf pan. Allow to rise again, uncovered, until doubled in bulk, approximately 45 minutes.

Preheat oven to 350 degrees. Bake 30 to 50 minutes, or until bread sounds hollow when removed from the pan and tapped on the bottom. Cool before slicing. It smells delicious!

Preparation Time: 3 hours, including rising time
Baking Time: 30 to 50 minutes
Yield: 1 loaf

HERBED FOCACCIA BREAD

A savory accompaniment to soups, salads, and Italian dishes

1/4 ounce package active dry yeast
1 cup warm water, 100 to 115 degrees
3 to 3 1/2 cups all-purpose, or bread flour
2 tablespoons fresh chopped rosemary,
 or oregano, or 2 teaspoons dried herbs
1 1/2 teaspoons salt

3 tablespoons olive oil
1/2 onion, finely chopped
2 cloves garlic, minced
1/2 cup grated Parmesan cheese
Additional extra virgin olive oil
Balsamic vinegar

Combine yeast and warm water and stir to dissolve. Let mixture stand until slightly foamy. In a large mixing bowl, combine 2 cups flour, herbs, and salt, using a wooden spoon. Add yeast mixture, stirring and adding additional flour to make the dough form a ball that pulls away from the sides of the bowl. Knead by hand or use a dough hook in your mixer until smooth and elastic, approximately 10 minutes. Place kneaded dough into an oiled bowl, turning so that the dough surface is oiled. Cover and let rise in a warm place until doubled in bulk, approximately 1 hour.

Preheat oven 450 degrees. Punch down dough. Turn onto a lightly floured surface and roll out to a 12-inch circle. Transfer to a 13-inch pizza stone or a large cookie sheet and brush with 1 1/2 tablespoons olive oil. Make indentations all over the surface of the dough. Spread with chopped onion and garlic; sprinkle with the Parmesan cheese and drizzle remaining olive oil over top. Let rise until doubled, approximately 1/2 hour.

Bake 30 minutes or until golden brown. Cut into pie-shaped wedges and serve warm. Extra virgin olive oil and balsamic vinegar puddled on a small plate makes an authentic accompaniment.

Note: Vary herbs to your taste; experiment and enjoy this recipe. Another favorite variation is 2 teaspoons fennel seeds and 1/8 to 1/4 teaspoon red pepper flakes.

Preparation Time: 2 hours
Baking Time: Approximately 30 minutes
Yield: 1 13-inch loaf

PEPPERONI AND CHEESE BREAD

Italian tomato sauce, recipe follows
1-pound loaf frozen white bread
   dough, thawed
3 tablespoons butter, softened
1 clove garlic, minced

8 slices Provolone cheese, about 1/2 pound
24 2-inch round slices pepperoni
1/2 green bell pepper, chopped
2 green onions, sliced
Sesame seeds

Prepare sauce. Preheat oven to 350 degrees. Grease a cookie sheet. On a lightly floured bread board roll dough out to a 12 x 18-inch rectangle. Saute garlic in butter for 2 to 3 minutes. Spread half of garlic butter mixture on top of dough. Arrange cheese, pepperoni, and green pepper over the dough; sprinkle green onion on top. Fold top third of dough over middle, then fold bottom third over top, enclosing filling, like folding a business letter. Pinch edges to seal. Spread remaining garlic butter over top and sprinkle with sesame seeds. Bake for 30 minutes, or until golden brown. Cool for 5 minutes; slice into servings and top with sauce. Serve warm.

Preparation Time: 1/2 hours
Baking Time: 30 minutes
Servings: 6

ITALIAN TOMATO SAUCE

2 tablespoons extra virgin olive oil
2 medium onions, finely chopped
3 medium carrots, finely chopped
2 cloves garlic, minced
1 12-ounce can tomato paste
10 Roma tomatoes, cut into fourths
1/4 teaspoon dry oregano leaves, or
   4 to 5 fresh oregano leaves, chopped

1/2 teaspoon dry basil leaves,
   or 8 to 10 fresh basil leaves, chopped
1 tablespoon sugar
1/2 cup sherry
1/2 cup water

In a medium saucepan, heat the oil and saute onions, carrots, and garlic until softened, but not brown, stirring frequently. Add all remaining ingredients and simmer uncovered over low heat for at least two hours. Sauce will be fairly thick.

Preparation time: 2 hours, 20 minutes
Cooking Time: 2 hours
Yield: 2 to 3 cups

Robert Mondavi Cabernet Sauvignon

BRAIDED EGG BREAD

Delectable with cream cheese and jam

2 1/4-ounce packages dry yeast
2 cups warm water
4 tablespoons sugar
2 teaspoons salt
1/4 cup vegetable oil

4 eggs, at room temperature,
   beaten, divided
6 to 7 cups all-purpose
   or white bread flour
Poppy seeds

Soften yeast in warm water in a large bowl. Add sugar, salt, oil, and 3 eggs, mixing together. Add 4 cups of flour and mix well. Slowly add enough of the remaining flour to form a sticky but firm dough. Knead on a floured board until smooth and elastic; or knead in a mixer with a dough hook, approximately 8 minutes. Turn into an oiled bowl. Cover with a dish towel. Set in a warm place and let rise until doubled in size, about 1 hour.

Preheat oven to 350 degrees. Punch dough down and divide in half. Cut each half into 3 pieces. Roll each piece into a 15-inch strip. Braid into two loaves, tucking ends under. Cover and let rise again until doubled in size. Brush top and sides with remaining egg. Sprinkle tops and sides with poppy seeds. Bake for about 40 minutes. Cool on rack before slicing.

Preparation Time: 4 hours, including risings
Baking Time: 40 minutes
Yield: 2 large loaves

SADDLEBACK BREAD

This bread is great served with chili. It does not require kneading.

1/4 ounce package dry yeast	1 tablespoon sugar
1 3/4 cups lukewarm water, divided	1 tablespoon garlic salt
4 cups flour	2 tablespoons melted butter

Dissolve yeast in one cup lukewarm water and put in a large bowl. Add flour, sugar, and garlic salt, combining well. Mix in the additional 3/4 cup water and stir until well blended. Dough will be very sticky. Cover bowl and allow to rise in a warm, draft-free location for one hour. Flour hands and breadboard. Divide dough in half. Shape into two round loaves and place into 2 greased 8 or 9-inch pie pans. Cover and let rise again in a warm place for 1 hour.

Preheat oven to 375 degrees. Brush loaves with melted butter. Bake for 45 minutes. Remove from pans and wrap in a clean cloth. Serve hot bread immediately with butter.

Note: Cooled loaves may be frozen. Reheat frozen loaves at 325 degrees for 20 minutes. Serve warm.

Preparation Time: 10 minutes; plus 2 hours rising time
Baking Time: 45 minutes
Yield: 2 round loaves

SOUTHWEST CORNBREAD MADELEINES

1/4 cup blue or yellow cornmeal	1 tablespoon cold shortening
1/3 cup flour	1 large egg
1 1/2 teaspoons sugar	1/4 cup milk
1 teaspoon baking powder	2 teaspoons chopped chives
Pinch cayenne pepper	

Preheat oven to 400 degrees. Combine cornmeal, flour, sugar, baking powder, and pepper. Blend in shortening, using a pastry blender or fork, to make a coarse meal. Whisk in the egg and milk to produce a loose batter. Stir in the chives. Generously grease madeleine pan and fill each cup 3/4 full. Bake for about 7 minutes, or until slightly browned. Remove from pan and cool on wire racks.

Preparation Time: 15 minutes
Baking Time: 7 minutes
Yield: 12 madeleines

CORNMEAL BUTTERHORN ROLLS

3/4 cup milk
1/4 cup sugar
1 teaspoon caraway seeds
1/2 teaspoon salt
3/4 cup butter or margarine, divided

1/4 ounce package dry yeast
1/4 cup warm water
3 cups flour, approximately
1 egg, beaten
1/2 cup plus 1 teaspoon cornmeal

In a small pan, scald milk, sugar, caraway seeds, salt, and 1/2 cup butter. Cool to lukewarm. Dissolve yeast in warm water. Combine until smooth 1 cup flour, egg, 1/2 cup cornmeal, yeast, and milk mixture. Add approximately 2 cups flour to make a stiff dough. Knead 3 or 4 minutes. Let rest for 10 minutes. Divide dough into two equal portions. Roll each part into a 9-inch round; cut each round into six wedges. Brush wedges with remaining melted butter and sprinkle with approximately 1 teaspoon of cornmeal.

Roll each wedge from the wide end to the narrow and bend to form butterhorns. Place on two cookie sheets. Let rise in a warm place until double in bulk, approximately 1 hour. Preheat oven to 425 degrees. Bake for 12 to 15 minutes.

Preparation Time: 3 hours, including rising time
Baking Time: 12 to 15 minutes
Yield: 12 large rolls

BLEU CHEESE BREAD STICKS

Yummy served with soup or salad and as a distinctive appetizer with drinks

3/4 pound bleu cheese, crumbled
1 3-ounce package cream cheese, softened
1/2 cup butter, softened
2 tablespoons milk

1/4 teaspoon freshly ground pepper
1/4 teaspoon salt
3 cups flour
1/2 cup finely chopped pecans

Preheat oven to 400 degrees. Cream the cheeses and butter together. Beat in remaining ingredients to form dough. Roll dough on a floured surface until 1/4-inch thick. Cut dough into strips approximately 1/4-inch wide by 4 inches long. Twist each strip several times and place on an ungreased cookie sheet. Bake until golden brown, approximately 5 to 7 minutes. Remove bread sticks and cool on a wire rack.

Preparation Time: 30 minutes
Baking Time: 5 to 7 minutes
Yield: 36 sticks

FLAKY DILL BISCUITS

2 cups flour
3 teaspoons baking powder
1/4 teaspoon salt
1 teaspoon dried dill

6 tablespoons cold unsalted butter,
   cut into small pieces
2/3 cup plus 1 tablespoon milk, divided
1 tablespoon fresh dill, optional
1/2 cup butter, softened, optional

Preheat oven to 450 degrees. Combine dry ingredients in a bowl. Cut in butter with a pastry blender or two knives until the mixture is crumbly. Add 2/3 cup milk and mix quickly. On a floured surface, roll dough with a floured rolling pin to about 3/8-inch thickness. With a biscuit cutter, cut dough and place biscuits on an ungreased cookie sheet. Brush the top of each biscuit with remaining milk. Bake for 10 minutes, or until golden brown. It is nice to serve with dill butter. Just stir fresh dill into softened butter until blended. Chill and serve with warm biscuits.

Preparation Time: 15 to 20 minutes
Baking Time: 10 minutes
Yield: 18 biscuits

TINY HERB ROLLS

These easy-to-make and attractive rolls make a good accompaniment to salad or could be used as an appetizer.

1/4 cup butter, or margarine
1 1/2 teaspoons parsley flakes
1/2 teaspoon dill seed
1/4 teaspoon onion flakes

1 tablespoon grated Parmesan cheese
1 8-ounce package refrigerated
   buttermilk biscuits

Preheat oven to 425 degrees. Melt butter; add parsley flakes, dill seed, onion flakes, and Parmesan cheese, stirring to blend ingredients. Cut each biscuit into quarters, using kitchen shears. Dip each piece in butter mixture and arrange in a buttered 8-inch round cake pan, pieces touching. Bake 12 to 15 minutes, or until lightly browned. Turn out in one piece onto a serving plate and serve as pull-apart rolls.

Preparation Time: 10 minutes
Baking Time: 12 to 15 minutes
Yields: 24 tiny rolls

PELICAN HILL PECAN ROLLS

These rolls never fail to get rave reviews.

2 cups pecan pieces
1 25-ounce package frozen white dinner
   rolls, the kind that need to rise
2/3 cup firmly packed brown sugar
1 teaspoon ground cinnamon

1/4 teaspoon nutmeg
1 3-ounce package vanilla pudding and
   pie filling; do not use instant pudding mix
1 cup butter, cut into pieces

Grease a 11 x 14-inch cookie sheet. Sprinkle the pecan pieces on bottom of greased cookie sheet. Arrange frozen rolls over nuts, and sprinkle with brown sugar. Combine cinnamon, nutmeg, and pudding mix and sprinkle over rolls. Top with butter pieces. Cover the pan with plastic wrap and place in refrigerator overnight. The next day, uncover and let rise in a warm place until doubled in bulk, approximately 1 1/2 hours. Preheat oven to 350 degrees. Bake for 15 minutes, or until golden brown. Cool 2 to 3 minutes and invert rolls onto waxed paper. Serve warm.

Note: Before beginning, dinner rolls can be cut for smaller-sized servings. Whole pecans are another alternative.

Preparation Time: 15 minutes, plus 1 1/2 hours rising time
Chilling Time: Overnight
Baking Time: 25 minutes
Yield: 24 pecan rolls

CINNAMON PUFFS

1/2 cup butter, divided
3/4 cup sugar, divided
1 egg
1 1/2 cups flour
2 1/4 teaspoons baking powder

1/4 teaspoon salt
1/4 teaspoon nutmeg
1/2 cup milk
1/4 teaspoon cinnamon

Preheat the oven to 350 degrees. Grease 18 muffin tins. Blend 5 tablespoons of butter with 1/2 cup sugar. Add the egg and mix well. Sift together flour, baking powder, salt, and nutmeg. Add to the butter and sugar mixture. Mix in the milk thoroughly. Fill muffin cups 2/3 full and bake for 20 to 25 minutes until golden brown. Combine 1/4 cup sugar and cinnamon. Gently roll cooked puffs in 3 tablespoons melted butter and then in the sugar and cinnamon mixture. Serve warm.

Preparation Time: 15 minutes
Baking Time: 20 to 25 minutes
Yield: 18 puffs

TEATIME RAISIN SCONES

2 1/2 cups all-purpose flour
2 teaspoons baking powder
1 teaspoon baking soda
1/2 teaspoon salt
1/2 cup sugar
6 tablespoons cold butter,
   cut into small pieces

1/2 cup raisins
1 egg, beaten
1/2 cup plain yogurt
Zest of 1/2 lemon
Milk, for brushing scones
Butter, jam, whipped cream,
   or Devonshire cream

Preheat oven to 425 degrees. Lightly grease a large baking sheet; set aside. Sift flour, baking powder, baking soda, and salt into a large bowl. Stir in sugar. Blend in the butter pieces until mixture is crumbly. Mix in raisins. With a fork, stir in egg, yogurt, and lemon zest, blending well to make a dough that barely holds together.

On a floured bread board, roll out the dough with a floured rolling pin to about 1/2-inch thick. Cut in rounds with a 1 1/2-inch biscuit cutter and place 1 to 1 1/2 inches apart on the baking sheet. Brush tops lightly with milk. Bake for 10 to 12 minutes, or until scones have risen and are golden brown. Cool on wire rack for 5 minutes. Serve warm with butter, jam, whipped cream, or Devonshire cream.

Preparation Time: 20 minutes
Baking Time: 10 to 12 minutes
Yield: 18 scones

APRICOT CLAFOUTI

1 29-ounce can apricot halves, drained
2 tablespoons apricot brandy
1/3 cup flour
1/4 teaspoon salt

3 eggs
1 cup milk
3 tablespoons butter, melted
Powdered sugar

Preheat oven to 375 degrees. Arrange apricot halves on the bottom of a 9-inch round cake pan or 9 x 9-inch square baking dish. Sprinkle with the brandy and set aside. Mix the flour, salt, eggs, milk, and butter in a bowl or processor. Pour the batter over the apricots and bake for about 40 minutes, or until brown and puffed. Sprinkle with powdered sugar. Serve hot or warm.

Preparation Time: 10 minutes
Baking Time: 40 minutes
Servings: 6

EGGS IN CREPE CUPS

Sensational presentation for a special brunch or luncheon

1 1/2 cups quick mixing flour
1 cup milk
1 cup plus 2 tablespoons cold water, divided
10 eggs, divided
1 teaspoon salt, divided
4 tablespoons melted butter

12 strips bacon, cooked crisp and crumbled
1/2 pound Monterey Jack pepper cheese, grated
1/4 teaspoon white pepper
1/4 cup sour cream
Cilantro or basil sprigs, for garnish

To make crepes, place flour in a medium mixing bowl; add milk, 1 cup water, 4 eggs, 1/2 teaspoon salt, and butter. Mix together with a whisk until well blended. Pour approximately 1/4 to 1/2 cup batter into a well-greased crepe pan to make 5-inch crepes. Cook until light brown on both sides. Cool crepes slightly. Place each crepe in a greased muffin cup, molding to fit the cup. The tops will stand up, or may be pinched and shaped attractively after filling the cups.

Preheat the oven to 350 degrees. Fill each crepe cup, layering with about a spoonful of bacon and a tablespoon of grated cheese. In a small bowl, beat 6 eggs with 2 tablespoons water; season with 1/2 teaspoon salt and pepper. Pour egg mixture into cups and top with a teaspoon of sour cream. Bake for 25 minutes, or until firm. Remove from oven and garnish with a cilantro or basil sprig. Place on serving dish and serve immediately.

Preparation Time: 35 to 40 minutes
Baking Time: 25 minutes
Yield: 12 1-cup servings

Robert Mondavi Brut Reserve Sparkling Wine

KIWI RELISH

Fresh, pretty, and distinctive with brunch and seafood entrees

4 kiwis, peeled and chopped
6 tablespoons chopped red onion
1 cup chopped pineapple, fresh or canned

Combine kiwis, onion, and pineapple to serve as a garnish.

Preparation Time: 5 minutes
Yield: 1 1/2 cups

ARTICHOKE SOUFFLE PIE

Pastry for 1 pie shell, unbaked
1/4 cup plus 1 tablespoon butter, divided
1/4 cup all-purpose flour
1 1/2 teaspoon dill weed
1/2 teaspoon salt
1/4 teaspoon pepper
1/4 teaspoon paprika
1 cup half-and-half or milk
1 1/2 cups shredded Monterey Jack cheese

2 14-ounce cans artichoke hearts,
 drained and quartered
1/4 cup chopped red bell pepper
1/4 cup sliced green onion
1 tablespoon butter
4 eggs, separated
1/2 teaspoon cream of tartar
Parmesan-chicken sauce,
 recipe follows

Preheat oven to 400 degrees. Place pastry dough into a 10-inch deep-dish pie plate; do not prick pastry. Bake for 10 minutes or until lightly brown. Remove crust and reduce oven to 300 degrees. In a medium saucepan, melt 1/4 cup butter. Blend in flour, dill weed, salt, pepper, and paprika. Place over medium heat and stir in milk, stirring constantly until mixture thickens and bubbles. Add cheese; remove from heat and stir until cheese is melted. Set aside. In a medium skillet, cook artichokes, pepper, and onions in 1 tablespoon butter until onion is tender. Drain; set aside.

In a large bowl, beat egg whites and cream of tartar with electric mixer on high speed until stiff peaks form. In a small bowl, beat egg yolks until eggs thicken and are lemon colored, about 5 minutes. Gradually beat cheese mixture into egg yolks. Gently fold yolk mixture into beaten egg whites. Spoon artichoke mixture into bottom of cooked pastry shell. Pour souffle mixture over artichoke mixture. Bake 45 to 55 minutes or until a knife inserted in center comes out clean. Serve immediately on individual plates. Spoon Parmesan-chicken sauce over each slice.

Preparation Time: 40 minutes
Baking Time: 45 to 55 minutes
Servings: 8

PARMESAN-CHICKEN SAUCE

3 tablespoons butter
3 tablespoons chopped green onion
2 tablespoons diced red bell pepper
3 tablespoons all-purpose flour
1/4 teaspoon salt

Dash white pepper
3/4 cup milk
1 cup chicken broth
1 1/2 cups diced cooked chicken
1/4 cup grated Parmesan cheese

In a saucepan, melt butter. Add onion and red pepper. Cook until tender. Blend in flour, salt, and pepper; stir in milk and chicken broth. Continue stirring until mixture thickens and bubbles. Stir in chicken and Parmesan cheese; heat through.

Preparation Time: 15 to 20 minutes
Yield: 3 1/2 cups

Vichon Chevrignon

ARTICHOKE HEART FRITTATA

Delicious! Serve for brunch or a light supper with fresh fruit and crusty French bread.

1 cup sliced frozen artichoke hearts,
   drained
2/3 cup chopped onion
2/3 cup chopped green or red bell pepper
1 cup chopped zucchini
1 teaspoon minced garlic
2 tablespoons vegetable oil
5 large eggs

1/3 cup milk
1/2 teaspoon salt
Dash pepper
1 1/2 cups soft bread cubes
1 8-ounce package cream cheese,
   cut in cubes
1 cup shredded Cheddar cheese

Preheat oven 350 degrees. Saute artichoke hearts, onion, peppers, zucchini, and garlic in the vegetable oil until tender crisp, about 5 minutes. In a mixing bowl, beat eggs with milk, salt, and pepper. Add the artichoke heart mixture, bread cubes, cream cheese cubes, and Cheddar cheese. Stir thoroughly but lightly, keeping cream cheese in cubes. Pour into a well-greased 9-inch pie plate. Bake for 45 minutes, or until frittata is set in the center and light brown. Cool 5 to 10 minutes before cutting into 6 wedges.

Preparation Time: 30 minutes
Baking Time: 45 minutes
Servings: 6

Robert Mondavi Brut Reserve Sparkling Wine

MUSHROOM AND ZUCCHINI TORTA

2 tablespoons vegetable oil
1 cup sliced fresh mushrooms
2/3 cup chopped onion
2/3 cup chopped zucchini
2/3 cup chopped green bell pepper
1 teaspoon minced garlic
5 eggs

1/3 cup light cream
Salt and pepper, to taste
1 1/2 cups fresh bread crumbs
1 8-ounce package cream cheese,
   cut into 1/2-inch cubes
1 cup shredded Cheddar cheese

Preheat oven to 350 degrees. In a saute pan, combine the oil, mushrooms, onion, zucchini, green pepper and garlic; cook stirring until tender but still crisp, about 5 minutes. In a large bowl, beat together the eggs, cream, salt, and pepper. Stir in the mushroom mixture, bread crumbs, cream cheese cubes, and Cheddar cheese; blend thoroughly, but lightly, so cream cheese cubes remain intact. Pour into a lightly greased 9 or 10-inch pie plate. Bake for 45 minutes, or until set and browned. Cool 5 to 10 minutes before cutting into wedges.

Preparation Time: 25 minutes
Baking Time: 45 minutes
Servings: 6 to 8

Robert Mondavi Pinot Noir

EGGPLANT AND MUSHROOM FRITTATA

2 tablespoons olive oil
2 cloves garlic, minced
1/3 cup chopped green onions,
   include tops
5 medium zucchini, thinly sliced
1 unpeeled eggplant, thinly sliced
3/4 pound mushrooms, thinly sliced

3 eggs
1 teaspoon Italian seasoning
1 teaspoon salt
1/2 teaspoon freshly ground pepper
3 cups grated Monterey Jack cheese
1 cup freshly grated Parmesan cheese
Lemon-Cheese sauce, recipe follows

Preheat oven to 350 degrees. Heat the olive oil in a large skillet and saute garlic until limp. Add onions, zucchini, eggplant and mushrooms. Saute, turning with a wooden spoon for about 6 to 7 minutes. Drain mixture.

Beat eggs until frothy. Add Italian seasoning, salt and pepper, combining well. Add eggs to vegetable mixture. Pour into a 13 x 9-inch baking dish. Cover with Monterey Jack cheese and sprinkle with Parmesan cheese. Bake for 40 minutes. Serve with lemon-cheese sauce.

Preparation Time: 20 to 30 minutes
Baking Time: 40 minutes
Servings: 12

LEMON-CHEESE SAUCE

4 tablespoons butter, or margarine
3/4 cup half-and-half, divided
1 egg
1/4 teaspoon salt
1/3 teaspoon freshly ground pepper

3 tablespoons freshly grated
   Parmesan cheese
1/4 teaspoon nutmeg
4 tablespoons fresh lemon juice

In a large saucepan, melt butter and add all but 2 tablespoons of the half-and-half. Cook over low heat for 5 minutes; remove from heat and set aside. In a bowl, beat together egg, salt, pepper, and remaining 2 tablespoons cream. Add the Parmesan cheese and nutmeg, stirring constantly with a wire whisk; slowly add the lemon juice. Combine the two mixtures and cook over medium heat, stirring until thickened. The sauce should coat the back of a spoon at the desired consistency.

Preparation Time: 10 to 15 minutes   Robert Mondavi Woodbridge Zinfandel
Sauce Yield: 1 1/2 cups

BASIL AND HAM STRATA

A new twist on a classic egg and cheese dish—a wonderful choice for a special breakfast for overnight guests.

1 cup milk	3 ripe tomatoes, sliced, and seeded
1/2 cup dry white wine	1/2 pound Monterey Jack cheese,
1 loaf French bread, cut into	thinly sliced
1/2-inch slices	4 eggs, beaten
1 8-ounce package thinly sliced ham	Salt and freshly ground black pepper,
2 bunches fresh basil leaves	to taste
3 tablespoons extra virgin olive oil	1/4 to 1/2 cup heavy cream

One day before serving, mix the milk and wine in a shallow bowl. Dip bread slices, one at a time, into the milk mixture and squeeze liquid back into the bowl without tearing the bread. In a buttered 12-inch oval or round au gratin or souffle dish, arrange the bread in an overlapping layer; cover with sliced ham and basil leaves which have been dipped in olive oil. Continue layering with tomato slices and cheese. Repeat layers, ending with the tomatoes. Beat the eggs with salt and pepper and pour evenly over the layers; cover with plastic wrap and refrigerate overnight.

The next morning, remove the dish from the refrigerator and let it stand 1 hour to reach room temperature. Preheat oven to 350 degrees. Drizzle the top with the cream and bake, uncovered, until puffy and browned, about 45 minutes. Serve warm.

Robert Mondavi Chardonnay Reserve Sparkling Wine

Preparation Time: 15 minutes plus 1 hour standing time
Chilling Time: Overnight
Baking Time: 45 minutes to 1 hour
Servings: 6

SPRING HAM AND SPINACH ROLL

1/4 cup plus 2 tablespoons butter,
   melted, divided
2 10-ounce packages frozen chopped
   spinach, cooked, and squeezed dry
3/4 cup chopped onion, divided
2 teaspoons salt, divided
Dash pepper
1/2 teaspoon nutmeg, divided
1 slice white bread crust removed,
   broken in pieces, and soaked in milk

6 eggs, dividing yolks; four in 1 cup,
2 in another, reserving egg whites
Pinch cream of tartar
1 teaspoon lemon juice
Pinch cayenne pepper
1/2 pound chopped mushrooms
3 tablespoons extra virgin olive oil
6 ham slices
1/2 cup grated Swiss cheese

Prepare a 11 x 15-inch jelly roll pan, lining with greased parchment or waxed paper. Preheat oven to 350 degrees. In a large bowl, combine 2 tablespoons melted butter, spinach, 1/4 cup onions, 1 1/2 teaspoons salt, pepper, 1/4 teaspoon nutmeg, bread, and 4 slightly beaten egg yolks. Mix well. In another bowl beat 6 egg whites, 1/2 teaspoon salt, and cream of tartar until stiff. Fold into spinach mixture. Using a rubber spatula, spread evenly in the prepared pan. Bake for 15 to 18 minutes, or until firm.

In a food processor, blend the remaining 2 egg yolks; add the lemon juice, 1/2 teaspoon salt, and cayenne pepper; keeping the processor running, slowly add 1/4 cup melted butter. Set aside.

In a saute pan, combine the mushrooms, onion, and olive oil. Saute until onions are translucent. Season with salt and add remaining 1/4 teaspoon nutmeg; add the seasoned egg mixture.

When the roll mixture is cooked, invert onto buttered sheet of foil and remove the parchment or waxed paper. Place ham slices on the roll, sprinkle with the Swiss cheese and spread the mushroom filling on top and roll up in jelly-roll fashion. Place roll, seam-side down, in pan and return to oven for 10 to 15 minutes, or until heated through.

Note: This roll can be refrigerated and the final heating completed just before serving time. Heating time will need to be longer.

Preparation Time: 1 hour
Baking Time: 25 to 35 minutes
Servings: 12 to 14

Robert Mondavi Chardonnay

CHILE RELLENO CASSEROLE

1 7-ounce can diced green chilies
1 7-ounce can green chili salsa
1/2 pound Monterey Jack cheese, grated
3/4 pound Cheddar cheese, grated
2 eggs

1/2 teaspoon salt
1 tablespoon flour
1 teaspoon ground cumin
1 cup evaporated milk

Preheat oven to 375 degrees. Combine diced chilies and chili salsa. Pour 1/2 of this mixture into an 8 x 8-inch baking dish. Top with both cheeses and cover with remaining chili mixture. Beat eggs with salt, flour, cumin, and milk. Pour egg mixture over the cheese-covered chilies. Bake, uncovered, for 35 to 40 minutes. Watch that casserole does not burn.

Note: This dish can be made an hour ahead of serving time.

Preparation Time: 20 minutes
Baking Time: 35 to 40 minutes
Servings: 6

SANGRIA

Especially nice with brunch or luncheon

1 large orange, thinly sliced
1/4 cup sugar
1 4/5-quart bottle Robert Mondavi
  Woodbridge Cabernet Sauvignon

2 cups fresh orange juice
1/2 cup Cointreau, or favorite
  orange liqueur
Orange slices, for garnish

In a large pitcher, stir together the orange slices and sugar. Add wine, orange juice, and Cointreau, blending well. Cover and chill. Serve over ice and garnish with orange.

Preparation Time: 10 minutes
Servings: 8 to 10

FROZEN BANANA SMOOTHY

1 banana, chopped
1 cup orange juice

Choice of 1/4 cup fruit

Peel and freeze banana in a ziplock bag. Combine frozen banana, orange juice, and another fruit such as peach, nectarine, fresh pineapple or berries. Put in blender and blend to desired consistency.

Preparation Time: 5 minutes
Servings: 1 or 2

THE CENTER'S TRIATHLON

Each year, the Orange County Performing Arts Center Triathlon attracts top athletes from around the world to a grueling endurance race in three sports: swimming, cycling, and running. Now recognized as one of the premier triathlons in the nation, the race, staged at Lake Mission Viejo, draws hundreds of participants and huge crowds of spectators.

More than a thousand volunteers from a cross-section of the community administer this event in support of The Center's ongoing activities. The festivities surrounding the race are almost an event in themselves. The Guilds sponsor a kick-off luncheon and a musical "Informance" for supporters of the Triathlon. Volunteers are recognized at a huge rally. A fitness expo is held along with athlete registration. More than a mere fundraiser, the Triathlon has become an opportunity each year for a cross-section of the community to work side by side, hour by hour, for a common purpose. The smiles on the faces of tired, but proud and satisfied volunteers after a successful race is one of the real rewards of the day.

Not a race for the faint of heart, the Mazda/Orange County Performing Arts Center Triathlon is a three-part test of skill and endurance as top athletes from around the world swim, cycle, and run in this international competition in picturesque Mission Viejo.

Who can resist a stroll on the beach with the sun shining on the water, the sea gulls and pelicans swooping the sea to catch their dinners, and the waves crashing on the shore? If you are lucky you may see some whales at play. Orange County's greatest bounty is its beaches, miles of picture-perfect coastline under a sunlit, deep blue sky.

SALADS

Some of Orange County's finest dining experiences are on the water. An assortment of fresh, flavorful salads could not have a prettier backdrop than the bay, the picturesque boats and homes, the blue sky, and the Newport Beach skyline.

FIELD SALAD WITH TOASTED WALNUTS

1/2 pound large white mushrooms, stemmed

1 tablespoon fresh lemon juice

1 tablespoon Dijon mustard

1/2 teaspoon salt, divided

1 teaspoon freshly ground pepper, divided

1/4 cup plus 1 1/2 teaspoons peanut oil

1 1/2 cups walnut pieces, approximately 6 ounces

1 1/2 tablespoons unsalted butter, melted

1/4 cup plus 2 tablespoons extra virgin olive oil

1 1/2 tablespoons red wine vinegar

6 ounces Roquefort or blue cheese, crumbled

9 cups mixed greens

Slice the mushroom caps horizontally about 1/4-inch thick. Stack the slices and cut them into 1/4-inch sticks. In a medium bowl, combine lemon juice, mustard, 1/4 teaspoon salt and 1/2 teaspoon pepper. With a fork, beat in peanut oil. Add mushrooms and toss to combine. Refrigerate. In a medium-size bowl, stir together olive oil, vinegar, remaining salt and pepper.

Preheat oven to 350 degrees. Toss walnuts with the melted butter and place on a baking sheets. Sprinkle with a pinch of salt and bake until golden brown, about 10 minutes. Cool.

Just before serving, put the greens in a large bowl and toss with the dressing. Arrange the salad on individual serving plates. Spoon equal amounts of the mushrooms in the center of each salad; scatter the walnuts and cheese over the top.

Note: This salad also makes a nice presentation served buffet style in a large serving bowl with a small bowl of nuts on the side.

Preparation Time: 30 minutes
Servings: 12 to 14

PECAN AND ROQUEFORT SALAD

1/3 cup sugar
1/4 cup unsalted butter
1/4 cup orange juice
1 1/2 teaspoon salt
1 1/4 teaspoon cinnamon
1/4 to 1/2 teaspoon cayenne pepper
1/4 teaspoon ground mace

2 cups pecan halves
2 heads Boston lettuce
2 6-ounce packages Roquefort cheese,
    crumbled
1 medium red onion, thinly sliced
3 green onions, thinly sliced
Raspberry vinaigrette, recipe follows

Preheat oven to 250 degrees. Line 15 x 10-inch jelly roll pan with foil. In a heavy sauce pan over low heat, combine and heat sugar, butter, orange juice, salt, cinnamon, cayenne pepper and mace until butter melts and sugar is dissolved. Increase heat to medium. Add nuts and toss until well coated. Spread nuts in a single layer on the foil-lined pan. Bake one hour, stirring every 15 minutes. Transfer nuts to another large sheet of foil. Separate nuts with a fork. Cool completely. Place lettuce, cheese, and onions in a salad bowl and chill. At serving time, toss all ingredients together.

Note: The cayenne-flavored nuts in this recipe may be stored in the refrigerator in an airtight container approximately one month. Bring to room temperature before serving. If nuts are sticky, bake on foil-lined pan at 250 degrees until crisp, approximately 20 minutes. These nuts are good as appetizers, too.

Preparation Time: 15 to 20 minutes
Baking Time: 1 hour
Servings: 8

RASPBERRY VINAIGRETTE

1/2 cup olive oil
3 tablespoons raspberry vinegar
1 tablespoon minced shallots

1/4 teaspoon salt
1/8 teaspoon white pepper

Combine oil, vinegar, shallots, salt and pepper, stirring until well blended.

Preparation Time: 5 minutes
Yield: 3/4 cup

SPINACH GREENS WITH FONTINA CHEESE

This spinach salad receives so many plaudits, you will serve it over and over again.

8 cups torn fresh spinach, cleaned,
   stemmed, and chilled
1 cup watercress, washed and chilled
Red wine dressing, chilled,
   recipe follows
1/4 cup olive oil

1/2 cup fine dry bread crumbs
2 teaspoons dried Italian seasonings,
   crushed
8 ounces Fontina cheese,
   cut into 16 wedges

Prepare salad greens and dressing and chill, separately, for several hours. At serving time, preheat broiler. Pour 1/4 cup olive oil into small shallow bowl. In another bowl combine bread crumbs and Italian seasoning. Dip each wedge of cheese in olive oil and roll in bread crumbs. Place cheese wedges on cool baking sheet. Do not let sides of cheese touch. Broil about 3 inches from heat for approximately 2 minutes or until brown and slightly softened. Do not overcook. Toss greens with dressing and place on 8 chilled salad plates. Place 2 warm cheese wedges on top the greens and serve at once.

Preparation Time: 25 minutes
Servings: 8

RED WINE DRESSING

1/4 cup olive oil
1/4 cup dry red wine
1 tablespoon lemon juice
1/2 teaspoon garlic powder

2 teaspoons Dijon mustard
1 teaspoon sugar
Salt and pepper, to taste

Combine all dressing ingredients and chill for several hours.

Preparation Time: 5 minutes
Chilling Time: 2 hours
Yield: 1/2 cup

GREENS WITH BAKED GOAT CHEESE AND ORANGES

1 3-ounce log of fresh goat cheese
1/2 cup olive oil
Salt, to taste
1 teaspoon dried thyme or oregano
1 cup dry bread crumbs

4 to 6 cups assorted garden lettuces
2 small oranges, peeled and sliced
1/4 cup sliced shitake mushrooms
Orange vinaigrette, recipe follows

Preheat oven to 400 degrees. Slice goat cheese into 1/4 to 1/2-inch thick rounds and place in a mixture of olive oil, salt, and thyme. Marinate for several hours or overnight. Roll in fine dry bread crumbs. Place cheese slices on a baking dish or cookie sheet. Bake in oven for about 5 to 6 minutes, until lightly heated through, but not melted.

Meanwhile, toss lettuces and mushrooms with orange slices and orange vinaigrette to lightly coat. Arrange on salad plates. Place the cheese in the center of the salad.

Preparation Time: 20 minutes
Serves: 8

ORANGE VINAIGRETTE

Juice of 2 oranges
Juice of 1 lemon
1/2 cup salad oil,
    or 1/4 cup salad oil
    and 1/4 cup olive oil

1 teaspoon salt
Freshly ground pepper
2 teaspoons vinegar
Zest of 1 orange

Combine orange juice and lemon juice. Blend with a whisk while adding oil, salt, pepper, and vinegar. Taste for seasoning. Add orange zest.

Preparation Time: 5 minutes
Yield: 1 cup

BACON AND CHIVE POTATO SALAD

6 cups quartered, unpeeled red potatoes
1/4 cup mayonnaise, sour cream
   or yogurt
2 tablespoons stone ground mustard
8 slices bacon, crisply cooked
   and crumbled

1/4 cup chopped chives
1 head butter lettuce, washed and dried
1 head radicchio leaves, washed and dried
1/4 cup chopped parlsey or chives

Place potatoes in boiling water, cook 15 minutes or until tender. Drain. Combine mayonnaise and mustard in large bowl. Add potatoes, bacon, and chives, mixing lightly. Refrigerate.

At serving time, arrange a border of alternating lettuce and radicchio leaves on a serving plate or in a bowl. Mound salad on the leaves and sprinkle with parsley.

Preparation Time: 20 minutes
Servings: 6

SALAD NICOISE

2 boiled potatoes, peeled and cubed
2 cups green beans, canned
   or fresh cooked beans
1 6-ounce can pitted black olives
Fresh onion rings, to taste
Italian, or garlic dressing, of choice
1 clove garlic, split
4 servings of salad greens

1/2 cup freshly chopped parsley
4 Roma tomatoes, cut in wedges
1 6-ounce can water-packed tuna, flaked
2 hard-boiled eggs, quartered
Anchovies, optional
Salt, to taste
Coarse-ground pepper, to taste

Combine potatoes, beans, olives, and onion rings in a bowl and toss with enough dressing to coat well. Set aside to marinate 2 to 4 hours at room temperature, or refrigerate overnight.

At serving time, rub a large bowl with garlic; add torn salad greens. Pour marinated vegetables over lettuce. Garnish with parsley, tomatoes, tuna, eggs, and anchovies. Sprinkle with salt and pepper. Toss salad at table, adding more dressing, if desired.

Preparation Time: 20 minutes
Marinating Time: 2 to 4 hours, or overnight
Servings: 4

CRYSTAL COVE COLESLAW

This is the perfect salad to take along to a barbecue or tailgate party. It may be prepared some hours ahead and chilled.

1 small head cabbage, shredded
1/4 cup chopped green onions
1/2 cup raisins
1 medium zucchini, shredded
1 to 2 medium carrots, shredded
1 cup mayonnaise, or less

Salt and pepper, to taste
Curry powder, to taste
1/2 cup dry roasted peanuts
2 tablespoons fresh chopped parsley,
   for garnish

Combine all ingredients except for the peanuts and parsley. At serving time, toss with peanuts. Place in a glass bowl for a pretty presentation and sprinkle with chopped parsley.

Preparation Time: 15 minutes
Servings: 8

FRESH ASPARAGUS SALAD

Here is another way to use that beautiful plant grown in the fields of Irvine!

2 pounds fresh asparagus
Yogurt salad dressing, recipe follows

Wash and trim asparagus. Put in a pan; cover with water and set aside for 10 minutes. Drain. Steam asparagus until tender but still crisp. Rinse immediately in cold water, drain, and pat dry. Refrigerate. This may be done a day ahead. To serve, arrange asparagus on a buffet platter, or individually on serving plates. Drizzle with dressing, or serve the dressing on the side.

Preparation Time: 20 minutes
Servings: 8 to 10

LIGHT YOGURT DRESSING

1 cup plain yogurt
1/4 cup mayonnaise
4 tablespoons Dijon mustard

2 tablespoons chopped fresh dill
2 teaspoons chopped fresh chives

Whisk all ingredients until well blended.

Preparation Time: 5 minutes
Yield: 1 1/4 cups

ARTICHOKE AND HEARTS OF PALM SALAD

1 6-ounce jar marinated artichoke hearts,
 reserve liquid
1 8-ounce can hearts of palm, drained
1/2 cup chopped green onions
1/2 cup cooked, crisp bacon
4 tablespoons finely chopped fresh parsley

4 medium sized garlic cloves, minced
6 to 8 ounces bleu cheese, crumbled
3 tablespoons lemon juice
Salt and pepper, to taste
Salad oil
2 heads romaine lettuce

Finely chop artichoke hearts and hearts of palm. Combine with green onions, bacon, parsley, garlic, bleu cheese, lemon juice, salt and pepper. To reserved marinade, add enough oil to make 8 tablespoons; add to vegetable mixture, combining well. These ingredients can be prepared ahead and refrigerated. Clean and tear romaine into pieces. At serving time, toss all ingredients together and serve on chilled plates.

Preparation Time: 30 minutes
Servings: 8 to 10

ZESTY EGGPLANT SALAD

2 medium eggplants, about 2 pounds
4 Roma tomatoes, seeded and
 coarsely chopped
1/2 cup minced red onion
1/4 cup walnuts, lightly toasted and
 coarsely chopped
1 clove garlic, minced
3 tablespoons lemon juice

2 teaspoons olive oil
1 tablespoon minced parsley
1 tablespoon minced fresh cilantro
3/4 teaspoon ground cumin
1/2 teaspoon paprika
1/4 teaspoon tumeric
Cilantro leaves, for garnish

Preheat oven to 400 degrees. Trim eggplants and cut in half lengthwise. Place on a cookie sheet, cut side down, and bake 45 minutes or until soft to the touch. Remove from oven and cool. Remove the pulp and chop coarsely. Place in a large bowl. Add tomatoes, onion, walnuts, garlic, lemon juice, oil, parsley, cilantro, cumin, paprika, and tumeric. Stir well to combine. Cover and chill. Garnish with cilantro just before serving.

Note: For best results, make this salad a day ahead.

Preparation Time: 1 hour
Chilling Time: 2 hours, or overnight
Servings: 6

Byron Pinot Noir

PARSLEY SALAD

Thanks to Gustaf Anders for donating this popular recipe. Garlic lovers will especially enjoy this unusual and delicious winter salad.

2 cups Italian parsley leaves
2 cups regular parsley leaves
4 ounces sun-dried tomatoes, chopped
1 cup grated Parmesan cheese

1 tablespoon minced fresh garlic
4 teaspoons Worcestershire sauce
Basil dressing, recipe follows

Make dressing and refrigerate. Toss together all ingredients except salad dressing. Drizzle with just enough dressing to moisten and flavor salad. Serve on individual salad plates.

Preparation Time: 10 minutes
Servings: 4

BASIL DRESSING

1 bunch fresh basil
2 whole shallots
2 garlic cloves
1 cup extra virgin olive oil

1/3 cup seasoned rice vinegar
Salt, to taste
White pepper, to taste

Put all ingredients in a blender and puree until smooth. Store in the refrigerator.

Preparation Time: 5 minutes
Yield: 1 1/4 cups

WATERCRESS AND ORANGE SALAD

2 heads butter lettuce
1 cup watercress leaves, washed
2 oranges, peeled and cut in segments
2 ripe avocados, peeled and sliced

3/4 cup slivered almonds, toasted
Spicy vinaigrette dressing, chilled,
  recipe follows

Prepare dressing. Wash lettuce, tear into bite-size pieces, and chill. At serving time, combine lettuce, watercress, orange segments, and avocado. Toss with desired amount of dressing. Sprinkle with the almonds.

Note: Canned Mandarin oranges are another choice in place of the fresh oranges.

Preparation Time: 15 minutes
Servings: 8

SPICY VINAIGRETTE

1/3 cup sugar
1/4 cup red wine vinegar
1 1/2 teaspoon lemon juice
1/4 cup olive oil
2 teaspoons chili sauce

1/2 teaspoon Worcestershire sauce
1/2 teaspoon dry mustard
1/4 teaspoon curry powder
4 to 5 dashes hot pepper sauce
1 clove garlic, crushed

Combine dressing ingredients and chill several hours. Shake well before serving.

Preparation Time: 5 minutes
Chilling Time: 3 hours or more
Yield: 1 cup

SPINACH AND STRAWBERRY PATCH SALAD

2 bunches fresh spinach, washed and
    dried
1 pint fresh strawberries, washed,
    stemmed, and halved

1/2 cup thinly sliced red onion, optional
Salad dressing of choice,
    recipe choices follow

In a salad bowl, toss all ingredients including salad dressing; or, arrange spinach, strawberries, and onions attractively on individual serving plates and drizzle with the dressing. Serve immediately.

Note: Diced avocados or other fruit can be substituted for the strawberries.

Preparation Time: 20 minutes
Servings: 6 to 8

CARMEN DRAGON DRESSING

1/2 cup sugar
2 tablespoons sesame seeds
1 tablespoon poppy seeds
1 1/2 teaspoons minced onions

1/4 teaspoon Worcestershire sauce
1/4 teaspoon paprika
1/2 cup vegetable oil
1/4 cup cider vinegar

Place sugar, sesame seeds, poppy seeds, onion, Worcestershire sauce and paprika in food processor or blender. With machine running, add oil and vinegar in a slow, steady stream until thoroughly mixed and thickened. Chill before serving.

Preparation Time: 5 to 10 minutes
Yield: 1 cup

CREAMY POPPY SEED DRESSING

1/2 cup mayonnaise
1 tablespoon white wine vinegar
1 tablespoon lemon juice

1/3 cup sugar
1/4 cup milk
1 tablespoon poppy seeds

Whisk all ingredients together until well blended.

Preparation Time: 5 minutes
Yield: 1 1/3 cups

PANTRY FRUIT SALAD

1 20-ounce can peach pie filling
1 16-ounce can mandarin oranges, drained
1 20-ounce can pineapple chunks, drained
3 bananas, sliced

1 16-ounce container fresh strawberries
  or raspberries
Yogurt or sour cream, for garnish
Zest of 1 orange, for garnish

Combine pie filling, oranges, and pineapple the night before serving. When ready to serve, add bananas and berries. Top with a dollop of yogurt or sour cream. Add orange zest.

Preparation Time: 10 minutes
Chilling Time: Overnight
Servings: 8

MESCLUN AND PEAR SALAD

Mesclun is a mixture of very young and tender greens. It may include arugula, nasturtium, mache, chervil, dandelion, oakleaf lettuce and herbs.

2 ripe pears, peeled, cored, and sliced
2 tablespoons lemon juice
3/4 to 1 pound mesclun, washed and dried

Balsamic vinaigrette, recipe follows
4 ounces bleu cheese

Sprinkle pear slices with lemon juice. Toss the greens with just enough of the vinaigrette to coat well. Serve greens on individual plates garnished with pear slices and crumbled bleu cheese.

Note: Other ingredients which may be used in this salad are celery, croutons, green onions, walnuts, and green grapes.

Preparation Time: 15 minutes
Servings: 6

BALSAMIC VINAIGRETTE

1 tablespoon red wine vinegar
2 tablespoons balsamic vinegar
Salt and freshly ground pepper, to taste

2 tablespoons olive oil
3 to 4 tablespoons salad oil

Whisk all ingredients until well blended.

Preparation Time: 5 minutes
Yield: 3/4 cup

SUMMER FRUIT SALAD

Very good and very pretty. A dessert or salad that is tasty with or without the dressing.

1/2 cup water
1/2 cup lime juice
1/2 cup sugar, or to taste
1 large banana, sliced diagonally
1 pint blueberries, divided
2 large nectarines, sliced
1 pint strawberries, stemmed, and halved

1 cup watermelon balls
1 cup seedless green grapes
1 kiwi, peeled, and sliced
Dark sweet cherries with stems,
   for garnish, optional
Creamy lime-honey dressing,
   chilled, recipe follows

Prepare creamy lime-honey dressing and chill. In a small bowl, combine water, lime juice, and sugar, stirring until sugar dissolves; add banana slices and set aside.

Set aside 1/2 cup blueberries. In a large glass bowl, add layers of blueberries, nectarines, and strawberries. Reserving banana syrup, continue layering with bananas, watermelon balls, grapes, the reserved blueberries, kiwi, and cherries. Pour banana syrup over all of the fruit. Cover, loosely, and refrigerate.

Note: You may refrigerate tightly covered leftovers up to 3 days.

Preparation Time: 30 minutes
Servings: 6 to 8

CREAMY LIME-HONEY DRESSING

1 cup sour cream
1/2 cup cottage cheese

1/4 cup lime juice
2 tablespoons honey

In food processor, mix sour cream and cottage cheese until smooth. Stir in lime juice and honey. Chill before serving.

Preparation Time: 5 minutes
Yield: 2 cups

PAPAYA AND CRAB SALAD

1 cup peeled and sliced papaya
12 ounces crabmeat or imitation
   crabmeat, squeezed dry
1/2 cup chopped celery
1/4 cup chopped red bell pepper
1/2 to 1 head iceberg lettuce, shredded
1/2 cup chopped Macadamia nuts

1/2 cup mayonnaise
1/2 teaspoon lemon peel
2 tablespoons lemon juice
1 tablespoon chopped chives
1/4 teaspoon pepper
Pinch of dried red pepper

Combine papaya, crabmeat, celery, red pepper, lettuce, and nuts in a salad bowl. Refrigerate. In a small bowl, combine mayonnaise, lemon peel, lemon juice, chives, and pepper seasonings. Refrigerate. Just before serving, toss well.

Preparation Time: 20 minutes
Servings: 4

Byron Sauvignon Blanc

JICAMA, ORANGE, AND RED ONION SALAD

1 head of romaine lettuce
1 1/2 pounds jicama, peeled and
   cut in paper-thin circular slices

6 seedless oranges, peeled and thinly sliced
2 red onions, sliced in thin rings
Orange-lime dressing, recipe follows

Line shallow bowl with lettuce. Alternate circles of jicama, orange and onion over top. Cover and refrigerate. Can be prepared 3 hours ahead. Just before serving, add dressing to salad and toss well.

Preparation Time: 15 minutes
Servings: 12

ORANGE-LIME DRESSING

1/2 cup olive oil
1/3 cup fresh lime juice
3 tablespoons red wine vinegar

3 tablespoons orange marmalade
1 teaspoon salt
Freshly ground pepper

Combine all ingredients in a container and shake well.

Preparation Time: 5 minutes
Yield: 1 cup

LIDO ISLE SEAFOOD SALAD

This elegant salad is best served very cold.

3 cups crab meat or fish pieces, cooked
3 cups small shrimp, cooked and shelled
5 green onions, minced, both green
  and white parts
1 cup diced pineapple
1 papaya, diced
1 cup diced jicama
2/3 cup Spanish peanuts or pine nuts
1/3 cup raisins
2 mangos, diced
Juice of 2 lemons

Juice of 1 lime
Zest from 1 lemon
Salt, to taste
Coconut salad dressing to taste,
  recipe follows
16 large lettuce leaves
2 tomatoes, each cut into 8 wedges
8 large shrimp, cooked and cleaned,
  for garnish
8 olives, of choice for garnish

Toss all ingredients except lettuce leaves, tomato wedges, large shrimp, and olives, reserving 3/4 cup dressing for garnish Set aside for 15 minutes.

Line 8 salad plates, or serving sea shells, with lettuce leaves. Spoon equal portions of salad into lettuce. Put a dollop of reserved dressing on top and garnish each with two tomato wedges, one large shrimp, and an olive.

Preparation Time: 1 hour
Servings: 8

COCONUT SALAD DRESSING

1/2 cup canned coconut
1/2 cup milk
1/2 cup cream
2 3/4 cups mayonnaise

1 cup sour cream
5 tablespoons curry powder
1/2 tablespoon salt

Put coconut and milk in blender or food processor. On high setting, process for 2 minutes. Add mayonnaise, sour cream, curry powder and salt; process for 15 seconds.

Preparation Time: 5 minutes
Yield: 5 1/2 cups

Robert Mondavi Chenin Blanc

BAY SHRIMP AND VEGETABLE SALAD

2 10-ounce packages petite peas, thawed
4 cups bay shrimp, cooked and drained
1 cup diced celery
1/2 cup chopped green onion, including
   some tops
1 6-ounce can sliced water chestnuts,
   drained
1 cup crisp cooked, crumbled bacon
2 6-ounce jars marinated artichoke hearts,
   drained and chopped

1 cup salted cashews
1 box cherry tomatoes
1/2 cup sliced radishes
1 head lettuce, shredded
1/2 small head purple cabbage,
   shredded
1 15-ounce can crispy Chinese
   noodles
Lemon cream dressing, recipe follows

Salad ingredients, except lettuce and cabbage, can be prepared 24 hours ahead and refrigerated in individual, sealed containers. When ready to serve, combine all ingredients with the desired amount of dressing in a large bowl.

Note: Chicken may be substituted for the bay shrimp.

Preparation Time: 30 minutes
Servings: 12

Robert Mondavi Chardonnay

LEMON CREAM DRESSING

1 cup sour cream
1 1/2 cups mayonnaise
2 tablespoons lemon juice

3 tablespoons fresh, chopped parsley
1/2 teaspoon paprika
Salt and pepper, to taste

Combine dressing ingredients and refrigerate.

Preparation Time: 5 to 10 minutes
Yield: 2 1/2 cups

CENTER STAGE LOBSTER SALAD

Oriental salads are popular in Orange County. Here is an elegant recipe.

1 to 2 tablespoons unsalted butter
1 pound uncooked lobster meat, diced
Dash of brandy
1/2 red cabbage, shredded
1 head iceberg lettuce, shredded
1 cup diced jicama
1/2 cup sesame seeds, toasted

1 3-ounce package slivered almonds, toasted
3 green onions, diced
1 package uncooked Oriental noodle soup mix, noodles only
Salt and pepper, to taste
Sweet and sour dressing, of choice

Melt butter in skillet, being careful not to burn; add diced lobster meat. Cook quickly on all sides. When all liquid has evaporated, remove from heat; add brandy and flame. When brandy is burned off, set aside.

In a bowl, toss cabbage, lettuce, jicama, sesame seeds, almonds, green onions, and crumbled noodles. Add lobster and dressing. Toss well and serve.

Note: Chicken or crab may be substituted for the lobster.

Preparation Time: 30 minutes
Servings: 8

Robert Mondavi Chardonnay

CAESAR SALAD DRESSING

A crisp Caesar salad is one of the most popular salads in restaurants in Orange County. Here is a wonderful Caesar salad dressing.

1 cup olive oil
1/2 cup fresh lemon juice
1 3-ounce can anchovies, drained
1 teaspoon Dijon mustard
1 teaspoon Worcestershire sauce

8 large cloves garlic, peeled
1/2 teaspoon fresh ground pepper
Tabasco to taste
Parmesan cheese

In a blender, whirl all ingredients together, adding enough Parmesan cheese to thicken.

Preparation Time: 10 minutes
Yield: 2 cups

CRACKED WHEAT SALAD

1 cup cracked wheat or bulgar wheat
1 3/4 cup chicken broth
1 cup chopped parsley
3/4 cup chopped onion
1/4 cup chopped mint
2 tomatoes, seeded and diced
4 basil leaves
1/2 cup lemon juice
1/4 cup olive oil

1 tablespoon balsamic vinegar
Salt and pepper, to taste
1 cup cooked and diced meat, of choice
1/2 cup cooked vegetables, of choice
1/2 cup diced celery or cucumber
1 avocado, peeled, seeded, and diced
8 radicchio or butter lettuce leaves,
   cup shaped

Combine cracked wheat and chicken broth in a quart-sized sauce pan. Cover and cook for 30 minutes. Drain and cool. Combine remaining ingredients with the bulgar, except for the lettuce leaf cups, and refrigerate for 2 hours. Serve on lettuce cups.

Note: Leftover beef, chicken, or pork may be used. It is fun to eat this salad in lettuce leaves like a taco.

Preparation Time: 1 hour
Refrigeration Time: 2 hours
Servings: 8

Byron Chardonnay

LIGHT COUSCOUS SALAD

1 1/2 cups couscous
1 1/2 cups boiling water
1 cup carrots, diced
1 green or red bell pepper, diced
1 cup frozen peas
1/2 cup green onions, chopped
2/3 cup currants

1/2 cup slivered almonds, toasted
1/2 cup vegetable oil
1/4 cup lemon juice
1/2 teaspoon ground cinnamon
3 tablespoons orange juice
1/4 cup chopped parsley
Salt, to taste

Pour boiling water over couscous. Cover and let sit 10 minutes. Fluff with fork to separate grains. Stir in carrots, sweet pepper, peas, onions, currants, and almonds. Whisk together oil, lemon juice, cinnamon, orange juice, and parsley. Pour over couscous and vegetables and mix well. Season to taste with salt. Chill overnight, or at least 1 hour.

Preparation Time: 25 minutes
Servings: 6 to 8

TABOULI SALAD

Thanks to Hans Loeschl, Executive Chef at the Westin South Coast Plaza, for sharing this recipe for The Guilds cookbook.

1 cup whole wheat
24 uncooked shrimp
1/2 cup chopped green zucchini
1/2 cup chopped carrots

1/2 cup chopped jicama
Sesame seeds
1/2 pound assorted baby lettuce
Oriental dressing, to taste, recipe follows

Cook whole wheat until soft and set aside. Blanch shrimp in salt water and chill. Make oriental dressing and set aside. In a mixing bowl, combine whole wheat, shrimp, vegetables, and sesame seeds. Add dressing to coat salad and serve immediately.

Preparation Time: 40 minutes
Servings: 4

ORIENTAL DRESSING

1 teaspoon minced fresh ginger
1/2 cup soy sauce
1 tablespoon plum sauce
2 sprigs chopped fresh tarragon
1 clove garlic, minced

1 egg, slightly beaten, optional
1 cup vegetable oil
1/2 cup sesame oil
Salt, to taste
Sugar, to taste

In a mixing bowl, combine ginger, soy sauce, plum sauce, tarragon, garlic, and egg. Whisk in the vegetable oil and sesame oil. Season with salt and sugar.

Preparation Time: 15 minutes
Yield: 2 cups

ORZO PASTA SALAD WITH SUN-DRIED TOMATOES

This salad is perfect to take to a picnic or a pot luck party.

6 cups orzo pasta
3 cloves garlic, peeled
1 teaspoon salt
1 teaspoon ground black pepper
1 tablespoon Dijon mustard
6 tablespoons balsamic vinegar
1 cup olive oil

2 cups sun-dried tomatoes in oil,
    drained and chopped
2 cups Calamata or oil-cured olives,
    pitted and halved
1 bunch fresh parsley, finely chopped
1/4 to 1/2 cup freshly grated
    Parmesan cheese

In a large sauce pan, cook orzo pasta in boiling salted water until just tender, about 8 to 10 minutes. Drain. Place garlic, salt, pepper, mustard, and vinegar into blender or food processor. Process to blend well. Pour into a container with cover. Add oil and shake to blend. Pour over the pasta while it is still warm. Toss well. Add tomatoes to pasta along with the olives and chopped parsley. Sprinkle with Parmesan cheese. Toss again and adjust the seasonings, if necessary. Serve immediately, or refrigerate for later use. Better served at room temperature.

Note: Orzo is a rice-shaped pasta. If you prefer to use dried tomatoes not in oil, pour boiling water over tomatoes and allow to soak 10 minutes before using.

Preparation Time: 30 minutes
Servings: 20

GREEK PASTA SALAD

3 cups shell, corkscrew or other
 uncooked pasta
2 tablespoons lemon juice
1/2 cup olive oil
1/2 teaspoon salt
1/4 teaspoon pepper
1 to 2 teaspoons fresh oregano, chopped
1 clove garlic, crushed

2 medium tomatoes, seeded and diced
1 green bell peppper, cut into thin strips
1 cucumber, chopped
12 black or Greek olives
1 1/2 cups Feta cheese, crumbled
1/2 cups fresh Italian parsley, chopped
4 green onions, sliced

Cook pasta according to package directions; drain well and cool. Combine lemon juice, oil, salt, pepper, oregano and garlic. Mix well until thick and creamy; chill. Combine pasta, tomatoes, green pepper, cucumber, olives, Feta cheese, parsley and green onion. Toss salad ingredients and dressing gently to coat. Serve immediately.

Note: Parmesan cheese may be substituted for Feta cheese; red onion may be substituted for green onion. Marinated artichoke hearts, cooked chicken pieces, shrimp, or salami can be added.

Preparation Time: 45 minutes
Servings: 6 to 8

Robert Mondavi Pinot Noir

TURKEY AND APRICOT SALAD

1/2 cup lemon juice
2 tablespoons honey
1/2 cup salad oil
1 tablespoon Dijon mustard
1 tablespoon poppy seeds
1/2 cup sliced green onions,
 including tops
1/2 teaspoon grated lemon peel

1/2 cup dried apricot halves
3 to 4 cups chopped cooked turkey
1/2 cup chopped slivered almonds,
 toasted
1 red apple, cored and thinly sliced
Salt, to taste
Lettuce, of choice

Combine lemon juice, honey, oil, mustard, poppy seeds, onions, and lemon peel. Add apricots; let stand at least 30 minutes. Add turkey to dressing mixture. Before serving, toss with almonds and apple slices. Sprinkle with salt. Serve salad on a bed of lettuce.

Preparation Time: 45 minutes
Servings: 6

Robert Mondavi Chenin Blanc

CHICKEN-VERMICELLI SALAD

4 boneless, skinless chicken
   breast halves
2 cups chicken broth
4 ounces vermicelli
1 teaspoon vegetable oil
2 medium red bell peppers
2 medium ripe tomatoes, peeled and
   seeded

1 6-ounce can marinated artichoke hearts
1/3 cup garlic vinaigrette, recipe follows
1/4 cup chopped fresh basil leaves
1/2 cup chopped fresh parsley
Curly endive or dark green lettuce

Poach chicken in broth 20 minutes, or until just cooked and no pink color remains. Cool chicken and shred coarsely. Set aside in refrigerator. Meanwhile, cook vermicelli; drain and toss with oil.

Roast peppers on a pan 5 to 6 inches below broiler, rotating 1/3 turn after each side blisters and turns black. Remove from broiler and place in a paper bag. Close the bag and allow peppers to steam in the bag for 5 minutes. When peppers are cool enough to handle, remove the skin, ribs, and seeds. Cut peppers in small strips. Cut tomatoes in small strips. Set peppers and tomatoes aside.

Place artichoke heart marinade in a large bowl. Slice hearts, discarding any tough leaves, and add to the marinade. Place chicken, vermicelli, and 1/3 cup Garlic Vinaigrette into the bowl, mixing well. Add more vinaigrette, if desired.

Just before serving, add tomatoes, red peppers, basil, and parsley, tossing to mix with the chicken-vermicelli. Arrange on a bed of endive or lettuce.

Preparation Time: 45 minutes
Servings: 4 to 6

GARLIC VINAIGRETTE

3 cloves garlic, peeled
3 tablespoons lemon juice
3 tablespoons red wine vinegar
2 teaspoons sugar

1/2 teaspoon salt
1/2 teaspoon pepper
1/3 cup extra virgin olive oil
2/3 cup vegetable oil

Using a food processor or a blender, pulse garlic cloves. Add lemon juice, vinegar, sugar, salt and pepper, blending well. Add oils and process until well mixed.

Preparation Time: 10 minutes
Yield: 1 1/2 cups

CHICKEN AND WILD RICE SALAD

The salad may be made a day ahead, but add greens just before serving.

Zesty chutney dressing, chilled,
   recipe follows
2 1/2 cups wild rice, rinsed
3 cups chicken broth
3 cups water
1 tablespoon white wine vinegar
2 tablespoons olive oil

Salt and pepper, to taste
1 cup chopped green onions
1 cup golden raisins
3 to 4 cups chopped cooked chicken
   breasts
3 cups mixed field greens

Prepare zesty chutney dressing. In a large sauce pan, combine the rice, chicken broth, and water. Bring to a boil; simmer, covered, for 50 to 60 minutes or until the rice is tender and most of the liquid is absorbed; drain. In a large bowl, combine rice, vinegar, olive oil, salt and pepper. Toss mixture and cool completely. Add the onions, raisins, and chicken; combine with dressing. Serve on top of the field greens, or toss all together.

Preparation Time: 15 minutes
Cooking Time: 50 to 60 minutes
Chilling Time: 2 hours
Servings: 10 to 12

Robert Mondavi Fumé Blanc

ZESTY CHUTNEY DRESSING

2 large garlic cloves, chopped
3 tablespoons white wine vinegar
4 tablespoons lemon juice
2 tablespoons curry powder
3 tablespoons bottled mango chutney

Salt and pepper, to taste
2/3 cup olive oil
3/4 cup sour cream
3 tablespoons water
1/2 cup finely chopped cilantro

In a blender or food processor, combine the garlic, vinegar, lemon juice, curry powder, chutney, salt and pepper; blend until smooth. With motor running, add the oil, sour cream, and water; mixing well. With a spoon, stir in the cilantro. Cover and refrigerate for up to 2 days.

Preparation Time: 15 minutes
Yields: 2 cups

SYMPHONIC CHICKEN SALAD

3 cups cooked chicken, cut in chunks
1 tablespoon grated onion
2 cups diced celery
1 cup chopped pecans
2 cups seedless green grapes
2 6-ounce cans water chestnuts,
   drained and chopped
2 cups peeled and diced apples
1/2 cup mayonnaise

1/3 cup white wine
1 teaspoon salt
1/8 teaspoon pepper
1 ripe avocado, peeled and sliced,
   for garnish
Lemon juice
8 large lettuce leaves, of choice
Pecan halves, for garnish

Combine chicken, onion, celery, pecans, grapes, water chestnuts, and apples. Set aside.
Combine mayonnaise, wine, salt and pepper; toss with chicken mixture. Refrigerate
until ready to serve.

At serving time, sprinkle avocado with lemon juice. Put lettuce leaves on serving plates;
spoon chicken salad in lettuce and garnish with sliced avocado and pecan halves.

Preparation Time: 1 hour
Servings: 8

Robert Mondavi Johannisberg Riesling

PAGODA CHICKEN SALAD

1 whole chicken breast, cooked,
   skinned, boned, and sliced
2 teaspoons chopped fresh ginger
2 cloves garlic, minced
1 tablespoon soy sauce
1/2 cup shredded radicchio
1 cup shredded iceberg lettuce

Salt and pepper, to taste
1 cup bean sprouts, washed
1 yellow bell pepper, thinly sliced
2 green onions, chopped
3 tablespoons red wine vinegar
1/4 cup sesame oil

Place chicken, ginger, garlic, soy sauce, radicchio, and iceberg lettuce in a bowl. Season
well with salt and papper. Add bean sprouts, yellow bell pepper, and green onions. Pour
in wine vinegar and oil. Toss well and serve.

Preparation Time: 25 minutes
Servings: 4

Robert Mondavi Chenin Blanc

MARINATED ANGEL HAIR AND CHICKEN SALAD

8 ounces uncooked angel hair pasta
6 chicken breast halves, cooked
  and cut in bite-sized pieces
1/8 cup rice wine vinegar
1/4 cup olive oil
1/8 teaspoon dry mustard
Salt and pepper, to taste
1/2 cup mayonnaise

1/2 cup sour cream
1/2 cup creme fraiche, see note
1 tablespoon tarragon
2 stalks celery, diced
1/4 cup chopped parsley
1 7-ounce jar marinated artichoke hearts,
  drained and cut into pieces
4 Roma tomatoes, seeded and diced

Cook and drain pasta. Place pasta and chicken in a quart-sized bowl. Combine vinegar, oil, mustard, salt and pepper. Pour over pasta mixture and let marinate 1 to 2 hours. Combine mayonnaise, sour cream, creme fraiche, and tarragon; pour over pasta and chicken ingredients. Add celery, parsley, and artichoke hearts. Mix all ingredients completely. Put in serving bowl. Before serving, garnish with diced tomatoes.

Note: Creme fraiche can be prepared at home. Use equal parts sour cream and whipping cream. Whisk together and let stand at room temperature for a couple of hours until thickened. Cover and refrigerate.

Preparation Time: 45 minutes
Chilling Time: 1 to 2 hours
Servings: 8

Vichon Chardonnay

CHICKEN-BROCCOLI SALAD

2 pounds broccoli, washed
1/2 teaspoon garlic salt
2 whole chicken breasts, poached,
  boned, and diced
4 hard boiled eggs, sliced
2 bunches green onions, chopped

1 pound Jack cheese, julienned
3/4 pound bacon, fried crisp and
  crumbled
1 basket cherry tomatoes, halved
Italian dressing, of choice
Salt and white pepper, to taste

Cook broccoli in garlic salted water until tender; allow to cool. Cut into bite-sized pieces. Combine broccoli with chicken, eggs, green onions, cheese, bacon, and tomatoes. Toss with dressing and season with salt and pepper.

Note: Shrimp may be substituted for the chicken.

Preparation Time: 1 hour
Servings: 6

Though snow doesn't fall and chestnuts don't roast over an open fire, holidays in Orange County have their own traditional magic. Every community, indeed, every street, decks itself out in colored lights and holiday finery and waterways sparkle with the twinkling lights of decorated boats. South Coast Plaza, perhaps the most beautiful shopping center in the country, is filled with strolling carolers and brilliant holiday displays, each year's more spectacular than the last. In this land of year-round sunshine, Thanksgiving and Christmas celebrations may include a walk on the beach or a traditional match-up of young and old in touch football or volleyball on the sand. For many, New Year's wouldn't be New Year's without an annual trip to nearby Pasadena for the thrilling pageanty of the Rose Parade and the Rose Bowl game.

SOUPS

Do you like to party before a ball game? Autumn leaves frame a lovely old mill house in North Orange County. Hearty soups are a perfect choice for this setting that has a feel of fall in New England.

FRESH CLAM GAZPACHO WITH AVOCADO

Our thanks to Alan Greeley, chef and owner of the Golden Truffle, for sharing this fresh clam gazpacho.

12 large clams, steamed, chilled,
  and minced
1 cucumber, peeled and diced
1 yellow bell pepper, seeded and diced
1 red bell pepper, seeded and diced
1/2 sweet onion, diced
3 ripe tomatoes, peeled and diced
3 tablespoons balsamic vinegar

6 tablespoons olive oil
Salt and freshly ground pepper, to taste
Pinch of sugar
Juice of 1 lemon
1 bunch cilantro, chopped
1 small Jalapeno chili pepper,
  seeded and minced
1 avocado, peeled, and diced

In a large bowl, combine all ingredients, except chili and avocado. Adjust seasoning; add chili to taste. Set aside in refrigerator 4 hours for flavors to blend. Just before serving, add avocado. Correct seasoning and serve in well-chilled bowls.

Preparation Time: 35 minutes
Chilling Time: 4 hours
Servings: 4 to 6

Robert Mondavi Fumé Blanc

SHOW-STOPPER PRESENTATION SOUP

Two soups, each wonderful alone, make a very special party presentation of two colors, half on each side of the bowl. They are balanced and will remain separate. Your guests will enjoy a tasting of the two soups as well.

Cream of pimento soup, recipe follows
Cream of asparagus soup, recipe follows
Herb sprig of choice, for garnish

Prepare soups separately, making sure they are the same consistency. Practice pouring at the time, on opposite sides of the bowl, to be sure your presentation will be beautiful to serve. When you use them together, they should be at room temperature, or just slightly chilled. Garnish with a small herb sprig in the center.

Preparation Time: 1 hour, 30 minutes
Servings: 16

CREAM OF PIMENTO SOUP

1/2 cup chopped onion
2 tablespoons butter
2 1/2 tablespoons flour
2 1/2 cups chicken broth

1 4-ounce jar whole pimentos
1 cup whipping cream
Salt and white pepper, to taste
Dill sprigs, for garnish

Saute onion in butter until soft. Stir in flour, and cook over low heat for 1 minute. Add broth and cook, stirring constantly, until thickened. Add pimentos, and puree until smooth. Return to pan and add cream, salt and pepper. Chill. Serve cold.

Note: This soup can be made up to 3 days in advance.

Preparation Time: 30 minutes
Servings: 8

CREAM OF ASPARAGUS SOUP

The secret ingredients to this soup are coriander and lemon juice.

2 10 1/2-ounce packages frozen asparagus
1/2 cup chopped onion
1/3 cup fresh minced parsley
1 3/4 teaspoons ground coriander
3 tablespoons butter

1 tablespoon flour
3 cups chicken broth
1 cup whipping cream
2 tablespoons fresh lemon juice
Salt and white pepper, to taste

Cook asparagus until tender. Rinse immediately in cold water and drain. Peel skin and cut the stalks into 1-inch pieces.

In a large saucepan, saute onion, parsley, and coriander in butter until vegetables are softened. Sprinkle in flour and cook for 2 to 3 minutes, stirring with a whisk. Remove from heat and stir in chicken broth. Return to heat and simmer, stirring occasionally for 5 minutes.

Combine asparagus and broth mixture in a food processor or blender. Puree, in batches, until smooth. Pour into a large, heavy saucepan and stir in cream. Over moderate heat, reheat soup but do not boil. Stir in lemon juice, then salt and white pepper to taste. Serve warm; or chill soup for several hours and serve cold. At serving time, garnish with thin lemon slices dusted with minced parsley or dollops of sour cream sprinkled with chopped chives.

Preparation Time: 30 minutes
Chilling Time: For cold soup, 2 hours or more
Servings: 8

WHITE GAZPACHO WITH CHICKEN

4 medium cucumbers, divided
1 large clove garlic, peeled and chopped
2 cups chicken broth, divided
2 cups sour cream
1 cup plain yogurt
3 tablespoons white vinegar
2 teaspoons salt
2 teaspoons pepper

1 teaspoon curry powder
3 chicken breast halves,
    cooked and shredded
5 Roma tomatoes, seeded and chopped
1/2 cup thinly sliced green onions
1 avocado, chopped
3/4 cup sesame seeds, toasted

Peel and dice 3 of the cucumbers. Place in blender; add garlic and a small amount of chicken broth. Puree ingredients. Add remaining broth and blend thoroughly.

In a large bowl, mix sour cream and yogurt and thin with 1/3 of the cucumber puree. Add vinegar, salt, pepper, and curry powder and remaining puree mixture. Peel, seed, and dice the remaining cucumber and add to the mixture. Add chicken and chill for 6 to 8 hours or overnight.

Serve soup in chilled bowls. On the side, fill separate bowls with the tomatoes, avocados, onions, and sesame seeds. Guests can spoon their choices on top.

Preparation Time: 1 hour   Vichon Chevrignon
Chilling Time: 6 to 8 hours
Servings: 6

CINCO DE MAYO GAZPACHO

The clams and seasonings make this an unique gazpacho.

8 cups clamato juice
3 tomatoes, seeded and chopped
4 green onions, thinly sliced
1/4 green bell pepper, diced
1/4 red bell pepper, diced
2 stalks celery, chopped
1/2 cucumber, seeded and chopped

1 6 1/2-ounce can minced clams, drained
1/2 cup ketchup
1 teaspoon horseradish
2 tablespoons Worcestershire sauce
2 tablespoons lemon juice
2 avocados, peeled, seeded, and diced

In a 3-quart container, combine all ingredients; stir to mix well. Chill at least 4 hours.

Preparation Time: 30 minutes   Robert Mondavi Fumé Blanc
Chilling Time: 4 hours or more
Servings: 8 to 10

VELVET VICHYSSOISE

3 leeks, rinsed and sliced
1 onion, chopped
1/2 cup butter, melted
1 tablespoon flour
6 cups water
1 1/2 teaspoons salt, divided

1 teaspoon white pepper, divided
3 large potatoes, peeled and cubed
Additional 1 tablespoon butter
1/2 cup whipping cream
Croutons or chopped chives, for garnish

In a large pot, saute leeks and onion in melted butter about 10 minutes, or until tender. Stir in flour. Slowly add water, 1 teaspoon salt, and 1/2 teaspoon pepper. Add potatoes; bring to a boil. Reduce heat and simmer until potatoes are tender, about 30 minutes. Allow to cool slightly.

In a blender, puree the mixture in batches, until creamy. Return to soup pot on low heat. Add additonal butter, cream, and remaining salt and pepper. Stir to blend. Heat, but do not boil. To serve, garnish with croutons or chopped chives.

Preparation Time: 35 minutes
Cooking Time: 30 minutes
Servings: 8

CARROT VICHYSSOISE

1 1/4 cups peeled and sliced carrots
2 cups peeled and diced potatoes
1 leek, cleaned and sliced, white only
3 cups chicken broth
1 teaspoon salt

1/8 teaspoon white pepper
1 cup cream
Shredded raw carrots, for garnish
Fresh or dried dill, chopped, for garnish

In a large saucepan, combine carrots, potatoes, leek, and chicken broth; bring to a boil. Reduce heat and simmer, covered, about 25 minutes, or until vegetables are tender. In a blender or food processor, puree the vegetables with their liquid. Place in a bowl, add the salt, pepper, and cream; stir to blend. Chill for several hours or overnight. Serve cold with a topping of shredded carrots and dill, if desired.

Preparation Time: 15 minutes
Cooking Time: 25 minutes
Chilling Time: 4 hours or more
Servings: 6

CHILLED CONFETTI SOUP

2 cups chicken broth
2 medium tart apples, cored,
   peeled, and chopped
2 cups chopped onion
1/2 teaspoon curry powder
1 large red bell pepper
2 cups plain yogurt

2 cups buttermilk
1/4 cup lime juice
1 1/2 cups corn kernels, cooked
   and divided
1/2 cup chopped cilantro, divided
1/3 pound small shrimp, cooked

In a large pot, combine broth, apples, onion, and curry powder. Cover and bring to a boil. Reduce to simmer and cook for 30 minutes or until apples are soft. Cool for at least 3 hours. Puree in a food processor. Cut a few thin slivers from the pepper for garnish and set aside. Dice the remaining pepper. Combine apple puree, diced pepper, yogurt, buttermilk, lime juice, 1 1/4 cups corn, and 1/4 cup cilantro. Chill 24 hours.

When ready to serve, ladle soup into bowls and top with shrimp, pepper strips, 1/4 cup corn, and 1/4 cup cilantro.

Preparation Time: 30 minutes
Cooking Time: 30 minutes
Chilling Time: 3 hours, plus 24 hours
Servings: 8 to 10

Vichon Chevrignon

SURFSIDE ZUCCHINI CREAMED SOUP

2 cups thinly sliced, unpeeled zucchini
3 cups chicken stock
1/4 cup minced onion
3 tablespoons uncooked rice
1/2 teaspoon dry mustard
1 1/2 teaspoons curry powder

1/2 teaspoon fresh minced ginger
1 teaspoon salt
1 teaspoon white pepper
1 1/2 cups half-and-half
Sour cream, for garnish
Mint leaves, for garnish

Place zucchini, chicken stock, onion, rice, dry mustard, curry, and ginger in a saucepan. Simmer 15 to 20 minutes or until squash is tender. Pour small amounts into a blender and whirl until smooth. Add half-and-half, salt, and pepper. Chill thoroughly and serve garnished with a dollop of sour cream and mint leaves.

Preparation Time: 25 to 30 minutes
Chilling Time: 2 hours
Servings: 6 to 8

SUMMER SQUASH SOUP

This soup uses fresh ingredients and contains no cream.

2 tablespoons butter or margarine
1 large onion, chopped
2 yellow crookneck squash, chopped
2 to 3 zucchini, chopped
4 large tomatoes, peeled, seeded,
  and chopped

2 teaspoons ground nutmeg
2 teaspoons cumin
1 teaspoon curry powder
3/4 cup brown sugar
6 cups chicken broth

In a large heavy pan, melt butter and saute onions until transparent. Add remaining ingredients, stirring to blend, and cook 30 minutes. Puree mixture in batches and return to pan. Serve warm.

Preparation Time: 20 minutes
Cooking Time: 30 minutes
Servings: 6 to 8

AVOCADO POTAGE IN SHELLS

This refreshing cold soup is presented in avocado shells to serve on plates as an accompaniment to a salad or a sandwich.

2 avocados, preferably Haas
2 tablespoons lemon juice, divided
3 tomatoes, peeled, seeded,
 and chopped
3/4 cup sour cream, divided
1 tablespoon chopped green onion

1 tablespoon chopped green bell pepper
1 tablespoon chopped celery
3 to 4 drops hot pepper sauce
Salt, to taste
1 1/4 cups chicken broth
1/2 cup vodka, optional

Cut avocados in half lengthwise; remove seeds and scoop out pulp with a spoon, leaving about 1/4-inch thick shell. Paint the inside of avocado halves with 1 tablespoon lemon juice. Freeze.

Blend avocado pulp, tomatoes, 1/2 cup sour cream, green onion, green pepper, celery, 1 tablespoon lemon juice, hot pepper sauce, and salt in blender or food processor. Add the broth. Correct the seasoning. Chill at least 4 hours.

When ready to serve, spoon soup into avocado shells. Top with small dollop of sour cream. Serve immediately. Pass a small pitcher of vodka to add to soup, if desired.

Note: These avocado shells are also appropriate for salad fillings.

Preparation Time: 35 minutes
Chilling Time: 4 hours or more
Servings: 4

CHEDDAR CHOWDER

1 cup water
2 small potatoes, pared and diced
1/2 cup diced carrot
1/2 cup diced celery
4 tablespoons butter
1/2 cup chopped onion
1/4 cup flour

2 cups chicken broth
1 1/2 cups milk
2 cups shredded Cheddar cheese
1/8 teaspoon baking soda
Salt and pepper, to taste
Minced fresh parsley, for garnish

In a large saucepan, combine water, potatoes, carrot, and celery. Bring to a boil; reduce heat and cook covered until vegetables are barely tender, about 10 minutes. Remove from heat and set aside. Meanwhile, in a large sauce pan over medium heat, melt the butter and saute the onion until transparent, 4 to 5 minutes. Stir in flour until smooth; cook and stir 1 minute. Gradually whisk in chicken broth; add milk; cook and stir until mixture thickens, about 1 minute. Stir in cheese, baking soda, salt and pepper. Add reserved vegetables and cooking liquid. Heat until just heated through. Garnish with fresh parsley and serve immediately.

Preparation Time: 20 minutes
Cooking Time: 20 minutes
Servings: 6 to 8

FENNEL FISH CHOWDER

The flavor of fennel is lovely in this soup. It brings out the sweetness of the fish.

1 tablespoon butter
1/2 cup finely chopped onion
1 large bulb fennel, cored and sliced,
    about 2 cups
1 pound white rose potatoes, diced
2 cups quartered carrots
2 8-ounce bottles clam juice

1 teaspoon salt
1/2 teaspoon white pepper
1/2 teaspoon thyme
1 pound cod fillet, cut into chunks
4 ounces peeled shrimp
1 pint half-and-half
1/4 cup chopped fresh parsley

Melt butter in a large heavy saucepan. Add onion and fennel. Saute until tender, about 10 minutes. Add potatoes, carrots, clam juice, salt, pepper, and thyme. Bring to a boil; reduce heat, cover, and simmer until vegetables are tender, about 10 minutes. Ladle 3 cups of soup mixture, mostly vegetables, into a blender; puree until smooth and return to saucepan. Add cod and shrimp; simmer covered until opaque, about 2 minutes. Gently stir in half-and-half and heat through. Do not boil. Sprinkle with parsley and serve.

Preparation Time: 30 minutes
Cooking Time: 35 minutes
Servings: 10 cups

Robert Mondavi Chardonnay Reserve

CRAB CORN CHOWDER

1/2 cup butter
4 ears fresh corn, kernels only
2 medium potatoes, finely diced
1 medium onion, finely chopped

4 cups half-and-half
Dash cayenne pepper
Salt and pepper, to taste
4 ounces crabmeat

In a large, heavy pan; melt the butter. Add corn kernels, potatoes, and onion; saute over medium heat until onion is translucent. Add half-and-half and simmer slowly until potatoes are tender, about 10 minutes. Add seasonings and crab, simmer just until meat is hot. Ladle into bowls.

Note: Serve with tortilla strips. Two cups frozen, thawed corn kernels may be substituted for the fresh corn.

Preparation Time: 20 to 30 minutes
Cooking Time: 20 minutes
Servings: 4 to 6

Robert Mondavi Chardonnay Reserve

CORN CHOWDER

4 slices bacon, diced
2 tablespoons butter
3 cups sliced onion
1 bay leaf
3/4 cup fresh bread crumbs
4 cups chicken broth

3 to 3 1/2 cups diced white rose potatoes
1/8 to 1/4 teaspoon red pepper flakes
Salt and freshly ground pepper, to taste
2 cups half-and-half
1 10-ounce package frozen corn
1 15-ounce can creamed corn

In a medium saute pan, saute bacon and drain; add butter, onion, and bay leaf. Cover and simmer for 10 minutes. Stir in bread crumbs.

In a large pot, mix broth, potatoes, pepper flakes, and onion mixture. Simmer for 30 minutes. Blend in half-and-half and corn. Simmer for 3 to 5 minutes. Puree 2 to 3 cups of the soup and stir it back into the pot; stirring to combine well. Serve warm.

Note: The chowder may be refrigerated and reheated at serving time.

Preparation Time: 30 minutes
Cooking Time: 45 minutes
Servings: 8

Vichon Chardonnay

CREAM OF ZUCCHINI AND BASIL SOUP

2 medium onions, chopped
2 cloves garlic, minced
1/3 cup chopped fresh basil
3/4 teaspoon dried thyme
2 tablespoons butter

8 cups chicken broth
8 cups chopped zucchini
3 1/2 tablespoons rice
1/3 cup cream cheese
Salt, to taste

In a soup pot, combine onion, garlic, basil, thyme, and butter. Cook over medium heat, stirring until onion is soft. Add broth and zucchini and bring to a boil. Stir in rice and simmer, covered, about 25 minutes. Add cream cheese and stir to blend. Puree soup and season with salt to taste. Serve warm.

Preparation Time: 25 minutes
Cooking Time: 25 minutes
Servings: 10 to 12

BUTTERNUT APPLE SOUP

A delightful blend of flavors!

1 medium red onion, chopped
1 tablespoon curry, or to taste
1 tablespoon butter
2 Granny Smith apples, divided
1 1/2 pound butternut squash,
   peeled, seeded, and cubed

3 14 1/2-ounce cans chicken broth,
   plus enough water to make 5 cups of broth
1 tablespoon lemon juice
1 teaspoon salt

In a large pot, saute onion and curry in butter. Peel, seed, and cube 1 apple. Combine apple, squash, and broth; add to onion mixture, simmer until tender, about 20 to 30 minutes. Meanwhile, peel, seed, and grate the remaining apple and cover with lemon juice. Set aside.

Add salt to the hot mixture and puree in blender, in batches, until smooth. Serve soup hot or chill several hours to serve cold. Garnish with the grated apple.

Preparation Time: 1 hour
Servings: 4 to 6

CREAM OF LEEK SOUP
WITH STILTON CRUST

3 tablespoons finely chopped shallots
4 cups chopped leeks
2 tablespoons unsalted butter
1 cup diced potatoes

4 cups chicken broth
3 cups cream
Salt, pepper, lemon juice to taste
8 slices of Stilton cheese

In a medium pan, saute shallots and leeks in butter until vegetables are limp. Add potatoes and chicken broth; cook, covered, until potatoes are done, about 30 minutes. Cool and puree. In a saucepan, bring cream to a gentle boil. Reduce heat to low; stirring frequently, cook until cream is reduced and slightly thickened, about 45 minutes.

Add cream to the leek and potato mixture, bring to a boil. Add salt, pepper, and lemon juice to taste. Serve in bowls and top with a slice of Stilton cheese.

Preparation Time: 1 hour, 45 minutes
Servings: 8

CREAM OF WATERCRESS-ZUCCHINI SOUP

2 cups chopped onion
4 tablespoons butter
3 cups chicken broth
4 medium zucchini, slice thickly

1 bunch watercress, rinsed, stemmed,
  and chopped
1 cup half-and-half
Salt and pepper

In a large heavy saucepan, cook onions in butter over low heat, stirring until onions are soft and lightly colored. Add broth and zucchini and bring to boil. Reduce heat; cover and simmer until zucchini are very tender, about 15 to 20 minutes. Add watercress, cook 5 minutes. Remove from heat and let stand 5 minutes. Pour soup through a strainer, reserving liquid. Process solids with 1 cup of the cooking liquid until smooth. Return to pot and add another cup of cooking liquid; add the half-and-half. Season with salt and pepper. Heat and serve.

Preparation Time: 30 minutes
Cooking Time: 15 to 20 minutes
Servings: 6 to 8

ONION SOUP GRATIN

This traditional soup is a meal in itself.

4 tablespoons butter
1 tablespoon extra virgin olive oil
8 medium yellow onions, thinly sliced
2 cloves garlic, minced
1 tablespoon sugar
Salt and pepper, to taste
3 tablespoons flour
4 cups beef broth, divided

4 cups water
1 cup dry white wine
3/4 teaspoon dried thyme
Pinch of nutmeg
6 toasted rounds of French bread
1 pound Gruyere, or Emmenthaler
   cheese, grated

In a large saucepan, heat the butter and oil; add onions and garlic; cook over moderate heat 5 minutes, stirring frequently. Add sugar, salt, and pepper; reduce heat and continue cooking 20 to 30 minutes, stirring occasionally until onions are lightly browned. Add flour; cook, stirring for 1 minute. Add 2 cups of the beef broth; bring to a boil; stir well. Add remaining broth, water, wine, thyme and nutmeg; return to a boil. Reduce heat and simmer, covered, 45 minutes, stirring frequently.

Preheat oven to 375 degrees. Divide soup among 6 ovenproof bowls. Place a toasted bread round in the center of each. Top with a generous sprinkling of cheese, place bowls on a baking sheet. Bake 25 minutes or until cheese is bubbly and beginning to brown.

Preparation Time: 15 minutes
Cooking Time: 1 hour, 15 minutes
Baking Time: 25 minutes
Servings: 6

GOLDEN LENTIL SOUP

Our thanks to Zov Karamardian, owner of Zov's Bistro in Tustin, for her popular soup recipe.

1 cup golden lentils, rinsed well
1/4 cup long grain rice
8 cups water, divided
1 1/2 carrots, diced
1 large yellow onion, diced

2 stalks of celery, diced
1 to 2 tablespoons salad oil
6 cups vegetable broth
Cumin, to taste
Salt, to taste

In a large pot, combine lentils, rice, and 4 cups water. Boil gently for about 15 minutes. In a skillet, saute carrots, onion, and celery in oil for 7 minutes; add to lentils, combining well. Add broth, remaining 4 cups water, and seasonings. Bring to a boil, stirring constantly. Reduce heat and simmer about 20 minutes. Serve warm.

Preparation Time: 1 hour
Servings: 10 to 12

LENTIL AND HAM SOUP

2 1/2 cups lentils
4 cups chicken broth
6 cups water
1 small bunch celery, including leaves,
    chopped
2 medium onions, chopped
4 carrots, chopped

1 ham hock, or 1/2 pound bacon, cubed
4 tablespoons unsalted butter, melted
4 tablespoons flour
1 10 1/2-ounce can consomme
Salt, to taste
Freshly ground pepper, to taste

In a large soup pot, combine lentils, broth, water, celery, onions, carrots, and ham hock. Heat to boiling. Reduce heat and simmer 1 1/2 to 2 hours. In a small saucepan, combine the butter and flour. Add the consomme, salt and pepper. Stir and cook until smooth and thickened. Gradually add to lentil mixture and simmer about 30 minutes. Serve warm.

Preparation Time: 20 minutes
Cooking Time: 2 hours, 30 minutes
Servings: 10

SPA TORTELLINI SOUP

1/4 pound bacon, cut into small pieces
2 cloves garlic, minced
4 cups fresh spinach, washed, dried,
   and chopped
6 to 8 cups chicken broth

1 28-ounce can tomatoes, with liquid
1 medium yellow bell pepper, seeded
   and cubed
1 8-ounce package fresh
   tortellini, of choice

In a saute pan, saute bacon and garlic for 5 minutes, or until bacon is cooked. Remove pieces from pan and set aside. Over medium-high heat, cook spinach in pan drippings for 2 to 3 minutes. Stir in broth, tomatoes, and pepper; bring to a boil. Stir in tortellini and bacon; simmer until pasta is al dente. Serve warm.

Preparation Time: 30 minutes
Cooking Time: 20 minutes
Servings: 10 to 12

SOUTH COUNTY TORTELLINI SOUP

2 tablespoons olive oil, divided
1 pound hot Italian sausage,
   casings removed
1 clove garlic, minced
1 onion, chopped
4 medium zucchini, sliced
1 red bell pepper, diced
1 28-ounce can Italian plum tomatoes,
   including juice, quartered

2 14 1/2-ounce cans chicken broth
1 6-ounce can tomato paste
1 8-ounce can tomato sauce
1 teaspoon dried oregano
1 teaspoon dried thyme
1 pound tortellini, flavor of choice
1/3 cup chopped fresh basil
Freshly grated Parmesan cheese

In a large skillet, heat 1 tablespoon oil and saute the sausage until crumbled and cooked. Remove with a slotted spoon and drain well on a paper towel. Add 1 tablespoon oil to pan; saute garlic and onion until transparent. Add zucchini and pepper; saute until softened. Add tomatoes, broth, tomato paste, tomato sauce, oregano, and thyme. Bring to a boil and simmer, covered, 15 minutes. Add tortellini and simmer 10 minutes. Stir in basil. Serve with Parmesan cheese.

Preparation Time: 30 minutes
Cooking Time: 30 minutes
Servings: 8

FETTUCINE AND ITALIAN SAUSAGE SOUP

This wonderful soup can be served at a Super Bowl or Boat Parade party.

2 pounds Italian sausage, sweet or hot
3 tablespoons olive oil
1 medium yellow onion, chopped
4 zucchini, sliced
3 ribs of celery, sliced
1 14 1/2-ounce can chopped tomatoes, undrained
1 6-ounce can tomato paste
3 14 1/2-ounce cans beef broth
3 cups water
1 cup burgundy wine, or any dry red wine

2 tablespoons fresh chopped parsley
1/2-ounce package fresh oregano, chopped
1/2-ounce package fresh basil, stemmed and chopped
4 cloves garlic, minced
2 bay leaves
1/2 teaspoon ground thyme
Salt and freshly ground pepper, to taste
1/4 pound green spinach fettucine
Freshly grated Parmesan cheese

In a large saute pan, brown sausage well. Drain on paper towels. Wipe out pan; add olive oil and saute onion, zucchini, and celery until just tender.

In a large stockpot, combine sausage, vegetables, tomatoes, tomato paste, beef stock, water, and burgundy. Bring to a simmer and add parsley, oregano, basil, garlic, bay leaves, thyme, salt and pepper. Simmer 5 minutes. Add fettucine and simmer for 30 minutes. Remove bay leaves. Adjust seasonings. Ladle into bowls, or mugs, and top with freshly grated Parmesan cheese.

Preparation Time: 25 minutes
Cooking Time: 35 minutes
Servings: 12

Robert Mondavi Woodbridge Cabernet Sauvignon

MISSION MINESTRONE

This is a hearty, main course soup; serve with salad and crusty French bread.

1/2 pound lean pancetta or bacon,
  cut into small pieces
1 tablespoon olive oil
2 large onions, chopped
1 cup diced potatoes
1 cup diced carrots
1 cup celery, sliced
6 cloves garlic, minced
1 bunch Italian parsley, chopped
1/2 pound zucchini
1 1-pound, 13-ounce can
  solid pack tomatoes
4 14 1/2-ounce cans chicken broth

4 quarts water
Thyme, to taste
Basil, to taste
Marjoram, to taste
2 bay leaves
Freshly ground pepper
2 cups broken spaghettini
  or other pasta
1/3 cup freshly grated Parmesan cheese
1 1-pound can lima beans, drained
Additional basil and Parmesan
  cheese, for garnish

In a large saute pan, cook pancetta until done but still limp. Drain. Combine olive oil and onion; saute until onions are translucent. Put pancetta and onion mixture in a large pot. Add all of the ingredients except the pasta, cheese, and beans. Bring to a boil; cover and simmer for 2 hours, stirring occasionally. Add pasta and cook until al dente. Just before serving, add lima beans and cheese. Ladle into bowls and garnish with fresh basil and more Parmesan cheese.

Preparation Time: 30 minutes
Cooking Time: 2 1/2 hours
Servings: 10 to 12

Robert Mondavi Cabernet Sauvignon

BEAN AND SAUSAGE SOUP

12 ounces turkey or pork sausage
2 15-ounce cans diced tomatoes,
  undrained
1 15-ounce can pinquito beans,
  undrained
1 15-ounce can black beans, undrained
1 15-ounce garbanzo beans, undrained

1 15-ounce can kidney beans, undrained
1/4 cup chopped cilantro, optional
1 teaspoon cumin
1/2 teaspoon ground pepper
Grated Parmesan or shredded
Monterey Jack cheese for garnish

In a soup pot, saute sausage 3 to 5 minutes, stirring constantly. Drain excess fat. Add tomatoes, beans, and seasonings. Bring to a boil; cover and reduce heat. Simmer 10 to 15 minutes, stirring occasionally. To serve, garnish with grated Parmesan or shredded Monterey Jack cheese.

Preparation Time: 25 minutes
Servings: 12

Robert Mondavi Cabernet Sauvignon

SANTA ANA ALBONDIGAS SOUP

1 cup chopped onion
1 tablespoon butter
5 10 1/2-ounce cans beef bouillon
4 cups water
2 7-ounce cans Ortega green chili salsa
1 28-ounce can tomatoes

1 teaspoon basil
1 teaspoon oregano
1 teaspoon salt
1/2 teaspoon pepper
Cornmeal meatballs, recipe follows
1/2 cup rice

In a large pot, saute onion in butter and add all other ingredients, except meatballs and rice; bring to a boil. Simmer for 20 minutes. Meanwhile, prepare meatballs. Add meatballs and rice to the broth and simmer gently, covered, 1 to 1 1/2 hours. Serve warm.

Preparation Time: 20 minutes
Cooking Time: 1 1/2 to 2 hours
Servings: 10 to 12

CORNMEAL MEATBALLS

1 1/2-pounds ground beef chuck
1/4 to 1/2-pound ground pork
1 onion, chopped
1 egg, beaten
1/2 teaspoon salt

1/4 teaspoon pepper
1/4 teaspoon garlic powder
1/4 cup milk
1/4 teaspoon basil
1/2 cup cornmeal

Combine ingredients and form into small walnut-sized balls. Brown meatballs or add uncooked meatballs to prepared albondigas broth.

Note: Meatballs can be browned lightly in the oven and drained before adding to the soup.

Preparation Time: 25 minutes
Yield: About 36 meatballs

Byron Pinot Noir

MUSHROOM BARLEY SOUP

1 pound lean ground beef
4 tablespoons butter
3 cloves garlic, chopped
1 medium yellow onion, chopped
3/4 cup celery, diced
3/4 cup carrots, diced
1 pound mushrooms, sliced
8 cups beef broth
1 cup burgundy wine
1/2 cup pearl barley

3 tablespoons chopped parsley
1 tablespoon Worcestershire sauce
1/2 teaspoon ground thyme
1/2 teaspoon ground marjoram
1/8 teaspoon nutmeg
Pinch of ground cloves
2 bay leaves
1 teaspoon salt
1 teaspoon black pepper
Chopped parsley, for garnish

In a large heavy saucepan, brown ground beef well. Drain on paper towels and set aside. Wipe out pan and add butter; saute garlic and onion. Add celery, carrots, and mushrooms; saute 5 minutes longer. Add remaining ingredients, except garnish, stirring to mix well. Add beef and bring to a boil. Reduce heat and simmer for 45 minutes. Skim fat and adjust seasonings. Ladle into bowls and garnish with chopped parsley.

Preparation Time: 30 minutes
Cooking Time: 45 minutes
Servings: 8

ZUCCHINI PEA SOUP

1 pound zucchini, chopped
1/2 cup finely chopped onion
1/3 cup chopped green onions
2 tablespoons vegetable oil
1/4 teaspoon dried thyme
7 cups chicken broth

1 cup water
1 10-ounce package frozen
   petite peas, thawed
Salt and pepper, to taste
Sour cream, for garnish

In a heavy saucepan or skillet, cook zucchini, onion, and green onion in vegetable oil for 3 minutes, or until vegetables are tender. Add thyme, broth, water, and peas. Simmer for 20 minutes. Puree soup and season with salt and pepper. Serve warm in individual soup bowls and garnish with a teaspoonful of sour cream.

Preparation Time: 25 minutes
Cooking Time: 20 minutes
Servings: 6

RED PEPPER SOUP WITH TOASTED CUMIN

1 1/2 medium onions, chopped
2 teaspoons butter
2 large red bell peppers, chopped
1 garlic clove, minced
1 1/2 tablespoons chili powder
2 cups vegetable broth, heated
8 tomatoes, seeded and chopped

1/2 teaspoon cumin seeds, toasted and diced
1/4 cup dry white wine
Salt, to taste
1/2 cup fresh or frozen corn kernels, thawed
Sour cream, for garnish
Cilantro, chopped, for garnish

In a large pot, saute onions in butter until transparent. Add red peppers and saute 2 to 3 minutes. Add garlic and chili powder and saute, stirring, until liquid has evaporated. Add broth and tomatoes; simmer, covered for 30 to 40 minutes. Remove from heat and add cumin seeds, wine, and salt. Puree mixture in batches. Return to pot and heat. Add corn and serve, garnished with a dollop of sour cream and chopped cilantro.

Preparation Time: 20 minutes
Cooking Time: 40 minutes
Servings: 4 to 6

COSTA MESA LIMA BEAN SOUP

1 10-ounce package frozen baby lima beans
2 tablespoons butter or margarine
1/2 cup chopped green onions
1 tablespoon curry powder
Salt, to taste

1 teaspoon fresh ground white pepper
1/2 teaspoon dried tarragon
1/4 cup fresh parsley
1/2 cup heavy cream
1 13 1/2-ounce can chicken broth
Sour cream and chopped chives, for garnish

Cook lima beans, following package directions. In a saute pan, melt butter and saute the green onions to soften; add curry powder. Place lima beans, onion mixture, seasonings, and cream in a food processor and puree until smooth. Return lima bean puree to pan and add chicken broth. Heat completely, about 20 minutes. Serve hot and garnish with a dollop of sour cream and chopped chives.

Preparation Time: 25 to 30 minutes
Cooking Time: 20 minutes
Servings: 6

Active, fit, and outdoorsy, residents of Orange County are always on the move. Exercise comes as naturally as breathing to most. Beaches, parks, and neighborhood streets are dotted with joggers and walkers. Cyclists in neon latex flash past on hilly inland byways, roller bladers of all ages skate down oceanfront boardwalks, and wetsuited stalwarts swim their distance come rain or shine. Horse-lovers explore the hilly inland canyons and miles of equestrian trails on horseback while golfers and tennis players meet the challenges of improving their games. The parking lot of every fitness center and gym is full.

VEGETABLES AND GRAINS

The Oaks in San Juan Capistrano, Joan Irvine Smith's private equestrian training facility known throughout the horse world for its premium string of hunters and jumpers, is an elegant location for a tailgate picnic in the shade of the stately oaks.
Photograph was underwritten by
THE OAKS

126

ARTICHOKE BOTTOMS WITH PUREE OF PARSNIPS

1 pound parsnips, peeled and
   sliced 1/2-inch thick
1/4 cup extra virgin olive oil
1/4 cup plus 1 tablespoon butter,
   softened, divided
1 teaspoon crumbled dried thyme
Salt and pepper, to taste

1 cup dry white wine
2/3 cup light cream
10 canned artichoke bottoms,
   rinsed and drained
2 tablespoons freshly grated
   Parmesan cheese, or to taste
Pimento, optional

In a saucepan, with salted water to cover, boil parsnips for 5 minutes; drain and pat dry. In a saute pan, heat olive oil and 1 tablespoon butter; add parsnips, thyme, salt, and pepper; cook and stir 2 to 3 minutes. Lower heat and add wine; simmer, covered, until very tender, about 10 minutes. In a processor or blender, puree the parsnips and any remaining liquid; add 1/4 cup butter and cream; blend. Season with additional salt and pepper, if needed. Preheat oven to 350 degrees. Put the artichoke bottoms in a buttered 11 x 7-inch baking dish. Mound puree into bottoms; or, fill a pastry bag with the puree and pipe into bottoms. Sprinkle with Parmesan cheese; bake 30 minutes. Garnish with pimento strips, if desired.

Preparation Time: 40 minutes
Baking Time: 30 minutes
Servings: 5 to 10

LIMA BEAN AND CORN CASSEROLE

1 10-ounce package frozen lima beans,
   thawed
1 14 1/2-ounce can vegetable broth
2 tablespoons butter
6 to 8 green onions, thinly sliced
1 10-ounce package frozen corn
2 tablespoons chopped fresh parsley

2 tablespoons finely chopped fresh basil
1 teaspoon minced fresh mint
1 large tomato, peeled, seeded,
   and coarsely chopped
Salt and pepper, to taste
3 tablespoons sour cream
3 tablespoons chopped cilantro

In a saucepan, combine the lima beans and vegetable broth; bring to a boil, reduce heat and simmer 10 to 15 minutes. Drain beans and reserve cooking broth. In a large saucepan, melt butter, add green onions. Cook, stirring occasionally, until softened, 3 to 5 minutes. Add the corn, parsley, basil, mint, reserved lima beans and broth. Bring to a boil, reduce heat and simmer 3 minutes. Add tomato, salt and pepper; cook an additional 5 minutes. Remove from heat, add the sour cream and cilantro, serve immediately.

Preparation Time: 25 minutes
Cooking Time: 25 minutes
Servings: 4 to 6

BAKED TOMATOES WITH BROCCOLI PUREE

This red and green combination is nice for holiday entertaining.

6 medium-size tomatoes
1 pound fresh broccoli
1/3 cup chopped onion
2 tablespoons butter
1/8 teaspoon nutmeg

1/3 cup cream
Salt and pepper, to taste
Freshly grated Parmesan
   cheese, for garnish

Slice tops from tomatoes; scoop out seeds and pulp; drain upside down over paper toweling. Cut broccoli into florets and cut stems into 1-inch pieces. Cook in boiling water, or steam until just tender, about 6 to 7 minutes. Drain and place in cold water.

Meanwhile, in a saute pan, combine the onion and butter. Cook, stirring until tender, about 5 minutes. Add the nutmeg and cream; cook, stirring another minute; set aside. In a blender or food processor, puree the drained broccoli with the onion mixture; season with salt and pepper.

When ready to serve, preheat oven to 350 degrees. Place tomatoes in a lightly greased baking dish. Fill the tomatoes with equal amount of the broccoli puree. Sprinkle a little Parmesan cheese over each tomato. Place in oven and bake, uncovered, 10 minutes, or until heated through.

Preparation Time: 20 minutes
Cooking Time: 10 minutes
Servings: 6

ONIONED NEW POTATOES

An easy version of oven-roasted potatoes

4 pounds baby new potatoes, washed and halved
1/2 cup butter, melted
3 1-ounce packages dry beefy-onion soup mix

Preheat oven to 350 degrees. In a large bowl, combine the potatoes, butter, and soup mix; toss to coat well. Transfer to a rimmed baking pan, about 15 x 11-inches. Bake for 45 to 60 minutes; stirring occasionally.

Note: Recipe easily cuts in half for fewer servings.

Preparation Time: 15 minutes
Baking Time: 45 to 60 minutes
Servings: 10

SAVORY SKILLET CARROTS

1/2 cup butter
2 tablespoons lemon juice
1 1/2 tablespoons brown sugar
2 teaspoons salt, optional

2 tablespoons chopped fresh basil,
   or 1 1/2 teaspoons dried basil
1/8 teaspoon powdered cloves
4 cups shredded carrots

In a saute pan, heat butter until foamy. Add the lemon juice, brown sugar, salt, basil, and cloves; stir to dissolve sugar. Add the carrots; toss until coated with butter mixture. Cover and cook over low heat, stirring once or twice, for 20 minutes, or until carrots are tender.

Note: Shred the carrots before you proceed with melting the butter. Turnips or parsnips can be substituted for the carrots.

Preparation Time: 30 minutes
Servings: 4 to 6

RED CABBAGE WITH GINGER AND BALSAMIC VINEGAR

2 tablespoons butter
1/4 cup extra virgin olive oil
3/4 cup chopped red onion
1 head red cabbage,
   shredded, about 3 pounds

1 teaspoon grated peeled fresh ginger
1 cup dry red wine
3 tablespoons brown sugar
Salt and pepper, to taste
1/4 cup balsamic vinegar

In a saute pan over medium heat, melt butter with oil; add onion and saute until tender, about 6 minutes. Increase heat to high and add cabbage and ginger; cook until cabbage is tender, stirring frequently, about 8 minutes. Reduce heat to medium and add the wine; boil until wine evaporates and cabbage appears dry, stirring occasionally, about 4 minutes. Reduce heat; cover and simmer 10 minutes. Add sugar and season with salt and pepper. Transfer to a bowl; cover and refrigerate overnight. When ready to serve, reheat the cabbage; add vinegar and stir to blend well.

Note: For the best flavor make this a day ahead; reheat briefly before serving.

Preparation Time: 10 minutes
Cooking Time: 30 minutes
Chilling Time: Overnight
Servings: 6

FIESTA CORN PUDDING

Straight from the pantry shelves for easy assembly

1 16-ounce can cream style corn
1 16-ounce can whole kernel corn, drained
1 cup sharp Cheddar cheese
1 cup crushed round buttery crackers
1 medium onion, finely chopped
1 7-ounce can chopped Ortega chilies,
  drained

1 egg, beaten
3 tablespoons sugar
2/3 cup evaporated milk
1/3 cup melted butter
3 dashes hot pepper sauce, or to taste
Salt and pepper, to taste
Additional sharp Cheddar cheese, grated

Preheat oven to 350 degrees. In a large bowl, combine the corn, cheese, cracker crumbs, onion, and chilies; stir to blend. Add the egg, sugar, milk, butter, hot pepper sauce, salt and pepper; fold together until well blended. Transfer to a buttered 3-quart casserole or 13 x 9-inch baking dish. Sprinkle top with additional Cheddar cheese; bake for 1 hour.

Preparation Time: 15 minutes
Baking Time: 1 hour
Servings: 6 to 8

CORN AND POTATO CAKES

1 pound russet potatoes,
  peeled and coarsely grated
3/4 cup finely chopped green bell pepper
1 1/2 cups fresh corn
4 to 5 green onions, thinly sliced

1 1/2 teaspoons ground cumin
3 tablespoons flour
Salt and pepper to taste
2 tablespoons olive oil or butter, divided
Sour cream, optional

Place the potatoes and green peppers in a kitchen towel, or several layers of paper towels; squeeze out the excess moisture. Place in a large bowl; add the corn, onions, cumin, flour, salt and pepper; toss to combine. In a saute pan, heat 1 tablespoon of oil; drop large spoonfuls of potato mixture into pan and flatten into 3 to 4-inch patties. Cook until patties are golden brown and crispy; turn and cook the other side, about 4 to 6 minutes each side. Remove and keep warm. Add the remaining tablespoon oil and repeat the process with remaining potato mixture. Serve warm with a dollop of sour cream, if desired.

Preparation Time: 30 minutes
Servings: 4 to 6

FRESH GREEN BEANS WITH GLAZED ONIONS

1 1-pound bag frozen pearl onions, thawed, or 1 pound fresh, skins removed

4 tablespoons seasoned rice vinegar, divided

1 tablespoon butter

3 tablespoons extra virgin olive oil, divided

2 teaspoons chopped fresh thyme or 1 teaspoon dried

3/4 teaspoon salt

1 teaspoon pepper

1 1/4 pounds fresh young green beans, trimmed

2 teaspoons Dijon mustard

Preheat oven to 400 degrees. Place onions in a medium-size bowl. In a small saucepan or cup, combine 2 tablespoons of the vinegar, butter, 2 tablespoons of the olive oil, thyme, salt and pepper; heat or microwave until butter melts. Stir and add to onions; toss. Place in a rimmed baking dish; bake, stirring frequently, 35 to 40 minutes, until evenly browned. Remove from oven and set aside.

Reduce oven to 350 degrees. Meanwhile, steam or blanch the green beans, until just tender, about 4 minutes. Drain and refresh under cold water; drain and set aside. In a large bowl, combine 2 tablespoons vinegar, 1 tablespoon oil, and mustard; add beans and onions; toss to mix. Transfer to a 2-quart baking dish; cover and bake 15 minutes, or until heated through.

Note: This can be made a day ahead and refrigerated; bake a little longer. Balsamic vinegar may be used in place of the seasoned rice vinegar.

Preparation Time: 50 minutes
Baking Time: 15 minutes
Servings: 4 to 6

ROASTED PEPPERS AND ONIONS

A simple, fresh, and interesting combination of flavors and colors

2 tablespoons extra virgin olive oil

3 bell peppers: 1 red, 1 green, and 1 yellow; cored, seeded, and thinly sliced

2 medium onions, thinly sliced

1 large garlic clove, minced

1 small piece fresh ginger, peeled, and grated, optional

1/2 cup chopped cilantro

Salt and pepper, to taste

Preheat oven to 425 degrees. In a rimmed baking sheet, combine the olive oil, peppers, onions, garlic, and ginger; bake, stirring frequently until cooked through and beginning to brown, about 15 minutes. Add cilantro, salt and pepper; cook an additional minute.

Preparation Time: 10 minutes
Baking Time: 15 minutes
Servings: 4

PEPPERS AGRODOLCE

8 bell peppers: 2 yellow, 2 red and
   4 green, seeded and sliced into
   1/2-inch pieces
4 tablespoons extra virgin olive oil,
   divided
Salt and pepper, to taste
2 cups herb seasoned bread stuffing mix

1 6-ounce jar or can pitted green olives,
   drained and sliced
1/4 cup pine nuts, toasted
1/4 cup drained capers
1/4 cup currants
1/2 cup cider vinegar
1/4 cup sugar

In a large saute pan, combine the peppers, 3 tablespoons of the olive oil, salt and pepper; cook, stirring until tender and softened; remove peppers to a large bowl. Add the remaining 1 tablespoon olive oil to the saute pan; add the stuffing mix; cook and stir until golden brown. Add olives, pine nuts, capers and currants; cook and stir about 1 minute. Add the vinegar and sugar; mix well. When blended, add peppers; cook and stir for another 1 to 2 minutes. Transfer to a serving bowl. Serve warm, or at room temperature.

Note: This colorful dish will keep several days in the refrigerator.

Preparation Time: 30 minutes
Servings: 8 to 10

PEPPERS GORGONZOLA

This is a wonderful accompaniment to grilled steaks or chops. These peppers may be served as a first course or as an appetizer on baguette slices.

4 red, yellow, or green bell peppers
   or a combination
1/2 cup crumbled Gorgonzola cheese

1/4 cup freshly grated Parmesan cheese
1 tablespoon lemon juice

Place peppers on a broiling pan; broil, turning often until all sides are blackened. Place peppers in a paper or plastic bag; set aside for 15 to 20 minutes. When cool enough to handle, remove skin, discard stems and seeds, and cut into 2-inch strips; place in a 1 quart, lightly greased baking dish. Preheat oven to 400 degrees. Sprinkle peppers with the Gorgonzola and Parmesan cheese; drizzle with lemon juice. Bake 10 minutes, or until bubbly and brown.

Preparation Time: 30 minutes
Baking Time: 10 minutes
Servings: 4

CARAMELIZED ONIONS

This is a delicious condiment with grilled or roasted meats, sandwiches, or as an appetizer on baguette slices.

2 large onions, thinly sliced,
   about 1 1/4 pounds
1 tablespoon vegetable oil
3 tablespoons brown sugar

3/4 cup red wine
3 tablespoons balsamic vinegar
Salt and pepper, to taste

In a large saute or saucepan, combine the onions, oil, and brown sugar; cook over moderate heat, stirring often, until onions begin to caramelize and turn golden, about 20 to 25 minutes. Add wine and vinegar, increase heat, and bring to a boil. Reduce heat to low and cook, stirring often, until most of the liquid has evaporated, about 15 minutes. Season with salt and pepper; cool. Serve warm or at room temperature. Onions will keep, refrigerated, up to 3 weeks.

Note: Baby white onions can be prepared this way for delicious appetizers. Just reduce cooking time. To serve; place in a bowl and provide toothpicks.

Preparation Time: 10 minutes
Cooking Time: 45 minutes
Yield: 2 cups

SUGAR SNAP PEAS SAUTE

1 pound sugar snap peas, trimmed
1 1/2 to 2 tablespoons extra
   virgin olive oil
1/3 cup chicken broth

Salt and pepper, to taste
2 tablespoons fresh dill,
   or 2 teaspoons dried dill

In a large saute pan, combine the peas, oil, and broth; cook over moderately high heat, covered, for about 4 minutes. Remove cover, season with salt, pepper, and dill; continue cooking stirring frequently, for 2 to 3 minutes, until the liquid is absorbed and a few of the peas begin to brown slightly.   Serve immediately.

Note: This preparation works well with other vegetables; asparagus is especially good, as well as the baby vegetables.

Preparation Time: 15 minutes
Servings: 4

EGGPLANT CASSEROLE

1 1/2-pound eggplant, peeled
  and cut in 2-inch pieces
2 tablespoons oil or butter
1/2 medium green pepper, chopped
4 green onions, thinly sliced

Salt and pepper, to taste
2 eggs, beaten
1/2 cup soda crackers or round buttery
  cracker crumbs
2 cups grated Cheddar cheese, divided

Preheat oven to 350 degrees. In a large saucepan, with water to cover, cook eggplant until tender, about 12 to 15 minutes; drain very well. In a saute pan, heat oil or butter; add green pepper and onions, cook, and stir until tender. Mash drained eggplant, add to onion mixture; season with salt and pepper. Remove from heat, add eggs and cracker crumbs; blend. Place half the mixture in a buttered 1 1/2-quart baking dish; sprinkle with 1 1/2 cups of the cheese. Cover with remaining vegetable mixture; top with remaining 1/2 cup cheese. Bake covered for 25 minutes; remove cover and continue baking for 15 minutes.

Note: This casserole can be made earlier in the day; bake just before serving.

Preparation Time: 40 minutes
Baking Time: 40 minutes
Servings: 10

Robert Mondavi Chardonnay

SPINACH AND SOUR CREAM CASSEROLE

1 10-ounce package frozen chopped spinach
1/3 cup grated onion
1/2 cup water
2 eggs, beaten
1/2 cup sour cream

1 cup freshly grated Parmesan cheese
1 tablespoon flour
2 tablespoons butter, melted
Salt and pepper, to taste
Pinch nutmeg

In a saucepan, combine spinach and onion with water; cook until spinach is thawed; drain well. Squeeze the spinach mixture in a towel to remove all liquid. Preheat oven to 350 degrees. Place spinach in a large bowl; add eggs, sour cream, Parmesan cheese, flour, butter, salt, pepper, and nutmeg; blend well. Transfer mixture to a greased 11 x 7-inch pan or baking dish. Bake 25 to 30 minutes or until a knife inserted in center comes out clean.

Preparation Time: 20 minutes
Baking Time: 25 to 30 minutes
Servings: 6

SWEET POTATO ORANGE CUPS

These attractive and fun cups are especially good with a holiday turkey.

4 large oranges
3 cups mashed sweet potatoes or yams,
   canned or freshly baked
3/4 teaspoon salt
1/4 cup brown sugar

1/4 cup brandy
1 tablespoon cream
2 tablespoons butter
1/3 cup chopped pecans

Preheat oven to 325 degrees. Cut oranges in halves and scoop out pulp. Cut pulp into small pieces, discarding seeds and membrane; fold into mashed sweet potatoes. Add salt and brown sugar; blend well. In a small pan, combine brandy, cream, and butter; heat until butter melts. Add to sweet potato mixture; beat until well blended and fluffy. Spoon into prepared orange shells; place in a greased shallow baking pan. Bake for 15 to 20 minutes. Sprinkle tops with the chopped pecans; return to oven and continue baking for another 15 to 20 minutes, until heated through.

Preparation Time: 30 minutes
Baking Time: 30 to 40 minutes
Servings: 8

CREAMY MASHED POTATO CASSEROLE

A delicious make-ahead mashed potato dish

2 1/2 pounds potatoes, peeled
   and cut in pieces
1 8-ounce package cream cheese,
   softened and cubed
1 medium yellow onion, minced

3 eggs, beaten
3 tablespoons flour
Salt and pepper, to taste
1 3-ounce can French fried onions

Preheat oven to 325 degrees. Cook potatoes in salted water to cover until tender, 15 to 20 minutes; drain well and mash. Add cream cheese cubes; beat until smooth. Add onion, eggs, flour, salt and pepper; beat until light and fluffy. Spoon into a lightly buttered 2-quart baking dish. Sprinkle top with French fried onions; cover. Bake for 30 minutes; remove cover and continue baking for another 30 minutes, or until top is golden.

Note: If potatoes are made ahead and refrigerated, bring to room temperature before baking.

Preparation Time: 30 minutes
Baking Time: 1 hour
Servings: 8

HERB POTATOES

2 pounds red or white new potatoes,
   cut into 4 to 6 pieces
1 1/2 to 2 pounds yellow onions,
   thinly sliced
2 to 3 tablespoons extra virgin olive oil
3 garlic cloves, crushed

1/2 cup fresh parsley, minced
3 tablespoons fresh minced dill,
   or 1 tablespoon dried dill
3 tablespoons fresh minced basil,
   or 1 tablespoon dried basil
Salt and pepper, to taste

Preheat oven to 425 degrees. In a rimmed baking pan, combine the potatoes, onions, olive oil, garlic, parsley, dill, and basil; toss well to combine. Bake for about 30 minutes, until cooked through and browned; stirring frequently. Season with salt and pepper and serve immediately.

Preparation Time: 10 minutes
Baking Time: 30 minutes
Servings: 8 to 10

BAKED POTATOES, TOMATOES, AND ONIONS

2 pounds baking potatoes, peeled
   and sliced 1/4-inch thick
2 cups thinly sliced onion
1 pound firm ripe tomatoes, peeled,
   seeded and cut in 1/2-inch dice,
   about 2 cups
1 cup freshly grated Asiago,
   Romano, or Parmesan cheese

1 tablespoon chopped fresh oregano
   or 1 teaspoon dried oregano
1/2 cup water
Salt and pepper, to taste
3 tablespoons extra virgin olive oil

Preheat oven to 400 degrees. In a large bowl combine the potatoes, onion, tomatoes, cheese, oregano, water, salt and pepper. Toss to mix well. Spoon mixture into a lightly oiled 13 x 9-inch baking dish; drizzle olive oil on top. Bake on top rack of the oven for 1 hour, stirring every 20 minutes. Set aside for 10 minutes and serve.

Preparation Time: 30 minutes
Baking Time: 1 hour
Servings: 6

SWEET POTATO CRESCENDO

A tasty version of the traditional Potatoes Anna. Good served with chicken, turkey, or pork.

4 medium sweet potatoes or yams,
   about 2 pounds
6 tablespoons melted butter, divided

3/4 cup Parmesan cheese
Salt and pepper, to taste

Peel potatoes and slice 1/8-inch thick; a food processor works well. Preheat oven to 425 degrees. Coat bottom of a 9-inch ovenproof skillet or a 9-inch cake pan with 1 tablespoon of the butter. Arrange 1/6 of the slices overlapping in bottom of pan. Drizzle with 1 tablespoon of the butter, sprinkle with 2 tablespoons Parmesan cheese, and season with salt and pepper. Repeat process 5 additional times. Cover wih foil, press down to compress potatoes. Bake for 30 minutes on lowest rack. Uncover and bake 45 minutes longer. Invert onto a serving platter.

Preparation Time: 25 minutes
Baking Time: 1 hour, 15 minutes
Servings: 6

STUFFED CHAYOTE SQUASH

2 chayote squash, halved vertically,
   and seeds removed
1 tablespoon butter
1/4 cup minced red bell pepper
1/4 cup minced onion
5 medium mushrooms, minced

2 tablespoons chopped fresh parsley
1/4 teaspoon ground allspice
1/2 teaspoon salt
1/4 teaspoon pepper
1 cup shredded Provolone cheese, divided
4 tablespoons chopped chutney

Place chayote in boiling water to cover; cook for 20 minutes. Drain in a colander; cool slightly. Scoop out the flesh, leaving shell intact; chop the flesh. In a large skillet combine the butter, red pepper, onion, mushrooms, parsley, allspice, salt and pepper. Saute for 4 to 5 minutes; add chopped chayote and 3/4 cup of the cheese. Preheat oven to 350 degrees. Place shells in a lightly greased 8-inch square baking dish. Fill with vegetable-cheese mixture; top with remaining cheese. Bake 7 to 8 minutes or until cheese melts and filling is heated through. Place a tablespoon of chutney on each squash half before serving.

Note: This squash may be prepared ahead and refrigerated. Increase baking time.

Preparation Time: 30 minutes
Baking Time: 7 to 8 minutes
Servings: 4

ZUCCHINI GRATIN

2 pounds zucchini, cleaned and
  coarsely grated
3 eggs, lightly beaten
6 green onions, thinly sliced
1/2 cup finely chopped fresh parsley
1/2 cup finely chopped fresh mint leaves
2 cups grated Gruyere cheese, divided
1/4 cup crumbled Feta cheese

1 teaspoon salt
1/4 teaspoon cayenne
1 cup flour
15 to 20 brine-cured black olives,
  pitted and halved
1 cup fresh bread crumbs
1/4 cup butter, cut into small pieces

Preheat oven to 375 degrees. In a large bowl, combine the zucchini, eggs, onions, parsley, mint, 1 cup of the Gruyere cheese, Feta cheese, salt, and cayenne; mix well. Fold in the flour and olives; spread in a lightly buttered 13 x 9-inch baking dish. Combine the remaining 1 cup Gruyere and bread crumbs; spread on the gratin; dot the topping with butter. Bake for 40 minutes, or until top is golden brown.

Note: This vegetable may be prepared a few hours ahead and refrigerated; it will need a few minutes longer baking time.

Preparation Time: 30 minutes
Baking Time: 40 minutes
Servings: 8 to 10

BUTTERNUT SQUASH GRATIN

3 pounds butternut squash or
  any yellow winter squash
1 teaspoon cinnamon

1 teaspoon salt
1 cup heavy cream

Preheat oven to 400 degrees. Peel and halve the squash; discard seeds and cut in chunks. In a food processor, coarsely grate the squash. Put in a large bowl; add the cinnamon and salt; toss to blend. Spread in a greased 13 x 9-inch baking dish. Pour the cream evenly over the squash; cover loosely with foil. Bake for 20 minutes; remove foil and bake 10 minutes longer, or until tender.

Note: This creamy squash may be prepared and baked early in the day and refrigerated. Reheat for 20 minutes before serving.

Preparation Time: 20 minutes
Baking Time: 30 minutes
Servings: 8 to 10

ROJAS CON QUESO

This chile dish is great with Mexican food or with most grilled meats.

4 fresh Anaheim or Poblanos chilies,
   3 to 4 ounces each
3 tablespoons oil
2 large yellow onions, peeled
   and thinly sliced
1/4 cup hot water

4 medium tomatoes, peeled,
   seeded, and chopped
1 1/2 teaspoons salt
1 8-ounce package cream cheese,
   cut in pieces

Preheat broiler. Cut chilies in half, remove stems and seeds. Place, cut side down, on broiler rack; broil until skins begin to blister and blacken, about 7 to 8 minutes. Cool slightly; remove skin and cut into strips. In a saute pan, heat oil; add onions and cook until lightly browned, 8 to 10 minutes. Add chilies, water, tomatoes, and salt; cook over moderately low heat until the liquid comes to a boil. Stir in cream cheese; simmer, stirring occasionally, for 10 minutes. Serve immediately or make ahead and reheat as needed.

Preparation time: 45 minutes
Servings: 4 to 6

ORZO AND BLACK BEANS

2 1/3 cups water
Salt, to taste
Pinch of saffron threads
1 cup orzo
1 tablespoon olive oil
1 small onion, chopped
1 large clove garlic, peeled and minced
1 teaspoon ground cumin

2 15-ounce cans black beans,
   drained and rinsed
1 cup chicken broth
1 small zucchini, diced
1 cup broccoli florets
1 cup diagonally sliced green beans
1/2 cup thinly sliced red bell pepper
Cilantro leaves, garnish

In a saucepan, combine the water, salt, and saffron; bring to a boil. Remove from heat for 10 minutes. Return to a boil, add orzo, cover, and remove from heat to let the liquid be absorbed, about 15 minutes. Meanwhile, in a saute pan, heat oil; add onion and garlic; cook until tender, about 5 minutes. Add cumin, beans, and broth; cook until beans are creamy, stirring frequently. If bean mixture becomes too dry, add additional broth. Steam zucchini, broccoli, green beans, and red pepper until just tender. Combine the orzo and vegetables; top with black bean mixture and garnish with cilantro.

Preparation Time: 50 minutes
Servings: 6

MEXICAN GREEN RICE

2 Poblano chilies, roasted, peeled,
    seeded, and chopped
1/2 cup chopped green bell pepper
3 cloves garlic
1/4 cup cilantro
1/4 cup Italian parsley
2 tablespoons vegetable oil

4 green onions, thinly sliced
1 cup rice, rinsed and drained
1 1/2 cups chicken broth
Additional cilantro or parsley, for garnish
Shredded Jack or Parmesan cheese,
    for garnish

In a blender or processor, combine the chilies, pepper, garlic, cilantro, and parsley. In a large saucepan, combine the oil, onions, and rice, cooking and stirring until onion is soft, about 3 to 4 minutes. Add the blended mixture and the broth. Cook, covered, over medium heat until liquid is absorbed and rice is tender, about 25 minutes. Serve with garnishes.

Note: This south-of-the-border rice is good with Mexican food, or with simply prepared chicken or meat. To save time, canned chilies can be used.

Preparation Time: 45 minutes
Servings: 4 to 6

BROWN RICE AND VEGETABLES MEXICAN STYLE

2 tablespoons butter or vegetable oil
1 medium green pepper, stemmed,
seeded, and coarsely chopped
1 medium crookneck squash,
    coarsely chopped
1 medium pattypan squash,
    coarsely chopped
2 small zucchini, halved lengthwise
    and sliced
12 fresh medium mushrooms, sliced

2 cloves garlic, minced
1 large yellow onion, coarsely chopped
4 cups cooked brown rice
1 16-ounce can tomato sauce
1 8-ounce can salsa
1 4-ounce can diced green chilies,
    drained
Salt and pepper, to taste
2 cups grated sharp Cheddar cheese
1/3 cup unsalted sunflower seeds

In a saute pan, melt butter or oil; add green pepper, crookneck, pattypan, zucchini, mushrooms, garlic, and onion; cook, stirring occasionally, until vegetables are soft and liquid has evaporated. Preheat oven to 350 degrees. In a buttered 13 x 9-inch dish, spread the cooked brown rice and cover with vegetable mixture. In a bowl, combine the tomato sauce, salsa, chilies, salt and pepper; pour over vegetables; top with cheese and sunflower seeds. Bake until heated through and cheese is melted, about 30 minutes.

Note: For a variation, add cooked shredded chicken.

Preparation Time: 30 to 40 minutes
Baking Time: 30 minutes
Servings: 4 to 8

CURRIED APRICOT RICE

1/4 cup butter
3/4 cup thinly sliced green onion
2 cups uncooked converted rice
4 cups chicken broth
1 tablespoon curry powder

3/4 teaspoon garlic salt
4 drops hot pepper sauce, or to taste
1 cup finely chopped dried apricots
1/3 cup chopped fresh parsley
1 cup pine nuts or slivered almonds, toasted

In a large saucepan, melt butter; add onion and saute for 2 minutes. Add rice, broth, curry powder, garlic salt, hot pepper sauce, and apricots; heat to boiling. Reduce heat and simmer, covered, for 20 to 25 minutes, or until liquid is absorbed. Let stand for 5 minutes; add parsley and nuts; stir to combine.

Preparation Time: 40 minutes
Servings: 10

LEMON RICE

1 cup rice
2 cups chicken broth
2 tablespoons butter
2 tablespoons lemon juice
1 teaspoon lemon zest or more, to taste

Salt and pepper, to taste
1/2 cup freshly grated Parmesan cheese
8 tablespoons finely chopped chives
    or green onions
8 tablespoons minced parsley

In a saucepan, combine the rice, broth, butter, lemon juice, lemon zest, salt and pepper. Bring to a boil; reduce the heat and simmer, covered, until the liquid is absorbed, about 25 minutes. Add Parmesan cheese, chives, and parsley; toss and serve.

Note: This rice is easy to prepare and very good with chicken or fish. The rice can be prepared ahead and reheated; add the Parmesan cheese, chives and parsley just before serving.

Preparation Time: 35 minutes
Servings: 4 to 6

QUINOA PILAF

Quinoa is a tiny grain that was a staple food in the Inca civilization. It is one of the best sources of complete protein in the vegetable kingdom. It has a light nutty taste; here is a nice change from the usual side dishes.

1 cup quinoa, rinsed and drained	2 medium carrots, finely chopped
1 3/4 cups chicken broth	1/3 cup chopped celery
1 tablespoon extra virgin olive oil	1 teaspoon minced garlic
1/3 cup diced green pepper	1/4 cup freshly grated Parmesan cheese
1/3 cup diced red pepper	Salt and pepper to taste
2 leeks, white part only, finely chopped	1/4 cup chopped Italian parsley

In a saucepan, combine the quinoa and broth; bring to a boil. Reduce heat and simmer, covered, until tender and all liquid is absorbed, about 5 minutes. Meanwhile, in a saute pan, heat oil; add the green and red peppers, leeks, carrots, and celery. Cook stirring until softened, 6 to 7 minutes; add garlic, continue cooking for a minute longer. Add cooked quinoa, Parmesan cheese, salt, pepper, and parsley. Serve immediately.

Note: This may be prepared ahead and refrigerated; reheat over low heat.

Preparation Time: 30 minutes
Servings: 6

ORZO WITH DRIED CHERRIES

A light side dish to serve with chicken or duckling

1 cup orzo	3 tablespoons extra vigin olive oil
6 cups water	1/3 cup dried cherries, chopped
1/4 teaspoon saffron	3 tablespoons slivered almonds, toasted
1 tablespoon orange zest	2 to 3 green onions, thinly sliced
2 tablespoons orange juice	Salt and pepper to taste

In a saucepan, combine the orzo, water, and saffron; bring to a boil for 8 minutes or until al dente; drain well. In a bowl, combine the orange zest, orange juice, and oil; whisk together until well blended. Add to the orzo, stir in the cherries, almonds, green onions, and season with salt and pepper; mix well.

Preparation Time: 20 minutes
Servings: 4

MANDARIN WILD RICE

Especially good with chicken or pork

1 cup wild rice, rinsed and drained
5 1/2 cups chicken broth
1 cup golden raisins
1 cup pecan halves
5 green onions, thinly sliced

Zest of 1 orange or 2 tangerines
1/3 cup fresh orange or tangerine juice
1/4 cup light oil
Salt and pepper, to taste

In a saucepan, combine the rice and broth; bring to a boil. Reduce heat; simmer uncovered 45 to 60 minutes or until rice is tender; drain. Transfer to a bowl. Add raisins, pecans, onions, orange zest, juice, oil, salt and pepper; toss together. Stand at room temperature for 2 hours. Warm slightly before serving, or serve at room temperature; best if it is not too hot.

Cooking Time: 1 hour
Marinating Time: 2 hours
Servings: 6 to 8

CORN RISOTTO WITH SAGE

3 medium-size ears fresh corn,
  husks and silk removed, or 2 1/2 cups
  frozen corn, divided
1 tablespoon butter
1 large onion, finely chopped
1 cup short-grain white rice,
  arborio, or pearl

3 1/2 cups warm chicken broth, divided
1/3 cup freshly grated Parmesan cheese
1/3 cup shredded Fontina cheese
3 tablespoons chopped fresh sage
  or 2 teaspoons dry sage leaves
Fresh sage leaves, for garnish

If using fresh corn, cut kernels from cobs; set aside. In a large skillet, melt butter; add onion; cook, stirring often until soft, about 5 minutes. Stir in 3/4 of the corn. Add 1 cup of the chicken broth; bring to a boil, stirring often. Add 1/2 cup more broth; reduce heat and simmer, uncovered. Continue adding broth, stirring often, until rice is tender and most of liquid is absorbed, 20 to 25 minutes. Lower heat and stir as mixture thickens. Remove from heat; fold in cheeses, and chopped sage; let stand until cheese melts, about 2 minutes. Transfer to a warmed bowl or platter. Meanwhile, cook the remaining corn and garnish with corn and sage leaves.

Preparation Time: 1 hour
Servings: 4

LENTILS, BULGUR, AND FRESH HERBS

1 tablespoon extra virgin olive oil
1 large onion, finely chopped
3 medium carrots, finely chopped,
   about 1/2 pound
2 celery ribs, finely chopped
1 cup lentils
1 cup bulgur

Salt and pepper, to taste
3 cups chicken broth
2 bay leaves
1/3 cup finely chopped Italian parsley
3 tablespoons finely chopped
   fresh cilantro
3 tablespoons finely chopped fresh mint

In a large saucepan, heat olive oil; add the onion, carrots, and celery. Cook over moderate heat, stirring, until soft, about 8 minutes. Add the lentils, bulgur, salt, pepper, bay leaves, and broth. Bring to a boil; reduce heat and cook tightly covered until liquid is absorbed, about 30 minutes. Add parsley, cilantro, and mint, stirring to blend; serve warm.

Preparation Time: 1 hour
Servings: 6

BARLEY PILAF

This pilaf is a good side dish with beef, lamb, or pork. It may be used to stuff a crown roast.

3 tablespoons extra virgin olive oil
3 tablespoons butter
2 medium-size leeks, cleaned
   and chopped, white part only
1 cup thinly sliced celery
2 cups pearl barley
1 bay leaf

1 teaspoon dried thyme
1 teaspoon salt
1/2 teaspoon freshly ground pepper
3 1/2 cups beef broth
1/2 cup dry red wine
1/2 cup minced fresh Italian parsley
1/4 cup minced fresh chives

Preheat oven to 350 degrees. In an ovenproof pan or casserole, heat the oil and butter over medium-low heat. Add leeks and celery; saute until soft, about 6 minutes. Add barley, bay leaf, thyme, salt and pepper; stir to coat. Add broth and wine, bring to a boil; cover tightly and place in oven. Bake until liquid is absorbed, about 40 minutes. Add parsley and chives; stir to combine.

Preparation Time: 15 minutes
Baking Time: 40 minutes
Servings: 8 to 10

From the historic mission town of San Juan Capistrano to the modern university community of Irvine, from the sprawling estates and horse property of Coto de Caza to the picturesque artists' colony of Laguna Beach, each of Orange County's communities has its own distinctive personality. The common thread running through them all? A rare kind of community spirit, the kind of spirit that causes ordinary citizens to volunteer to pose, night after night, in the living tableaux of famous artworks of the Pageant of the Masters in Laguna. The kind of spirit that causes owners of long sleek sailing vessels and ramshackle rowboats to decorate them from bow to stern and join the annual boat parades at Huntington Harbour and Newport Beach. The kind of spirit that causes schoolteachers and accountants, homemakers and research scientists from Fullerton to San Clemente to volunteer their time and personal resources to the dream of building and maintaining a world renowned performing arts facility for their children's children.

PASTA

Flowers seem to be brighter at the beach and food always tastes better outdoors. This Emerald Bay photograph was underwritten by the FRIENDS OF STERLING PERFORMANCES

SEA SCALLOPS WITH BROCCOLI
AND RED PEPPER WITH PASTA

A beautiful dish! The red and green colors with the yellow of the saffron sauce makes a lovely pasta presentation.

2 large red bell peppers
1 pound broccoli, cleaned
12 ounces penne, fusilli or ziti
4 tablespoons extra virgin olive oil,
  divided
2 shallots, finely chopped
3/4 cup dry white wine
1 teaspoon white wine vinegar

3/4 cup heavy cream
3/4 cup butter, melted
Salt to taste
Freshly ground pepper to taste
1/4 teaspoon saffron threads
12 firm, sea scallops, rinsed and horizontally
  sliced 1/8-inch thick, about 1 pound
Chopped parsley for garnish

Under a hot broiler, broil peppers, turning until charred on all sides, about 15 minutes. When cool enough to handle, remove the skins and seeds and cut into 1 1/2-inch long thin strips. Separate broccoli florets from stems and cut stems into thin slices. Steam broccoli until tender, about 8 to 10 minutes. Refresh under cold water and drain. Set aside.

Cook pasta until al dente. Drain, toss with 2 tablespoons olive oil, and arrange on serving platter. Keep warm, covered, off the heat.

Meanwhile, combine shallots, white wine, and vinegar in a small, heavy saucepan. Cook over medium heat until the liquid has evaporated. Whisk in the cream, lower the heat and simmer until reduced by one-half. Remove the pan from heat and slowly whisk in the melted butter. Season to taste with salt and pepper and stir in the saffron. Keep sauce warm off the heat over a saucepan of hot water.

Season scallops with salt and pepper and saute with remaining 2 tablespoons olive oil until opaque. Add pepper strips, broccoli and toss until warm. Add more olive oil, if needed. Take care not to overcook scallops or vegetables. Combine with saffron sauce. Spoon over the pasta and garnish with parsley. Serve immediately.

Preparation Time: 45 minutes to 1 hour
Servings: 6

Robert Mondavi Woodbridge Sauvignon Blanc

THAI CHICKEN ANGEL HAIR PASTA

1 tablespoon peanut butter
1 cup peanut oil
1 tablespoon sesame oil
1/2 cup rice wine vinegar
3 tablespoons soy sauce
2 tablespoons chopped fresh cilantro
2 jalapeno peppers, seeded and chopped
3 to 4 green onions, thinly sliced
4 cloves garlic, peeled and minced
Juice of 2 limes
1 teaspoon red pepper flakes

1/4 teaspoon hot pepper sauce
1/2 teaspoon white pepper
1 1/2 pounds chicken breasts, boned
    and skinned
1 teaspoon salt
1 pound angel hair pasta
1/2 pound fresh snow peas, strings removed
3 medium carrots, julienned,
    about 1/2 pound
1/2 cup salted peanuts
2 tablespoons chopped cilantro

In a large glass or stainless steel bowl, combine the peanut butter, peanut oil, sesame oil, vinegar, soy sauce, cilantro, jalapeno peppers, green onions, garlic, lime juice, red pepper flakes, hot pepper sauce, and white pepper. Rub the chicken breasts with the salt and slice into thin strips. Add to marinade; set aside for 2 hours. Drain chicken; pat dry and reserve marinade. Grill or pan-fry chicken strips until cooked through.

Meanwhile, cook pasta according to package directions until al dente; drain. In a large saute pan, bring reserved marinade to a boil, add snow peas and carrots; cook and stir for 2 minutes. Combine with the chicken strips and pasta; sprinkle with peanuts. Garnish with cilantro and serve.

Preparation Time: 25 minutes
Marinating Time: 2 hours
Cooking Time: 20 minutes
Servngs: 4 to 6

Vichon Chevrignon

ROASTED ONION AND TURKEY LASAGNA

3 1/2 pounds thinly sliced
   yellow onions
3 thick slices bacon, diced
3 tablespoons balsamic vinegar
1 1/2 pounds ground turkey
3 tablespoons finely chopped fresh
   thyme, or 1 tablespoon dried thyme

12 wide lasagna noodles, about 6 ounces
2 cups chicken broth
1 1/2 cups milk
2 tablespoons cornstarch,
   dissolved in 1/4 cup water
1 1/2 cups freshly grated Parmesan cheese

Preheat oven to 400 degrees. In an 11 x 17-inch roasting pan, combine the onions, bacon, and vinegar; bake, stirring occasionally until onions and bacon are browned, about 1 hour.

Add the turkey and thyme, stirring to combine. Bake an additional 12 to 15 minutes until turkey has turned white. Place mixture in a bowl, set aside pan. Meanwhile, cook lasagna noodles according to package directions, until al dente, about 8 minutes. Drain; place in cold water; set aside.

To roasting pan, add the broth and milk; place over high heat and bring to a boil. Add cornstarch mixture; stirring until it comes to a boil; remove from heat. Drain noodles well, blotting dry. Place 6 noodles, overlapping, in bottom of a greased 13 x 9-inch pan. Top with half of the onion mixture, sauce, and cheese; repeat layers to use remaining ingredients. Reduce oven temperature to 375 degrees. Bake lasagna, uncovered, until hot and bubbling about 40 to 45 minutes. Let stand 10 minutes before serving.

Preparation Time: 45 minutes
Baking Time: 1 hour, 45 minutes
Servings: 8

BLACK BEAN LASAGNA

4 pounds Italian style Roma tomatoes, cored and cut in half lengthwise
2 tablespoons extra virgin olive oil
2 to 3 garlic cloves, minced
1 cup firmly packed fresh cilantro, chopped
10 dry lasagna noodles, about 5 ounces
3 15-ounce cans black beans, drained and rinsed

1/3 cup chicken broth
2 teaspoons ground cumin
1 teaspoon chili powder
Salt and pepper, to taste
2 15-ounce cartons ricotta cheese
5 cups Jack cheese, shredded

Preheat oven to 425 degrees. Place tomatoes, cut side up, in a 10 x 15-inch baking pan, it will be crowded. Sprinkle with oil and garlic. Bake until well browned, about 1 1/4 hours; set aside and cool. Peel and discard skins; place in a colander and press to remove liquid.   Combine in a blender or processor with cilantro; blend until smooth. Meanwhile, cook lasagna noodles according to package directions until al dente; drain and place in cold water.

In a bowl, combine the black beans, broth, cumin, and chili powder; mash to incorporate the liquid; season with salt and pepper. In another bowl, combine the ricotta cheese and 2 cups of the Jack cheese.

Drain noodles, pat dry, and arrange 5 noodles in the bottom of a 13 x 9-inch greased baking dish. Top with half the bean mixture, ricotta mixture, and the tomato sauce. Repeat layers to use remaining ingredients. Sprinkle with remaining 3 cups of Jack cheese. Reduce oven to 375 degrees. Bake, uncovered, 45 minutes or until warmed through and bubbly. Remove from oven, let stand 10 minutes; serve.

Preparation Time: 80 minutes
Cooking Time: 45 minutes
Servings: 8

FETTUCCINI WITH ARTICHOKES AND PEAS

1/2 cup butter, divided
3 tablespoons flour
2 1/2 cups hot milk
1 cup freshly grated Parmesan cheese, divided
Salt and pepper, to taste
2 large garlic cloves, minced
2 9-ounce packages frozen artichoke hearts, thawed and drained

1 10-ounce package frozen petite peas, thawed and drained
1 1/2 pounds Roma tomatoes, peeled, seeded, and coarsely chopped
3/4 cup chopped Italian parsley
1 pound fettuccini
1 cup shredded Fontina cheese, divided

In a saucepan, melt 1/4 cup of the butter. Over low heat, whisk in the flour, cook, stirring, for 2 minutes. Gradually add the hot milk, stir well to avoid lumps; bring to a boil. Reduce heat and simmer for 10 minutes, stirring often. Blend in 1/4 cup of the Parmesan cheese and season with salt and pepper. Remove from heat, cover and keep warm.

In a saute pan, cook the garlic in remaining 1/4 cup butter for 1 minute. Add the artichoke hearts; cook until lightly browned, about 5 minutes. Add the peas, cook an additional 3 minutes. Add tomatoes and parsley, cook until tomatoes are tender about 5 to 6 minutes; season with salt and pepper. Meanwhile, cook fettuccini according to package directions until al dente; drain.

Preheat oven to 350 degrees. In a lightly buttered 13 x 9-inch baking dish, spread 1/3 of the sauce. Add half of the fettuccini; top with half the vegetables. Sprinkle with half the remaining Parmesan cheese and half the Fontina cheese. Spread with another 1/3 sauce, remaining fettuccini, and vegetables; top with remaining sauce and remaining Fontina cheese. Bake 20 to 30 minutes.

Note: This dish can be prepared a few hours ahead; bake just before serving.

Preparation Time: 40 minutes
Baking Time: 30 minutes
Servings: 4 to 6

Robert Mondavi Woodbridge Chardonnay

PENNE ALL'ARRABBIATA

6 ounces bacon, chopped
1 onion, chopped
3 to 4 cloves garlic, peeled and chopped
1 28-ounce can ready cut tomatoes
Salt and pepper, to taste

1/4 teaspoon cayenne pepper, or to taste
1 pound penne
1 cup chopped fresh basil leaves
1 cup freshly grated Parmesan cheese

In a skillet, brown bacon until almost crisp; remove and drain bacon on paper towels. Discard all but 2 tablespoons of the drippings. Add the onion and garlic; cook until soft, about 7 minutes. Crumble reserved bacon; add to onions along with undrained tomatoes, salt, pepper, and cayenne. Simmer 20 minutes. Meanwhile, cook penne according to package directions, until al dente; drain well. Put pasta on a warmed platter. Spoon sauce over pasta; top with basil leaves and Parmesan.

Preparation Time: 45 minutes
Servings: 4, as a side dish

Robert Mondavi Pinot Noir

PENNETTE WITH MUSHROOMS

This pasta is cooked like risotto. Though unusual, browning the dry pasta creates an exceptionally good taste.

3 tablespoons extra virgin olive oil,
    divided
1/2 pound mushrooms, sliced
2 cloves garlic, minced
4 tablespoons minced parsley, divided
Salt and pepper, to taste

1 cup beef broth
3 1/2 cups water
12 ounces pennette
1 tablespoon sherry
1/2 cup heavy cream
1 cup freshly grated Parmesan cheese

In a skillet, heat 2 tablespoons of the olive oil. Add the mushrooms, garlic, and 2 tablespoons of the parsley; cook, stirring until mushrooms are tender, about 3 to 4 minutes. Season with salt and pepper; set aside. In a saucepan, combine the broth and water; bring to a simmer over low heat.

In a skillet or large saucepan, heat the remaining tablespoon of olive oil over medium high heat. Add the pennette; cook, stirring, until pasta turns a golden brown, 5 to 8 minutes. Add the sherry; cook until evaporated. Reduce heat and add about 1 cup of the hot broth. Cook, stirring frequently, and continue adding broth as it evaporates until all the broth is used and pasta is al dente, 15 to 25 minutes. Add the cream; cook 1 minute longer. Add reserved mushrooms, Parmesan cheese, and remaining 2 tablespoons parsley. If necessary, season with salt and pepper and serve at once.

Preparation Time: 40 minutes
Servings: 4, as a side dish

Robert Mondavi Chardonnay

SUMMER VEGETABLE AND PASTA BOWL

A quick and colorful way to use the summer vegetables

1 pint cherry tomatoes, halved
1 pint yellow pear tomatoes, halved
4 tablespoons extra virgin olive oil
1 medium red onion, finely chopped
1 large ear of corn, kernels removed,
   or 1 1/3 cup frozen corn
6 to 8 green onions, thinly sliced on
   diagonal, white and green separate

2 large garlic cloves, peeled and minced
12 ounces tiny pasta shells
5 ounces Feta cheese, crumbled
1/2 cup fresh basil, finely shredded,
   or 1/4 cup dry basil leaves
3/4 cup freshly grated Parmesan cheese
Salt and pepper, to taste
Additional Parmesan cheese

Place tomatoes in a nonmetal colander. Sprinkle lightly with salt; let drain for 30 minutes. In a saute pan over medium heat, heat 3 tablespoons of the oil. Add the red onion, corn kernels, white part of sliced onions, and garlic; saute until onions begin to wilt, about 7 minutes.

Meanwhile, cook pasta according to package directions until al dente; drain well, reserving 1 cup of cooking liquid. Return pasta to same pan, add onion mixture, tomatoes, green onion slices, Feta cheese, basil, 1/2 cup Parmesan cheese, remaining tablespoon oil, and 1/2 cup of the reserved cooking liquid. Toss over medium heat, adding more liquid and Parmesan cheese as necessary to form a light sauce. Season with salt and pepper. Serve, passing additional Parmesan cheese.

Preparation Time: 45 minutes
Servings: 4 to 6

SPICED COUSCOUS

A brightly colored side dish; attractive to serve with lamb or chicken

1 large yellow pepper, chopped
1 medium onion, chopped
3 tablespoons vegetable oil
2 1/2 cups corn, freshly cut, or frozen
Salt and pepper, to taste

1 1/2 cups chicken broth
1 cup couscous
2 teaspoons tumeric
1 teaspoon cumin

In a saute pan, combine the yellow pepper, onion and 1 tablespoon of the oil; cook and stir for 3 to 4 minutes. Add corn and remaining oil; cook for another 4 minutes and season with salt and pepper; set aside. In a saucepan, combine the broth, couscous, tumeric, and cumin; bring to a boil, cover, and remove from heat. Let set for about 5 minutes until liquid is absorbed. Combine the couscous with the pepper mixture and serve.

Preparation Time: 25 minutes
Servings: 6

PASTA, GARBANZOS, AND ROASTED RED PEPPERS

This combination of tastes and textures is wonderful.

2 15-ounce cans garbanzo beans,
  rinsed and drained
2 medium red onions, diced, about 1 pound
1/2 cup balsamic vinegar
5 red bell peppers, cored, seeded,
  and diced
2 cups fresh Roma tomatoes,
  seeded, and diced

1 cup fresh basil, chopped, divided
1/2 cup extra virgin olive oil
4 large garlic cloves, peeled and minced
Salt and pepper, to taste
1 1/2 pounds fusilli or rotini pasta
2 cups freshly grated Parmesan cheese,
  divided

In a large bowl, combine the garbanzo beans, onions, and balsamic vinegar; set aside. Preheat broiler. In a bowl, combine the red peppers, tomatoes, 1/4 cup of the basil, olive oil, garlic, salt and pepper. Spread evenly on a large rimmed cookie sheet. Broil until peppers soften and begin to blacken, stirring occasionally, about 15 minutes. Add to the garbanzo mixture.

Meanwhile, cook the pasta according to package directions until al dente; drain well. Combine with garbanzos and peppers; add remaining 3/4 cup basil and 1 cup of the Parmesan cheese; toss to blend. Serve immediately with remaining cup of Parmesan.

Preparation Time: 15 minutes
Cooking Time: 30 minutes
Servings: 8

Robert Mondavi Fumé Blanc

PASTA GRATIN PROVENCAL

Give your meal a Mediterranean flavor. This pasta is good with simply prepared lamb or veal.

3 1/2 cups small tubular pasta
1 1/2 cups brine-cured Nicoise olives,
  pitted and chopped
5 medium tomatoes, peeled, seeded,
  and coarsely chopped

1 tablespoon minced fresh thyme,
  or 1 teaspoon dried
1/4 cup extra virgin olive oil
Salt and pepper, to taste
1 cup freshly grated Parmesan cheese

Preheat oven to 400 degrees. Cook pasta according to package directions until al dente. Meanwhile, in a large bowl, combine the olives, tomatoes, thyme, olive oil, salt and pepper. Drain the cooked pasta; add to bowl with olive mixture and toss together. Place in a slightly oiled 13 x 9-inch baking dish. Cover the top with the Parmesan cheese. Bake for 10 minutes, or until heated through.

Preparation Time: 20 minutes
Baking Time: 10 minutes
Servings: 6

Byron Pinot Noir

BAKED PASTA AND GORGONZOLA

1 pound mushrooms, sliced
3 to 4 garlic cloves, peeled and minced
5 tablespoons butter
1/4 cup fresh sage leaves, chopped,
   or 1 tablespoon dried
8 cups shredded radicchio, divided

1 pound penne or other tubular pasta
2 cups light cream
2 cups freshly grated Parmesan cheese
2 cups crumbled Gorgonzola cheese
Salt and pepper, to taste

In a large saute pan, over low heat, combine the mushrooms, garlic, and butter; cook until liquid from mushrooms evaporates, about 15 minutes. Add sage and 7 cups of the radicchio, stirring to blend; remove from heat and set aside. Preheat oven to 400 degrees. Cook pasta according to package directions until al dente, drain well. In a large bowl, combine pasta, cream, Parmesan cheese, Gorgonzola cheese, salt, pepper, and mushroom mixture; blend well. Turn into a lightly greased 9 x 13-inch baking pan. Bake for 25 minutes, or until heated through. Sprinkle remaining cup of radicchio over the top and serve.

Preparation Time: 40 minutes   Robert Mondavi Woodbridge Cabernet Sauvignon
Baking Time: 25 minutes
Servings: 6 to 8

RIGATONI WITH FRESH HERBS

1/3 cup extra-virgin olive oil
2 teaspoons minced garlic
1/4 teaspoon dried hot red pepper flakes
1/2 cup finely chopped pitted
   green olives
2 tablespoons capers, drained
   and finely chopped
1/2 cup finely chopped Italian parsley
   or cilantro

1/2 cup finely chopped fresh basil leaves
Salt and pepper, to taste
12 ounces rigatoni, or any tubular pasta
2 cups chopped arugula leaves
3/4 cup freshly grated Parmesan cheese,
   plus addtional for garnish

In a skillet, heat oil over moderately low heat. Add garlic and red pepper flakes; cook, stirring 1 to 2 minutes until garlic is soft, but not browned. Add olives and capers; cook an additional 1 minute. Stir in the parsley and basil; remove from heat and season with salt and pepper. Cook rigatoni according to package directions until al dente; drain well. In a large bowl, toss together the pasta, reserved sauce, arugula, and Parmesan cheese. Serve as a side dish with additional cheese.

Preparation time: 30 minutes   Robert Mondavi Cabernet Sauvignon
Cooking Time: 20 minutes
Servings: 4

ANGEL HAIR PASTA WITH TOMATOES AND BASIL

6 medium tomatoes, peeled, and seeded
1 cup fresh, coarsely chopped basil
3 large garlic cloves, thinly sliced
1 teaspoon salt or more, to taste

1 teaspoon pepper
3/4 cup extra virgin olive oil
1 pound angel hair pasta
Freshly grated Parmesan cheese

Cut tomatoes into 1/4-inch dice; place in a bowl. Add the basil, garlic slices, salt, pepper, and olive oil; stir to blend. Set aside for 15 to 30 minutes. Meanwhile, cook the angel hair pasta according to package directions until al dente; drain. Combine the pasta and tomato mixture. Place the serving dish over a large pan with a little boiling water. Let set 15 minutes before serving to allow the pasta to absorb the sauce. Sprinkle with a generous amount of Parmesan cheese; serve. Pass additional Parmesan at the table.

Preparation Time: 30 to 45 minutes
Servings: 4 to 6

Vichon Chardonnay

PASTA AND WHITE BEANS
WITH TOMATO AND HERB SAUCE

1 pound dried white great northern beans
1/3 cup extra virgin olive oil
5 cloves garlic, minced
1/3 cup chopped Italian parsley
3 tablespoons coarsely chopped
   fresh sage leaves
2 bay leaves
1/2 teaspoon crushed red pepper,
   optional

Salt and pepper, to taste
1/2 teaspoon dried oregano
1 cup water
8 Roma tomatoes, peeled, seeded,
   coarsely chopped
1 pound pasta, of choice
1 large red onion, chopped
1 cup fresh basil leaves, chopped
2 cups grated Parmesan cheese

Cook beans according to package directions. Meanwhile, in a saucepan, combine oil, garlic, parsley, sage, bay leaves, red pepper, salt, pepper, and oregano; cook over low heat, stirring for 2 to 3 minutes. Add water; bring to a boil. Add tomatoes; reduce heat and simmer 7 to 8 minutes. Combine beans and the tomato mixture; simmer until heated through, about 5 minutes; discard the bay leaves. Cook pasta according to package directions. To serve divide the pasta in shallow soup or pasta bowls. Ladle the bean mixture over the pasta. Garnish with red onion and basil; sprinkle generously with Parmesan cheese and serve.

Note: Six cups canned white beans may be substituted for the dried beans.

Preparation Time: 1 hour 15 minutes
Servings: 6 to 8

CLASSICAL MUSIC ABOUNDS

Nothing can compare to the sweep and grandeur of classical music as it expresses ideas and emotions where words fail. What gifted composers have put into music comes to life as The Center hosts classical music of every type, from chamber music to full symphony to chorus with more than 200 voices. The spectacular acoustics of Segerstrom Hall contribute to a clear and natural sound. It's music as music is meant to be!

The Orange County Philharmonic Society, founded in 1953, presents the world's finest classical touring orchestras including The Philadelphia Orchestra, The Radio Symphony Orchestra Berlin, The Leningrad Philharmonic, The London Philharmonic, The Israel Philharmonic Orchestra, The Cleveland Orchestra, The Los Angeles Philharmonic, Orchestre National de France, and many more. The Center's own Chamber Music Series offers internationally renowned ensembles performing in the intimate surroundings of Founders Hall.

The Center is also home to many regional performing arts organizations, among them Orange County's own Pacific Symphony Orchestra. When the orchestra moved to The Center in 1986, its subscription base immediately increased by 1,000 percent; it has since grown to national stature. Under the baton of Carl St.Clair, Pacific Symphony brings the magic of great music—classical and pops as well as a family series—to Orange County audiences during its Center seasons. Throughout the year, the Master Chorale of Orange County and Pacific Chorale perform the world's great choral works at The Center.

Sergerstrom Hall comes alive with the special magic of classical music. Committed to presenting internationally acclaimed classical musicians and nurturing classical music groups here at home, The Center was the site of this Orange County Philharmonic Society presentation of The Chicago Symphony conducted by Sir Georg Solti.

Wine has been produced in California for over two hundred years, since the padres introduced the cultivation of grapes to the missions they established here. Today California wines are known and enjoyed throughout the world. Anyone who has ever sipped a crisp, chilled Chardonnay or a perfect, fruity Chenin Blanc with an elegant picnic lunch on a fragrant fall day knows how much wine can complement a meal.

POULTRY

**An elegant luncheon overlooking the lovely sculpture garden of the
Robert Mondavi Wine and Food Center
is sure to include the perfect wine.
Photograph underwritten by
ROBERT MONDAVI WINE AND FOOD CENTER, COSTA MESA**

CHICKEN ARTICHOKE RING IN FILO

A spectacular luncheon dish served with a salad or fresh fruit.

1/2 cup plus 2 tablespoons unsalted
   butter, divided
1 large onion, chopped
2 whole chicken breasts,
   skinned and cooked
1 6-ounce jar marinated artichoke
   hearts, chopped
12 ounces Fontina cheese, grated
1 cup grated Parmesan cheese

4 green onions, chopped
1 1/2 teaspoons dried thyme
1 tablespoon choppped parsley
4 eggs
1/2 cup heavy cream
3/4 teaspoon grated nutmeg
1/2 teaspoon salt
1/4 teaspoon pepper
1/2 pound filo dough

Melt 2 tablespoons butter and saute onions until soft. Cool. Chop cooked chicken into 1-inch cubes.

In a large bowl, mix chicken, artichoke hearts, cheeses, green onions, thyme, parsley, and onions. In another bowl, beat eggs and cream together. Add nutmeg, salt, and pepper. Pour egg mixture into the chicken mixture and toss to combine. Set aside.

Preheat oven to 350 degrees. Melt 1/2 cup butter, and brush bottom and side of a 10-inch bundt or tube pan. Cut the filo sheets in half. Line the pan by pressing the filo sheets inside the pan so they drape over the edges. Each new sheet should overlap the previous one. Brush melted butter on the sheets. Circle the pan 2 or 3 times with layers of filo. Pour chicken mixture into filo-lined pan and bring overlapping sides up over the mixture to cover. Brush filo with remaining butter. This dish may be made serveral hours ahead and refrigerated until ready to bake.

Bake for 1 hour, until the filo is crisp and golden. Cool in the pan for 15 minutes; invert and slice into wedges. Can be served warm, room temperature, or cold.

Preparation Time: 30 minutes
Baking Time: 1 hour
Servings: 8 to 10

Vichon Chevrignon

CHICKEN DIJON

The Guilds thank Disneyland and Executive Chef, Alfred Boll, for sharing this delightful recipe.

6 chicken breasts, about 6 ounces each
1 cup plus 1 1/2 tablespoons
  Dijon mustard, divided
1 cup seasoned bread crumbs
3 tablespoons butter, divided
4 tablespoons white wine

1 tablespoon finely chopped shallots
1 cup heavy cream
1/2 teaspoon salt
1/8 teaspoon white pepper
1 tablespoon flour

Preheat oven to 375 degrees. Dip the chicken breasts into 1 cup mustard; then, coat with bread crumbs. Melt 2 tablespoons butter in saute pan. Saute chicken breasts in butter until golden brown. Arrange chicken breasts in 8 x 8-inch baking dish. Place in oven for 15 to 20 minutes. Meanwhile, in a saucepan, combine the wine and shallots. Bring to a boil; reduce heat, and simmer until reduced by half. Strain sauce to remove the shallots. Add cream, remaining 1 1/2 tablespoons mustard, salt and pepper. In a small pan, combine remaining tablespoon butter and flour to make a roux; add to sauce, and simmer until thickened, about 5 minutes. To serve, pour sauce over baked chicken breasts.

Preparation Time: 25 minutes
Baking Time: 15 to 20 minutes
Servings: 6

Robert Mondavi Chardonnay

CHICKEN ITALIANO

1 pound Italian sausage
2 tablespoons butter
2 broiler/fryer chickens,
  cut in pieces
1 16-ounce can tomato puree
1/4 pound fresh mushrooms,
  sliced and sautéed
1 10 1/2-ounce can pitted ripe olives,
  sliced, reserve 1/4 cup liquid

3 tablespoons Italian parsley
1 1/2 teaspoons celery flakes
1 1/2 teaspoons Italian seasoning
1 teaspoon minced onion
Salt and pepper to taste
1/4 teaspoon garlic salt
1 bay leaf

Cut sausage into bite-size pieces; brown in a large skillet. Remove and drain sausage. Discard grease. Melt butter in the same skillet. Saute chicken pieces until browned; remove and drain. Add tomato puree to pan drippings and blend. Add remaining ingredients, mixing well. Return chicken and sausage to the pan; combine with sauce. Cover and simmer for 1 to 1 1/2 hours or until chicken is tender. Remove bay leaf and serve.

Preparation Time: 30 minutes
Cooking Time: 1 to 1 1/2 hours
Servings: 8 to 10

Woodbridge Zinfandel

CHICKEN WITH SUN-DRIED TOMATOES

8 boned and skinned chicken breast halves
6 tablespoons unsalted butter
1 teaspoon salt
1/2 teaspoon freshly ground pepper
2 large shallots, minced

1 1/3 cups heavy cream
1 cup dry white wine
1/4 teaspoon marjoram
1/2 cup coarsely chopped
   sun-dried tomatoes

Cut each chicken breast, on the diagonal, into 5 to 6 equal strips. In a skillet, over moderately high heat, melt the butter and add the chicken, sprinkling with salt and pepper. Saute, turning until the chicken is just opaque, 4 to 5 minutes.

Remove chicken with a slotted spoon and set aside. Add the shallots to the skillet and saute, stirring until softened. Add the cream, wine, marjoram, and sun-dried tomatoes. Bring to a boil. Cook until sauce is slightly thickened. Return the chicken to the skillet and simmer gently, spooning sauce over the chicken until heated through.

Preparation Time: 25 minutes
Cooking Time: 15 minutes
Servings: 8

Robert Mondavi Chardonnay

TAILGATE LEMON CHICKEN

Lemon Chicken travels well and makes excellent picnic fare.

12 chicken pieces, of choice
Fresh lemon juice, to cover
   chicken pieces
1 cup flour
1 teaspoon salt

1/2 teaspoon white pepper
2 tablespoons chopped parsley
1 cup grated Parmesan cheese
1/4 to 1/2 cup oil
2 tablespoons lemon zest

Marinate chicken pieces in lemon juice, covered, 1 hour in the refrigerator. Preheat oven to 350 degrees. Drain chicken, reserving marinade, and pat dry. Place flour, salt, pepper, parsley, and cheese in a bag, and shake well to mix. Shake chicken pieces in a bag, coating completely. Heat oil in a frying pan and brown the chicken. Arrange chicken in a large shallow baking pan. Drizzle the lemon marinade on the top. Sprinkle with lemon zest. Bake, covered, 20 minutes; then, bake uncovered, 15 minutes, or until tender. Chill about 2 hours.

Marinating Time: 1 hour or longer
Preparation Time: 30 minutes
Baking Time: 30 to 35 minutes
Servings: 6 or more

Robert Mondavi Fumé Blanc

CHICKEN WITH AUTUMN FRUIT

12 pieces chicken
1/2 cup flour
1/2 teaspoon salt
Dash pepper
1/4 cup plus 2 tablespoons oil, divided
1 tablespoon brandy
3 cloves garlic, minced
1 medium onion, minced

2 cups sliced mushrooms
1 1/2 cups apple wine
2 apples
2 fresh pears
Lemon water
2 teaspoons cornstarch
1/4 cup water
6 servings rice, or pasta

Preheat oven to 350 degrees. Coat chicken with flour and season with salt and pepper. In a frying pan, saute chicken in 1/4 cup oil. Pour brandy over chicken and flame. Set aside. In a separate skillet, saute the garlic and onion in 2 tablespoons oil. Place chicken, onion mixture, mushrooms, and apple wine in a large baking pan. Peel, core and quarter pears and apples and dip into lemon water; add to the chicken pan. Bake, covered, for 40 minutes or until chicken is done. Remove chicken, mushrooms, and fruit to a heated platter. Mix cornstarch and water; add to pan juices and cook until thickened. Serve gravy in a separate bowl.

Preparation Time: 20 to 25 minutes
Cooking Time: 40 minutes
Servings: 6

Robert Mondavi Chenin Blanc

CITRUS CHICKEN WITH PEACHES

8 chicken pieces, about 3 pounds
2 teaspoons salt
1/4 teaspoon pepper
1/2 teaspoon paprika
1/2 cup vegetable oil
1 cup orange juice
2 tablespoons white wine vinegar

2 tablespoons firmly packed brown sugar
1 teaspoon grated nutmeg
1 teaspoon dried basil
12 small potatoes
3 peaches, peeled and quartered
Parsley for garnish

Wash and dry chicken. Season with salt, pepper and paprika. Saute in oil until lightly browned on all sides and place in a large baking pan. Combine orange juice, vinegar, sugar, nutmeg, and basil. Pour over chicken. Place potatoes between chicken pieces and cook, covered, over medium heat until tender, about 25 minutes. Add peaches and heat 5 minutes. Spoon onto 4 serving plates; garnish with parsley.

Preparation Time: 20 minutes
Baking Time: 25 minutes
Servings: 4

Robert Mondavi Chenin Blanc

CHICKEN AND MUSHROOMS
WITH SHERRY ORANGE SAUCE

An elegant brunch or luncheon chicken entree

6 chicken breast halves
1/2 teaspoon salt
1 medium onion, sliced
1/4 cup green bell pepper, chopped

1 cup sliced mushrooms
Sherry orange sauce, recipe follows
Orange slices, for garnish
Paprika

Broil chicken breast skin side up about 10 minutes, or until brown. Do not turn. Reduce oven to 375 degrees. Place browned chicken in a shallow baking pan or casserole. Sprinkle with salt and place the onion, green pepper and mushrooms on top. Make sherry orange sauce and pour over the chicken and vegetables. Bake for 45 minutes or until tender. Baste several times during cooking. At serving time, sprinkle with paprika and garnish with orange slices.

Preparation Time: 20 to 30 minutes
Cooking Time: 45 minutes
Servings: 6

Robert Mondavi Chenin Blanc

SHERRY ORANGE SAUCE

1 cup orange juice
1/4 cup dry sherry
1/2 cup water
1 tablespoon firmly packed brown sugar
1 teaspoon salt

1/4 teaspoon pepper
1 teaspoon fresh orange zest
1 tablespoon flour
2 teaspoons chopped parsley

Combine all sauce ingredients and simmer until slightly thickened.

Preparation Time: 20 minutes
Yield: 2 cups

PURPLE CHICKEN

A welcome change from everyday chicken, especially when plums are at their best. This plum sauce bursts with flavor.

8 chicken breast halves,
  skinned and boned
1/4 cup flour
1/2 teaspoon paprika
1/2 teaspoon salt

Pinch cayenne pepper
1/4 teaspoon ground black pepper
1/4 cup unsalted butter
2 cups dry white wine
Plum sauce recipe follows

Wash and dry chicken. Coat with flour. Season with salt, cayenne pepper, and black pepper. In a large skillet, melt the butter and saute the chicken breasts about 5 minutes on each side or until lightly browned. Add the wine. Cover and simmer for 5 minutes. Transfer chicken to an 11 x 7-inch casserole. Pour pan juices over the chicken; set aside.

Preheat the oven to 350 degrees. Meanwhile, make the plum sauce. Pour sauce over chicken. Cover and bake 30 minutes, or until chicken is tender and no longer pink.

NOTE: You can garnish with additional plum slices.

Preparation time: 45 to 50 minutes
Baking time: 30 minutes
Servings: 6 to 8

Byron Pinot Noir

PLUM SAUCE

8 Italian plums, pitted or 1 cup
  drained canned plums
2 slices fresh ginger root, peeled
2 tablespoons brown sugar
2 tablespoons rice vinegar or
  wine vinegar

2 tablespoons soy sauce
1/2 cup cold water
1 tablespoon cornstarch
1/2 teaspoon cinnamon

In a food processor, chop plums and ginger. In a medium saucepan combine plums, ginger, brown sugar, vinegar, and soy sauce. Cook over medium heat, stirring for about 5 minutes until soft. Combine water, cornstarch, and cinnamon; stir until smooth. Add to the plum mixture and cook, stirring constantly about 2 minutes or until thickened.

Preparation Time: 20 minutes
Yield: 1 1/2 cups

WINTER CHICKEN IN ORANGE SAUCE

1/4 cup plus 1 tablespoon flour, divided
1 teaspoon salt, divided
1/8 teaspoon ground cinnamon
1/8 teaspoon ground cloves
Dash garlic powder
8 skinned and boned chicken
   breast halves
2 tablespoons oil

1 6-ounce can frozen orange juice
   concentrate, thawed
1 cup water, divided
1 tablespoon minced dried onion
Salt, to taste
4 cups hot cooked rice
Chopped parsley for garnish

Combine 1/4 cup flour, 1/2 teaspoon salt, cinnamon, cloves, and garlic powder in a paper or plastic bag; add chicken pieces, a few at a time; shake bag to coat evenly. In a 12-inch skillet, heat oil. Brown chicken breasts over medium heat 15 to 20 minutes.

In a small mixing bowl, combine orange juice, 1/2 cup water, and minced onion; pour over the chicken in the skillet. Cover and simmer about 30 minutes until chicken is tender, turning occasionally to glaze.

Meanwhile, blend 1/4 cup cold water, 1 tablespoon flour, and 1/2 teaspoon salt to made a roux; set aside. Remove chicken to heated serving platter and keep warm. Add the roux to orange juice mixture in skillet. Cook and stir until thickened and bubbly. At serving time spoon orange sauce over chicken and hot cooked rice; garnish with chopped parsley.

Preparation Time: 30 minutes
Cooking Time: 1 hour
Servings: 6 to 8

Robert Mondavi Chenin Blanc

CHINESE CHICKEN IN LETTUCE LEAVES

3 tablespoons oil
1 1/3 cups finely chopped chicken breast
1 cup seeded and finely chopped
   green or red bell pepper
1/2 tablespoon sugar
1/2 tablespoon salt
Freshly ground pepper to taste
2 1/2 tablespoons minced fresh ginger
1 1/2 tablespoons soy sauce
3 tablespoons water

1 tablespoon lemon juice
1 large scallion, sliced
1/2 cup chopped walnuts
1/2 cup rice wine vinegar
1 1/2 tablespoons soy sauce
1 teaspoon sesame oil
Dash hot sauce or chili oil
8 to 12 iceberg lettuce leaves,
   washed, dried, and chilled

Heat the oil in a skillet or wok over medium high heat. Add the chicken, green or red pepper, sugar, salt and pepper. Cook, stirring constantly until the peppers turn a deeper color and the chicken is cooked, about 3 to 5 minutes. Add the ginger, soy sauce, water, and lemon juice to the chicken mixture, stirring well. Cook for 1 more minute. Remove the chicken from the heat. Sprinkle with the scallion and walnuts. Set aside and keep warm.

Make a sauce for dipping, mixing vinegar, soy sauce, sesame oil, and hot sauce in a small bowl until well blended. To serve, place 2 or 3 tablespoons of the chicken mixture on a lettuce leaf, roll up; and place on serving dish. Pass the sauce separately.

Preparation Time: 30 to 35 minutes
Cooking Time: 4 to 6 minutes
Servings: 4

Vichon Chevrignon

SESAME CHICKEN

1/4 cup sesame seeds, toasted
1/2 cup soy sauce
1/4 cup packed brown sugar
1 teaspoon ground ginger
1/2 teaspoon pepper

4 cloves garlic, minced
4 green onions, thinly sliced, divided
8 skinned, boned, whole chicken breasts,
   cut in bite-sized pieces
4 to 6 cups cooked parsleyed rice

Make a marinade mixture by combining the sesame seeds, soy sauce, brown sugar, ginger, pepper, garlic, and 1/2 of the green onions. Stir chicken into marinade mixture; cover and chill 1 to 4 hours.

Arrange the chicken in a single layer in a baking pan; pour the marinade over the chicken. Broil 6 inches from heat until golden, about 10 minutes. Turn chicken and broil 5 minutes longer or until meat is no longer pink. Serve with parsleyed rice, garnishing with the remaining sliced green onions.

Preparation Time: 20 to 30 minutes
Marinating Time: 1 to 4 hours
Cooking Time: 15 minutes
Servings: 6 to 8

Vichon Chevrignon

STIR-FRY CHICKEN WITH VEGETABLES

1 cup chicken broth, heated
1 tablespoon cornstarch
2 tablespoons soy sauce
4 teaspoons oil
3 whole chicken breasts, cut in slivers
1 cup Chinese pea pods
1 green bell pepper, cut in strips

10 mushrooms, sliced
4 green onions, sliced
1 8-ounce can sliced water
   chestnuts, drained
2 cups jullienned carrots
2 cups steamed rice

Mix chicken broth with cornstarch and soy sauce until smooth. Set aside. Heat oil and stir fry chicken for 2 to 3 minutes. Add all vegetables and cook until tender and still crisp. Add the cornstarch mixture and cook to make a thickened sauce, about 2 minutes. To serve, spoon rice on plates and spoon chicken mixture over rice.

Preparation Time: 20 to 30 minutes
Cooking Time: 20 minutes
Servings: 4 to 6

Robert Mondavi Fumé Blanc

PARTY PERFECT CHICKEN WITH CURRY GLAZE

Exotic curry glaze, recipe follows
6 tablespoons flour
1 1/2 teaspoons salt
1 tablespoon ground ginger

2 fryers, quartered,
   or 8 chicken breast halves
6 tablespoons butter

Preheat oven to 400 degrees. Prepare the curry glaze and set aside. Combine flour, salt, and ginger in a bag. Add chicken, one piece at a time, and shake to coat. Melt butter in a large flat baking pan and roll floured chicken pieces in the butter. Place chicken skin side up in the pan; do not overlap pieces. Bake 20 minutes.

Spoon half of the curry glaze over the meat and bake 20 minutes longer. Spoon on remaining glaze and bake a final 20 minutes or until chicken is tender and slightly browned.

Preparation Time: 10 minutes
Baking Time: 1 hour
Servings: 8

Robert Mondavi Chenin Blanc

EXOTIC CURRY GLAZE

1/2 cup chopped onion
6 slices bacon, uncooked and diced
2 tablespoons flour
1 to 3 teaspoons curry powder
1 14 1/2-ounce can condensed beef broth

1 tablespoon sugar
2 tablespoons applesauce
2 tablespoons ketchup
2 tablespoons lemon juice
2 tablespoons shredded coconut

In a frying pan, over medium heat, cook onion and bacon, stirring for 3 or 4 minutes. Blend flour and curry into pan ingredients. Stir in broth and sugar; add applesauce, ketchup, lemon juice, and coconut. Simmer for 10 minutes.

Preparation Time: 20 minutes
Yield: 2 to 2 1/2 cups

CILANTRO-STUFFED CHICKEN BREASTS
IN PINK PEAR SAUCE

This recipe will please the microwave cooks.

Pink pear sauce, recipe follows
6 boned and skinned chicken
   breast halves

4 to 5 tablespoons chopped fresh cilantro
2 tablespoons dry white wine
Strawberries, for garnish

Prepare pink pear sauce. Cut 3 diagonal slashes in each chicken breast. Stuff each slash with chopped cilantro. Place breast in baking dish; pour wine around them; cover with plastic wrap and microwave on high for 5 minutes.

Spoon a few tablespoons of the sauce on a platter. Arrange cooked chicken over the sauce in a spoke pattern. This can be done a day ahead. Chill remaining sauce in refrigerator.

Just before serving, place platter that is covered with plastic wrap, back in the microwave and cook on high for 2 minutes to reheat. Garnish plate with fresh strawberries and serve with the remaining sauce.

Preparation Time: 10 minutes
Microwave Time: 7 to 10 minutes
Servings: 6

Robert Mondavi Chenin Blanc

PINK PEAR SAUCE

1 16 ounce can unsweetened juice-packed pears, drained
1 cup fresh strawberries, washed and stemmed
2 tablespoons raspberry vinegar

Puree all ingredients in blender or food processor. Chill until ready to use.

Preparation Time: 10 minutes
Yield: 3 cups

CRESCENT BAY STUFFED CHICKEN

8 skinned and boned large chicken
   breast halves
Pinch of salt
1/4 cup light cream
1 cup fresh bread crumbs
1/3 cup finely chopped onion
1 5-ounce can water chestnuts,
   drained and finely chopped
6 tablespoons butter, divided

1 teaspoon ground ginger
1/4 pound ground veal
1/2 pound ground pork
1 egg, beaten
3 tablespoons soy sauce, divided
1/8 teaspoon cayenne pepper
2 tablespoons honey
3 tablespoons sesame seeds

Flatten chicken breasts. Sprinkle lightly with salt; set aside. To make stuffing, pour cream over bread crumbs and let soak. In a large pan, saute onion and water chestnuts in 2 tablespoons butter. Add soaked bread crumbs, ginger, veal, pork, egg, 1 tablespoon soy sauce, and cayenne pepper; mix well.

Preheat oven to 325 degrees. Top each piece of chicken with some stuffing. Roll up and place seam side down in a greased baking dish. To make a honey butter sauce, cream 4 tablespoons butter and honey together and beat in 2 tablespoons soy sauce. Spread sauce over the chicken rolls. Bake, basting with the juices, until the chicken is fully cooked and tender, about 35 to 45 minutes.

Change oven to 450 degrees. Sprinkle chicken rolls with sesame seeds. Bake 10 minutes or until well browned. Watch to prevent burning.

Preparation Time: 1 hour
Baking Time: 45 to 55 minutes
Servings: 6 to 8

Woodbridge Cabernet Sauvignon

STUFFED CHICKEN LEGS

4 strips bacon, chopped
1/2 cup chopped onion
2 cloves garlic, minced
1/2 cup chopped broccoli

3/4 cup shredded mozzarella cheese
1/2 cup dry bread or cracker crumbs
4 chicken legs, including thighs

Preheat oven to 375 degrees. In a frying pan, saute bacon until crisp; remove from pan; saute onion and garlic in drippings until tender. In a saucepan cook broccoli until tender; drain well. Puree bacon, onion, garlic, and broccoli along with cheese and crumbs in blender. Loosen skin from meat of chicken legs and stuff mixture under the skin. Bake, covered for 30 minutes; remove cover, and bake another 30 minutes.

Preparation Time: 45 to 55 minutes
Baking Time: 1 hour
Servings: 4

Robert Mondavi Pinot Noir

CHICKEN BREASTS IN MUSHROOM CHIVE SAUCE

8 skinned and boned chicken
  breast halves
6 tablespoons butter, divided
3 green onions, chopped
1 clove garlic, minced
3 to 4 cups sliced mushrooms
1 cup chicken broth

Dash lemon juice
1 cup heavy cream
2 tablespoons flour
2 tablespoons finely chopped
  fresh chives
Salt and pepper to taste
Parsley for garnish

Wash and dry chicken. Melt 2 tablespoons butter and saute chicken until lightly browned. Remove and set aside. Melt 2 tablespoons butter and saute onions, garlic, and mushrooms over high heat until lightly browned. Remove and set aside. Add broth to same pan; boil until reduced by half. Reduce heat; add lemon juice and cream. In a small pan, combine 2 tablespoons butter and flour to make a roux. Add roux to the cream sauce; simmer until thickened. Add chicken and simmer until tender. Add mushroom mixture and chives and heat through. Serve on individual plates with parsley garnish.

Preparation Time: 30 minutes
Cooking Time: 20 to 30 minutes
Servings: 4 to 8

Robert Mondavi Chardonnay

CHICKEN ROLLS WITH YOGURT TOPPING

12 to 14 skinned and boned
  chicken breast halves
2 cups plain non-fat yogurt
1/4 cup lemon juice
4 teaspoons Worcestershire sauce
4 teaspoons celery salt, or to taste

1/2 teaspoon pepper
2 teaspoons paprika
4 cloves garlic, chopped or
  1 teaspoon garlic powder
1 1/2 to 2 cups dry bread crumbs
1/2 cup butter, melted

Wash and dry the chicken. Combine yogurt, lemon juice, Worcestershire sauce, and seasonings. Dip chicken in the yogurt mixture, making sure each piece is well coated. Refrigerate chicken, covered, overnight. Reserve remaining yogurt mixture. Preheat oven to 350 degrees. Spray a shallow baking pan with non-stick vegetable spray. Dip the smooth side of the chicken in packed, dry bread crumbs. Roll up, starting at the pointed end. Arrange in a single layer in baking pan. Drizzle melted butter over each piece. Bake uncovered for 1 hour. Spoon reserved yogurt mixture over the chicken. Bake 15 minutes longer until nicely browned. Sprinkle with paprika and parsley.

Marinating Time: Overnight
Preparation Time: 45 minutes
Baking Time: 1 hour, 15 minutes
Servings: 12 to 14

Robert Mondavi Fumé Blanc

LEMON AND HERB ROASTED CHICKEN

1 5-pound roasting chicken
1 teaspoon salt
1/2 teaspoon pepper

Juice of 1 lemon
3 tablespoons herb of choice,
   suggest rosemary

Preheat oven to 400 degrees. Combine salt, pepper, and lemon juice; rub the chicken with mixture, inside and out. Loosen skin from the meat on the breasts and the legs. Place the rosemary under the skin.

In a roasting pan with a rack, place the chicken in the oven, breast-side up. Roast for 15 minutes. Lower the oven to 350 degrees and continue cooking, about 1 hour 20 minutes. Chicken is done when the juices run clear from piercing the thigh with a sharp knife or tester. Let the chicken rest at least 10 minutes before carving.

Preparation Time: 15 minutes
Roasting Time: 1 hour 35 minutes
Servings: 4

Robert Mondavi Fumé Blanc

HERBED CHICKEN ROLLS

6 skinned, boned, and flattened
   chicken breast halves
1/3 cup melted butter, divided
Salt and pepper, to taste
6 slices mozzarella cheese
1/2 cup flour
1 egg, beaten

1 cup fresh bread crumbs
2 tablespoons chopped parsley
1/4 teaspoon rubbed sage
1/4 teaspoon ground rosemary
1/4 teaspoon dried thyme
1/2 cup dry white wine

Preheat oven to 350 degrees. Brush chicken with butter. Season with salt and pepper. Place one slice of cheese on each piece of chicken and roll up, tucking in edges. Coat each lightly with flour; dip into beaten egg and roll in bread crumbs. Arrange chicken in a shallow baking dish. Add herbs to remaining melted butter and drizzle over the chicken; bake 30 minutes. Pour wine over chicken and bake 20 more minutes, basting several times.

Preparation Time: 20 to 30 minutes
Cooking Time: 50 minutes
Servings: 6

Robert Mondavi Fumé Blanc

CORNISH GAME HENS WITH RASPBERRY MARINADE

3/4 cup seeded puree of fresh raspberries
1 cup raspberry vinegar
Zest of 1 lemon
1 tablespoon minced garlic
2 tablespoons minced fresh mint
Freshly ground black pepper, to taste

Salt, to taste
1/3 cup olive oil
4 Cornish game hens
Fresh raspberries, for garnish
Mint, for garnish

To make marinade, combine puree, vinegar, lemon zest, garlic, mint, black pepper and salt. Whisk olive oil into mixture until well blended. Place game hens in a shallow glass, or ceramic container, and pour marinade over them. Marinate at room temperature 2 hours, or in the refrigerator at least 4 hours. Preheat oven to 350 degrees. Roast hens for about 40 minutes. Serve hot or at room temperature. Garnish with fresh berries and mint.

Note: Unsweetened frozen raspberry puree can be substituted. Chicken breasts can be an option to the cornish game hens.

Preparation Time: 15 minutes
Marinating Time: 2 to 4 hours
Roasting Time: 40 minutes
Servings: 4

Robert Mondavi Pinot Noir

CHICKEN ROLLS AU GRATIN

16 boned and skinned chicken
  breast halves
2 pounds Jarlsberg cheese, divided
2 eggs, beaten
2 tablespoons milk
2 cups dry bread crumbs

1 cup Parmesan cheese, freshly grated
4 tablespoons chopped parsley, divided
Pepper to taste
1/2 cup oil
4 cups heavy cream
1/4 cup dry vermouth

Preheat oven to 350 degrees. Flatten the chicken breasts and set aside. Cut 1 1/2 pounds of cheese into 1 x 3-inch pieces. Place one piece of cheese in each breast; roll and secure with a toothpick. In a medium bowl, whisk the eggs and milk. In another bowl, combine bread crumbs, Parmesan cheese, 1 tablespoon chopped parsley, and pepper. Dip the chicken pieces first in the egg mixture, then in the crumb mixture to coat completely. Brown chicken in hot oil in frying pan and arrange in a single layer in greased 13 x 9-inch baking dish.

Shred remaining 1/2 pound cheese; divide in half. In a saucepan, heat the cream, remaining parsley, vermouth, and half the shredded cheese. Pour this over the chicken and top with the remaining shredded cheese. Bake for 30 to 35 minutes.

Preparation Time: 30 minutes
Cooking Time: 30 to 35 minutes
Servings: 8 to 12

Robert Mondavi Chardonnay

ROAST QUAIL WITH CRANBERRY MADEIRA GLAZE

Cranberry Madeira Glaze, recipe follows
12 quail
1/2 cup chicken broth

12 slices of white bread,
    crusts removed and toasted

Preheat oven to 450 degrees. Prepare glaze. In a skillet, heat 2 tablespoons butter over low heat. Brown the quail and arrange breast sides up. Transfer 1/2 cup of glaze to a small bowl and set aside. Baste generously with some of the remaining glaze. Roast the quail in the top third of the oven for 10 minutes. Lower heat to 400 degrees and roast, basting with some of the remaining glaze, for another 40 minutes or until the leg meat is no longer pink. Transfer quail to a plate. Pour off any fat in skillet.

Deglaze skillet with remaining 1/2 cup broth, scrape up the brown bits, and stir in the reserved 1/2 cup of glaze. Boil mixture, whisking, until thickened. Season with salt and pepper, if necessary.

To serve, place quail on top of toast. Spoon sauce over top. Pass any remaining sauce in a sauceboat.

Note: If quail legs begin to brown too much, cover them with foil to complete the roasting time. Uncover to check for doneness.

Preparation Time: 20 minutes
Cooking Time: 50 minutes
Servings: 12

Robert Mondavi Cabernet Sauvignon

CRANBERRY MADEIRA GLAZE

1 12-ounce bag fresh or frozen
    cranberries, thawed
2/3 cup firmly packed dark brown sugar
1/2 cup apple juice
1/2 cup cranberry juice
1/3 cup Madeira, Marsala, or red wine
1/2 teaspoon nutmeg

1/4 teaspoon ground ginger
1/2 teaspoon dry mustard
1/2 cup chicken broth
Zest of 1 orange
1/4 cup unsalted butter, divided
Salt and pepper to taste

Combine cranberries, brown sugar, apple juice, cranberry juice, wine, nutmeg, ginger, mustard, 1/2 cup of the chicken broth, orange zest, 2 tablespoons of the butter, salt and pepper to taste. Bring to a boil, and simmer for about 20 minutes, or until it is thickened and the berries have burst. Strain the glaze through a sieve into a bowl.

Preparation Time: 35 minutes
Yield: 2 1/2 cups

CURRIED CHICKEN BREASTS

8 skinned and boned chicken
   breast halves
1 cup flour, seasoned with salt,
   pepper, and ginger
1/3 cup butter or margarine, melted
2 onions, finely chopped
2 green peppers, finely chopped
1 garlic clove, minced
3 teaspoons curry powder, or to taste

2 1/2 16-ounce cans chopped tomatoes
1 teaspoon chopped parsley
1/2 teaspoon thyme
2 to 3 cups cooked rice
3 heaping tablespoons currants
Salt and white pepper, to taste
1/2 cup almond slivers, toasted
Parsley, for garnish

Preheat oven to 375 degrees. Wash and dry chicken; coat with seasoned flour and brown in butter in a frying pan. Remove; drain and place in a large casserole or roaster, keeping chicken warm. In the same frying pan, add onions, peppers, garlic, and curry powder; simmer, stirring constantly. Add tomatoes, parsley, and thyme; pour mixture over chicken. Add remaining tomatoes if liquid is needed to cover chicken. Bake, uncovered, about 40 minutes, or until the chicken is tender.

Place chicken in the center of a large serving platter and surround with rice; keep warm. Add the currants to the roaster and stir; adjust seasonings and pour over rice. Sprinkle almonds over the top and garnish platter with parsley.

Preparation Time: 40 minutes
Baking Time: 40 minutes
Servings: 8

Robert Mondavi Pinot Noir

TURKEY CHILI

1 slice bacon, diced
1 pound ground turkey
1 large onion, chopped
1 large red bell pepper,
   seeded and diced
3 cloves garlic, minced
2 tablespoons chili powder
1 7-ounce can diced green chilies,
   undrained
1 10 1/2-ounce can chicken broth

1 14-ounce can diced tomatoes,
   undrained
1/4 cup ketchup
1 teaspoon ground cumin
1 teaspoon dry oregano leaves
1 teaspoon ground coriander
1 15-ounce can kidney beans, drained
Salt and pepper, to taste
Shredded cheddar cheese, for garnish

In a 5-quart saucepan, over medium heat, stir bacon and turkey until turkey is lightly browned, about 10 minutes. Add onion, bell pepper, and garlic, stirring frequently until onion is limp, about 10 minutes. Add remaining ingredients, except the cheddar cheese. Simmer for about 45 to 55 minutes. Garnish with cheddar cheese, or serve with cheese in a bowl on the side.

Preparation Time: 30 minutes
Cooking Time: 45 to 55 minutes
Servings: 6

Woodbridge Zinfandel

JAMBOREE CHICKEN

An ideal "prepare-ahead" recipe

3 to 4 pounds cut-up chicken
Olive oil
1 onion, sliced
2 cloves garlic
1 green bell pepper, cut in pieces

1 15-ounce can tomato sauce
1/2 cup white wine
1 to 2 tablespoons whole allspice
2 bay leaves
Salt and pepper to taste

Preheat oven to 375 degrees. Place chicken in a large ovenproof casserole and lightly coat with olive oil. Add onion, garlic, and green bell pepper. Brown, uncovered, in the oven for 25 minutes. Meanwhile, combine tomato sauce, white wine, allspice, bay leaves, salt and pepper. Reduce oven temperature to 350 degrees. Pour sauce over the chicken and bake, covered, an additional 30 minutes, or until tender.

Preparation Time: 20 to 30 minutes
Baking Time: 55 minutes
Servings: 4

Robert Mondavi Fumé Blanc

TURKEY CUTLETS WITH CHILIES

8 turkey cutlets
1 1/2 teaspoons salt, divided
Pepper, to taste
1/4 cup butter
1/4 cup oil
1 onion, chopped

2 4-ounce cans whole Ortega chilies
4 fresh Ortega chilies, or 2 fresh
   poblanos chilies
1 cup milk
2 cups sour cream
1/2 cup Monterey Jack cheese

Preheat oven to 350 degrees. Cut each cutlet into 4 fillet pieces. Season with 1/2 teaspoon salt and pepper. Heat the butter and oil together and saute the turkey cutlets for a few moments on both sides until lightly browned. Set aside. In the same pan, saute the onion until soft. Cut canned chilies into strips and add to pan; cook for 5 minutes. Set aside.

In a food processor or blender puree the fresh chilies; add milk and 1/2 teaspoon salt, blending well. Add sour cream, stirring to combine. Set aside.

In a 2-quart casserole, arrange half the turkey cutlets. Cover with half of the chili strips and half the sauce. Repeat layers. Sprinkle with cheese and bake until cutlets are done and the cheese is melted, about 30 minutes.

Preparation Time: 30 minutes
Baking Time: 30 minutes
Servings: 8

Woodbridge Chardonnay

CAPISTRANO ENCHILADAS

1 cup diced cooked chicken or turkey
1 1/2 cups shredded Cheddar
   cheese, divided
1 1/2 cups sour cream
3 green onions, sliced

1 2 1/2-ounce can sliced olives,
   drained, divided
1/4 cup oil
6 7-inch flour tortillas
2 cups salsa, divided

Preheat oven to 375 degrees. Combine chicken, 1/2 cup cheese, sour cream, green onions, and 1/2 of the olives. Set aside. In a saute pan, heat oil and soften each tortilla. Press between paper towels to remove excess oil. Dip tortillas in salsa. Spoon about 1/2 cup filling in center of each tortilla and roll. In a flat 11 x 7-inch buttered casserole, place rolls seam-side down. Sprinkle with olives and cheese. Pour remaining salsa on top. Bake, uncovered, for 15 minutes or until bubbly.

Note: This recipe can be doubled easily.

Preparation Time: 30 minutes   Vichon Chevrignon
Baking Time: 15 to 20 minutes
Servings: 3 to 6

TURKEY SOFT TACOS

2 tablespoons butter
2 cloves garlic
1 cup water
6 black peppercorns
Dash of cumin seed
6 turkey cutlets
Salt, to taste
Vegetable oil

8 flour tortillas
2 cups shredded Cheddar cheese
1 cup guacamole
2 cups shredded lettuce
2 cups chopped tomatoes
1 cup sour cream
1/2 cup sliced ripe olives
1/2 cup salsa, or hot sauce, optional

In a saute pan over medium heat, melt the butter and add the garlic, water, pepper corns, and cumin. Heat to a simmer and add the turkey; cover and simmer until turkey is tender, adding water if necessary, about 10 minutes. Remove turkey from heat; when turkey is cool enough to handle, shred and sprinkle with salt.

Wipe saute pan clean; heat vegetable oil and lightly brown the tortillas, one at a time, and drain on paper towels. When ready to serve, spread turkey across the center of each tortilla and cover with cheese. Fold the taco and fill with guacamole, lettuce, tomatoes, sour cream, and olives. Drizzle with salsa or hot sauce, if desired.

Preparation Time: 30 minutes   Vichon Chevrignon
Cooking Time: 30 minutes
Yield: 8 tacos

OLD TUSTIN TURKEY CURRY

This is almost like a flavorful stew with condiments.

3 tablespoons oil
3 tablespoons butter
6 carrots, peeled and chopped
6 ribs celery, chopped
1 large onion, chopped
1 medium apple, chopped
4 1/2 tablespoons curry powder
1 cup chicken broth
1/4 cup flour
4 cups water, divided

1 clove garlic, minced
1/2 cup applesauce
1/2 teaspoon ginger
1 tablespoon red currant jelly
1/2 teaspoon allspice
Pinch of salt
2 pounds cooked turkey, shredded
4 cups steamed rice
Condiments: raisins, peanuts,
   coconut, chutney

Heat oil and butter in a Dutch oven; saute chopped carrots, celery, onion and apple. Cook over low heat 10 minutes; add curry, stirring 2 minutes. Add chicken broth and cook 15 minutes. Make a roux of flour and 1/4 cup water. Stir in remaining water, a little at a time. Add garlic, applesauce, ginger, red currant jelly, allspice, salt, and curry mixture. Simmer 1/2 hour. Strain to make a smooth sauce. Put sauce into a double boiler; add shredded turkey; simmer until turkey is heated through. Serve with rice and condiments in separate dishes.

Preparation Time: 30 to 45 minutes
Cooking Time: 1 hour, 15 minutes
Servings: 8 to 10

Byron Pinot Noir

DAY-AFTER TURKEY CASSEROLE

2 tablespoons butter
1 cup chopped celery
1 teaspoon chopped onion
1/2 cup mushrooms
1 cup cooked rice

2 cups cooked bite-size pieces of turkey
1/4 cup mayonnaise-style salad dressing
1 teaspoon curry powder
1 tablespoon lemon juice

Preheat oven to 350 degrees. Melt butter and saute celery, onion, and mushrooms. Combine cooked rice, turkey pieces, salad dressing, curry powder, and lemon juice. Stir in sauted vegetables. Pour into a lightly greased 11 x 7-inch casserole dish. Bake, uncovered, about 20 minutes.

Preparation Time: 15 to 20 minutes
Baking Time: 20 minutes
Servings: 4

Vichon Coastal Chardonnay

BROADWAY AT THE CENTER

Top hats and tails, high-stepping dancers and lilting love songs—nothing beats the exuberant charm of a splashy Broadway musical. Every year the best of Broadway comes to The Center, attracting large audiences and sending them home after the performance smiling and humming one of those memorable tunes.

The Phantom of the Opera, Fiddler on the Roof, Cabaret, Cats, Me and My Girl, The Who's Tommy, Les Misérables, My One and Only, Evita, Crazy for You—The Center presents them all, and many more, making Broadway a local street right here in Orange County. Ranging from timeless classics to recent international hits, the musicals feature celebrated composers like George Gershwin, Cole Porter, and Rodgers and Hammerstein, the contemporary talents of Stephen Sondheim and Andrew Lloyd Webber, and artists like Liza Minnelli, Richard Chamberlain, Sarah Brightman, Chita Rivera, Joel Grey, Tommy Tune, and Tim Curry.

Fabulous settings fill The Center's stage and serve as spectacular backdrops for the larger-than-life stories told so effectively and evocatively through music. Is there a more exhilarating moment in the theater than a toe-tapping Broadway musical full of singable songs and ablaze with energy and life?

The Center's national touring productions of Broadway standouts have always drawn large, enthusiastic audiences. The stirring musical *Les Misérables* conquered the Segerstrom Hall stage, breaking all Center box office records in 1991.

A dramatic, twelve-story high arch of Napoleon red granite graces the facade of the Orange County Performing Arts Center. As the sun sets, the light from the lobbies shines through the Grand Portal. Patrons begin to stream through the Carriage Circle and the Arrival Gardens, and they can't help but note The Center's striking angles, its soaring spaces, and its immense, gleaming metal sculpture, "The Fire Bird." The Center is an architectural jewel and a fitting site for the finest artists in the world.

SEAFOOD

"The Fire Bird" and the Grand Portal with its familiar Arch act as a dramatic background for a splendid seafood buffet.

LAGUNA LOBSTER TAILS

Lobster tails are always enjoyed and are wonderful party fare.

Chunky Tomato Vinaigrette,
  recipe follows
4 lobster tails
1 tablespoon balsamic vinegar

1 tablespoon water
1 teaspoon extra virgin olive oil
1 teaspoon dried tarragon

Prepare vinaigrette at least one hour before serving time and chill. Cut lengthwise through tops of lobster shell and pry shell apart. Starting at the cut end of the tail, carefully loosen lobster meat from the bottom of the shell, keeping the meat attached at the end of the tail. Lift meat through the top shell opening and place on top of the shell. Repeat procedure with all lobster tails. Place lobster tails on a rack in a shallow roasting pan.

Combine vinegar, water, olive oil, and tarragon; stir well. Brush lobster tails with half of the mixture.

Broil lobster tails approximately 6 inches from the heat for 10 minutes, or until the flesh turns opaque, basting with remaining vinegar mixture. Serve with vinaigrette.

Preparation Time: 20 minutes
Cooking Time: 10 minutes
Servings: 4

CHUNKY TOMATO VINAIGRETTE

2 cups finely chopped tomato, seeded
2 tablespoons chopped green onion
2 tablespoons chopped fresh parsley
2 tablespoons balsamic vinegar
1 teaspoon water

1 teaspoon extra virgin olive oil
1 teaspoon dried tarragon
1/4 teaspoon salt
1/2 teaspoon freshly ground pepper

In a bowl, combine all ingredients and mix well. Cover and chill for at least 1 hour.

Preparation Time: 10 minutes
Chilling Time: 1 hour
Yield: 2 1/2 cups

Robert Mondavi Chardonnay Reserve

SHRIMP ETOUFFEE

This is an excellent Cajun recipe.

1 teaspoon dried basil
1/2 teaspoon dried thyme
2 teaspoons salt
2 teaspoons cayenne pepper
1 teaspoon freshly ground white pepper
1 teaspoon freshly ground black pepper
1/4 cup chopped onions
1/4 cup chopped celery

1/4 cup chopped green bell pepper
1/2 cup extra virgin olive oil
3/4 cup flour
3 cups chicken broth, divided
1 cup unsalted butter, divided
1 cup finely chopped green onions
2 pounds medium-size shrimp, cooked

Combine the basil, thyme, salt and pepper seasonings in one bowl. In another bowl, combine the onions, celery, and bell pepper.

In a saute pan, heat the oil over high heat until just ready to smoke. Add the flour to make roux, stirring until smooth. Continue cooking, whisking constantly, until the flour is lightly browned. Remove from heat and stir in the vegetables and 1 teaspoon of the seasoning. Continue stirring while the mixture cools.

In a large saucepan, bring 2 cups of broth to a boil over high heat. Add to the vegetable mixture and whisk until well blended. Place on low heat.

In a large pan, melt 1/2 cup butter and stir in the green onions; add the shrimp. Saute briefly; add remaining butter and pour into the vegetable mixture. Stir in remaining cup of broth and seasoning; serve hot in a bowl or soup tureen.

Preparation Time: 45 minutes
Servings: 4 to 6

Byron Pinot Noir Reserve

SHRIMP STROGANOFF

2 pounds shrimp, shelled and deveined
2 tablespoons flour
1 1/2 teaspoons salt
1/4 teaspoon fresh ground pepper
1/4 teaspoon tarragon
1/3 cup butter or margarine

1/2 cup finely minced onion
1 pound mushrooms, thinly sliced
1 14 1/2-ounce can chicken broth
1 cup sour cream
Chopped parsley, for garnish

Cut shrimp in half lengthwise. Combine flour, salt, pepper, and tarragon. Dredge the shrimp in the flour mixture, reserving any remaining seasoned flour.

Melt the butter in a large skillet and cook until shrimp turns pink and onion is golden. Reserve some shrimp for garnish. Add remaining seasoned flour and mushrooms, whisking gently to avoid lumps. Blend well. Add chicken broth and simmer for 10 minutes; do not overheat or shrimp will be tough. Remove from heat and stir in sour cream.

Serve in a warm dish, garnished with parsley and reserved shrimp. Accompany with hot pasta.

Preparation Time: 30 minutes
Servings: 4 to 6

Vichon Chardonnay

SEAFOOD IN PASTRY SHELLS

This is a great brunch or luncheon dish.

4 frozen puff pastry shells
1/4 cup butter
12 medium shrimp, peeled
  and deveined
12 medium scallops
8 mushrooms, sliced

2 tablespoons chopped shallots
1/2 cup dry sherry
2 cups heavy cream
Salt and freshly ground white pepper,
  to taste
2 tablespoons chopped parsley

Prepare the pastry shells as directed on package and keep warm. In a large pan, melt butter and saute the shrimp, scallops, and mushrooms for 5 minutes. Remove from pan with slotted spoon and keep warm. Add shallots and sherry. Deglaze pan by cooking quickly over high heat, scraping the bottom of the pan to loosen flavorful bits. Add heavy cream and continue cooking until reduced by half. Season with salt and pepper; add parsley. Return seafood to the sauce. Spoon mixture into warm pastry shells and serve immediately.

Preparation Time: 30 minutes
Servings: 4

Robert Mondavi Chardonnay Reserve

SHRIMP AND ARTICHOKE CASSEROLE

2 14-ounce cans artichoke hearts,
  drained, divided
2 pounds cooked shrimp
1/2 pound fresh mushrooms, sliced
6 tablespoons butter, divided
5 tablespoons flour
3/4 cup milk

3/4 cup heavy cream
Salt and white pepper, to taste
1/4 cup dry sherry
1 tablespoon Worcestershire sauce
1/4 cup freshly grated Parmesan cheese
  or to taste
Paprika

Preheat oven to 375 degrees. Arrange 1 1/2 cans artichoke hearts on the bottom of a buttered 9 x 13-inch glass baking dish; divide shrimp evenly over artichokes. In a medium saucepan, saute sliced mushrooms in 2 tablespoons of butter, stirring for 5 minutes. Spoon mushrooms over the shrimp and artichoke hearts. In the same saucepan, melt remaining 4 tablespoons butter and stir in flour. When blended, gradually add milk and cream, stirring constantly with wire whisk. When mixture is thickened and smooth, season with salt and pepper. Add sherry and Worcestershire sauce. Pour sauce over the shrimp, artichokes, and mushrooms. Sprinkle with Parmesan cheese and paprika. Bake until heated through, about 20 to 30 minutes. Garnish with remaining artichokes.

Preparation Time: 10 to 15 minutes
Baking Time: 20 to 30 minutes
Servings: 4 to 6

Vichon Chevrignon

SEAFOOD BUFFET CASSEROLE

1 pound crab meat, cooked
1 pound shrimp, cooked
1/4 cup chopped red pepper
1/4 cup chopped green pepper
1/4 cup finely chopped scallions
1/2 cup finely chopped celery
1 4-ounce can water chestnuts, sliced
1/2 5-ounce package frozen
  baby peas, thawed

1 1/2 cups cooked rice
2 teaspoons Worcestershire sauce
1 cup mayonnaise
1 teaspoon coarsely ground
  black pepper
Salt, optional
2 cups crushed cashews

Preheat oven to 350 degrees. In a large bowl, combine all ingredients except cashews. Place mixture in a 13 x 9-inch casserole or oven-to-table serving dish and top with cashews. Bake for approximately 30 to 45 minutes until quite hot.

Preparation Time: 30 minutes
Cooking Time: 30 to 45 minutes
Servings: 8 to 10

SPICY SEAFOOD PAELLA

Magnifico!

2 tablespoons extra virgin olive oil
1 pound Chorizo sausage,
   casings removed and thickly sliced
1 green bell pepper, chopped
1 red bell pepper, chopped
1 medium red onion, chopped
4 cloves garlic, finely minced
1 teaspoon crushed dried red pepper
2 1/2 cups long grain rice, uncooked
3 cups clam juice
1/2 cup water

1 cup dry white wine
1/4 teaspoon saffron
Salt and freshly ground pepper, to taste
1/2 teaspoon dried basil
1 10-ounce package frozen artichoke
   hearts, thawed and drained
1 pound medium-size raw shrimp,
   shelled and deveined
1 pound small to medium-size scallops
1 pound firm white fish, cut into
   1-inch pieces

Preheat oven to 350 degrees. In a large frying pan or Dutch oven, heat olive oil over medium heat; saute sausage until just cooked through. Add peppers, onion, garlic, and crushed red pepper. Stir and cook for about 5 minutes. Add rice, clam juice, water, wine, saffron, salt, pepper, basil, and artichoke hearts. Bring mixture to a boil, stirring constantly.

Transfer mixture to a Paella pan or 4-quart baking pan; cover with a lid or foil. Bake for 30 minutes, stirring occasionally to mix ingredients.

Remove pan from oven and artfully arrange seafood, gently pushing partway into rice with the bowl of a spoon. Do not stir or mix. Cover and continue baking for 15 minutes or until the rice is tender and the seafood is cooked. Serve immediately.

Note: Well-scrubbed clams in shells or cooked, cracked crab in shells can be included. Italian or pork sausage can be substituted for the Chorizo sausage.

Preparation Time: 30 minutes
Cooking Time: 45 minutes
Servings: 8

Byron Pinot Noir

DIRECTOR'S FISH STEW

1 pound red snapper
1 pound sea bass
24 medium size shrimp
18 black mussels, cleaned
12 clams
3 sweet Italian sausages
3 hot Italian sausages
1/2 cup olive oil
1 cup chopped parsley
1 large onion, chopped
1 green or red bell pepper, sliced
3 cloves garlic, chopped

6 tomatoes, peeled, seeded
  and chopped
2 cups of tomato sauce
2 cups water
1 cup white wine
1 tablespoon sweet basil
1/2 tablespoon oregano
1 large bay leaf
Freshly ground pepper
1 teaspoon salt, optional
Juice of one lemon

Cut the sea bass and red snapper into pieces about 1 1/2-inches thick. Steam cleaned clams and mussels in 1 cup of white wine until they are open. Discard any shellfish that fails to open. Strain the broth and reserve it. Cut the sausages into 1 1/2-inch pieces and cook in a pan until brown. Set aside.

Heat 1/2 cup of olive oil in a large kettle or stewing pan. Add the parsley, onions, peppers, and garlic. Cook over low heat for approximately 4 to 5 minutes. Add the chopped tomatoes, tomato sauce, basil, oregano, and reserved mussel and clam broth. Cover the kettle and simmer for about 5 to 6 minutes. Add the sea bass, red snapper, shrimp, and sausages; cover kettle and simmer for 30 minutes. Just before serving, add the mussels and clams and simmer for another 5 minutes.

Serve in large soup bowls with crusty sourdough bread.

Preparation Time: 1 hour 30 minutes
Servings: 6 to 8

CHOPIN CIOPPINO

1 1/4 cups chopped onion	Pepper to taste
2 cloves garlic, chopped	Salt to taste
3/4 cup chopped green bell pepper	1 cup dry red wine
1 cup chopped celery	1/4 pound shelled shrimp, cut in half
1/4 cup olive oil	1 pound firm white fish, cut in
1 14-ounce can tomatoes	1-inch cubes
1 16-ounce can tomato sauce	1 cup clam juice or water
1 teaspoon thyme	1/2 pound crab pieces
1 teaspoon basil	1/2 pound small scallops
1 teaspoon oregano	Fresh parsley for garnish

In a stock pot or Dutch oven, saute onion, garlic, green pepper and celery in oil until soft but not brown. Add tomatoes, tomato sauce, herbs and spices, wine and clam juice. Heat to boiling, then simmer 30 minutes. Add shrimp, fish, crab, and scallops to sauce. Simmer 10 to 15 minutes. Add water if needed. Serve in large soup bowls; garnish with fresh parsley.

Preparation Time: 1 hour
Servings: 6 to 8

BAKED SWORDFISH WITH ITALIAN SAUCE

6 swordfish, tuna or other firm fish	1/3 cup sliced pimento-stuffed olives
Salt and pepper, to taste	1/3 cup pine nuts or slivered almonds,
2 tablespoons olive oil	toasted
1 medium onion, thinly sliced	1/3 cup raisins
4 small tomatoes, peeled and chopped	3 teaspoons capers
or 1 16-ounce can whole peeled	2 garlic cloves, minced
tomatoes, drained and chopped	

Preheat oven to 350 degrees. Rinse fish and dry on paper towel. Season with salt and pepper, if desired. In a flat casserole dish, arrange fish in a single layer. Bake for 25 to 30 minutes until cooked.

To make sauce, heat oil in a small skillet; add onions and saute for 2 to 3 minutes. Add tomatoes, olives, nuts, raisins, capers, and garlic. Cook for 5 minutes over medium-low heat, stirring occasionally. Season to taste with salt and pepper. To serve, spoon sauce over fish.

Note: This sauce is also delicious with baked chicken.

Preparation Time: 35 to 35 minutes
Servings: 6

SWORDFISH WITH AVOCADO BUTTER

4 swordfish or shark steaks
1/3 cup soy sauce
1 teaspoon grated lemon peel
1/2 cup lemon juice

1 teaspoon Dijon mustard
1/2 cup corn oil
Avocado butter, recipe follows

Combine soy sauce, lemon peel, lemon juice, mustard, and oil. Marinate swordfish steaks, covered, in the refrigerator for 1 to 3 hours. Prepare avocado butter.

About 10 to 15 minutes before serving time, broil or barbeque swordfish steaks. While steaks are still hot from the grill, top each one with a large dollop of avocado butter and serve.

Preparation Time: 10 minutes
Marinating Time: 1 to 3 hours
Cooking Time: 10 to 15 minutes
Servings: 4

Vichon Chevrignon

AVOCADO BUTTER

1/2 cup butter or margarine, softened
1 large avocado, mashed
2 tablespoons finely chopped
   fresh cilantro

1 tablespoon Worcestershire sauce
1 teaspoon garlic salt
4 tablespoons lemon juice
Dash of red pepper sauce

Blend all ingredients and chill in the refrigerator.

Preparation Time: 10 minutes
Chilling Time: 1 to 2 hours
Yield: 1 1/2 cups

BAKED SALMON BEURRE BLANC

Beurre Blanc Sauce
3 to 4 pounds of salmon filet,
   1 to 1 1/4 inch thick

Salt and freshly ground white pepper
Lemon slices
Fresh basil sprigs

Make the Beurre Blanc sauce ahead. Preheat oven to 350 degrees. Line baking dish with foil and place salmon on the foil, skin side down. Sprinkle generously with salt and freshly ground white pepper. Bake until the fish is just opaque in center, about 15 minutes.

To serve, transfer salmon to a platter and garnish with lemon slices and fresh basil sprigs. Pass the Beurre Blanc sauce.

Preparation Time: 20 minutes
Servings: 6

BEURRE BLANC SAUCE

3 tablespoons white wine vinegar
3 tablespoons dry white wine
2 shallots, finely chopped
1 cup chilled, unsalted butter,
   cut into 16 pieces
1/2 cup seeded and diced tomatoes

1/2 cup diced cucumber
Salt and freshly ground white pepper,
   to taste
3/4 cup loosely packed fresh basil
   leaves, chopped

Combine vinegar, wine, and shallots in a small saucepan. Boil until reduced to 1 tablespoon, approximately 5 minutes. Remove pan from heat and whisk in 2 pieces of butter. Set pan over low heat and whisk in remaining butter 1 piece at a time, removing pan from the heat briefly should drops of melted butter appear. If the sauce breaks down at any time during preparation, remove from heat and whisk in 2 pieces additional cold butter.

Remove sauce from heat and fold in tomato and cucumber. Season with salt, freshly ground white pepper, and add basil. The sauce can be prepared as much as 1 hour ahead of serving time.

Preparation Time: 30 minutes
Cooking Time: 45 minutes
Servings: 6

Robert Mondavi Chardonnay

SALMON WITH CHAMPAGNE-BASIL CREAM

2 tablespoons unsalted butter
1/4 cup finely chopped shallots
2 cups dry champagne
2 cups heavy cream
Salt and white pepper, to taste
1 cup pine nuts

1 cup fresh basil leaves
2 tablespoons extra virgin olive oil
4 8-ounce salmon steaks or filets
Extra virgin olive oil
1/2 cup finely chopped fresh chives

In a heavy saucepan, melt butter over medium heat. Add shallots and saute for 3 minutes. Increase heat to high and add champagne. Bring to a boil and reduce liquid to about 1/2 cup, approximately 10 minutes. Add cream and simmer until thickened to sauce consistency, stirring occasionally, approximately 8 minutes. Season to taste with salt and white pepper and set aside.

Blend pine nuts, basil leaves, and olive oil in a food processor until finely chopped. Season with salt and white pepper.

Preheat broiler. Brush salmon steaks with olive oil and season with salt and white pepper. Broil 3 minutes on each side, or until cooked through. Remove from the broiler and coat each piece of fish with pine nut mixture, pressing gently to adhere pesto to fish.

Bring cream sauce to a simmer and stir in chives. Spoon sauce onto serving plates and top with the broiled salmon steaks.

Preparation Time: 40 minutes
Servings: 4

Robert Mondavi Chardonnay Reserve
Sparkling Wine

FISH SAUCES AND SALSAS

We can not resist sharing the following versatile sauces and salsas to spark up all kinds of fish, including red snapper, swordfish, halibut, salmon, and tuna. They are wonderful in appearance for parties.

TOMATO CAPER SAUCE

8 Roma tomatoes, seeded and chopped
1/2 onion, chopped
4 tablespoons capers, drained
1/2 cup chopped ripe black olives

1/2 teaspoon chopped fresh thyme
1/2 teaspoon chopped fresh oregano
4 small garlic cloves, finely chopped
2 tablespoons chopped fresh parsley

In a medium bowl, combine all ingredients and refrigerate, covered, for several hours before serving. This sauce is best served on chilled fish.

Preparation Time: 20 minutes
Yield: 2 cups

Robert Mondavi Pinot Noir

RED PEPPER SAUCE

1 large red bell pepper,
   seeded and chopped
1 small onion, chopped
2 celery ribs, chopped

1 small zucchini, chopped
2 tablespoons lime juice
4 tablespoons extra virgin olive oil
1/4 teaspoon cayenne pepper

In a medium bowl, combine all ingredients and refrigerate, covered, for several hours before serving. Serve this sauce on chilled fish.

Preparation Time: 25 minutes
Yield: 2 cups

Robert Mondavi Fumé Blanc Reserve

FRESH PINEAPPLE SALSA

This salsa is wonderful with any grilled fish!

2 cups seeded and diced tomatoes
1 3/4 cups diced fresh pineapple
1/4 cup chopped green onion
2 tablespoons diced green chilies

3 tablespoons minced fresh cilantro
2 tablespoons balsamic vinegar
1 tablespoon olive oil

In a large bowl, combine all ingredients and stir well. Let stand at room temperature 1 hour before serving. Refrigerate for longer holding time. Keeps for several days in the refrigerator.

NOTE: If you like a spicier salsa, add minced jalapeno peppers to taste.

Preparation Time: 30 minutes
Standing Time: 60 minutes
Yield: 3 1/2 cups

Robert Mondavi Fumé Blanc

MANGO SALSA

1 1/2 cups peeled, chopped mango
1/4 cup chopped red bell pepper
3 tablespoons chopped green onions

1 teaspoon brown sugar
1/2 teaspoon minced garlic

Combine mango, red pepper, onions, brown sugar, and minced garlic in a small saucepan. Cook over medium heat 5 minutes or until thoroughly heated, stirring frequently.

Preparation Time: 20 minutes
Yield: 2 cups

Robert Mondavi Fumé Blanc Reserve

AVOCADO-PAPAYA SALSA

1 large avocado, peeled, seeded,
  and chopped
1 papaya, peeled, seeded, and chopped
1/2 cup chopped fresh cilantro

1 small tomato, peeled, seeded,
  and chopped
1/4 cup lemon juice
1/4 cup orange juice

In a bowl, combine all ingredients and refrigerate, covered, for several hours. Bring sauce to room temperature if serving on hot fish.

Preparation Time: 25 minutes
Yield: 2 cups

Vichon Chevrignon

CHILLED POACHED SALMON

Cucumber dill sauce, recipe follows
Dry white wine, see directions
Water, as needed
1 teaspoon salt
10 peppercorns, crushed
8 sprigs thyme
4 sprigs parsley

1 6-pound salmon, cleaned, with
  head and tail left on
3 lemons, thinly sliced, for garnish
1 bunch dill, washed and dried,
  for garnish
1 cucumber, thinly sliced, for garnish

Make the cucumber dill sauce and chill. Pour enough wine into poacher to fill it 1/4 full. Add water to make it 1/2 full. Add salt, peppercorns, thyme, and parsley. Bring the liquid to a boil and simmer for 15 minutes.

Before lowering salmon into the poaching liquid, measure fish at the thickest part. Place salmon in liquid, bring to a boil and simmer for 10 minutes per inch. Transfer fish to a large platter and carefully peel off the skin. Cover and chill. Garnish with lemon, dill, and cucumber before serving.

Preparation Time: 35 minutes
Cooking Time: 10 minutes per inch at thickest part of salmon, or until done.
Chilling Time: 2 hours or more
Servings: 10 to 12

CUCUMBER DILL SAUCE

1 1/2 cups peeled, seeded and chopped
  cucumbers, well drained
2 cups chopped fresh dill
1 clove garlic, peeled and chopped
1 cup sour cream

1 1/2 cups mayonnaise
1/2 teaspoon freshly ground pepper
1/2 teaspoon cayenne pepper
1/2 teaspoon salt

Place all sauce ingredients in a bowl and mix thoroughly. Chill until ready to use. Serve sauce in a pretty serving bowl on the side.

Preparation Time: 20 minutes
Yield: 5 to 6 cups

Robert Mondavi Fumé Blanc Reserve

SALMON IN A POTATO CRUST
WITH THREE VEGETABLE SAUCES

Thank you to the highly acclaimed chef, John McLaughlin from JW's, in the Anaheim Marriott, for sharing one of his signature dishes with us.

2 large carrots, peeled and chopped
Salt, divided
Pinch of sugar
1/2 cup clarified butter, divided

1 bunch spinach, cleaned and stemmed
1 red bell pepper, roasted, peeled, and seeded
4 or 5 russet potatoes, peeled
1 1/2 pounds salmon, cut in 4 portions

Make pureed sauces of 3 colors for flavor and presentation, each thick enough to avoid runniness. Cook carrots in water with salt and sugar; drain, reserving the liquid; adjust consistency if necessary. Blend carrots until smooth. Saute spinach in 1 teaspoon butter. Drain, reserving liquid. Blend spinach until smooth. Chill. Blend red pepper until smooth. Adjust consistency of sauces with reserved liquid or water, if necessary. Set aside.

To make potato crust; slice the potatoes, as thinly as possible. Preheat a nonstick 7-inch skillet, brushed with a little clarified butter. Arrange potato slices in the skillet in overlapping rows. Cook the potatoes lightly without browning them; they should hold together in one piece. Make sure the potatoes are cooked completely to retain a nice color. Slide potato crust out onto a wax paper-lined tray. Prepare 3 more potato crusts. Crusts can be set aside up to 3 hours.

Preheat oven to 450 degrees. Sprinkle salmon with salt. Wrap each portion in the potato crusts. Saute briefly in the remaining clarified butter. Put in baking pan; bake two minutes and turn; bake 5 more minutes. Drain and keep warm.

To serve, salt sauces to taste and lightly reheat. Arrange a dollop of each sauce on 4 individual plates. Place the crusted salmon on top.

Note: Clarified butter is made by slowly melting butter and skimming off the foamy white particles that can burn, leaving the tasty, clear yellow portion.

Preparation Time: 1 hour, 40 minutes
Baking Time: 7 minutes
Servings: 4

Robert Mondavi Fumé Blanc Reserve

STEAMED CHILEAN SEA BASS
WITH TAPENADE AND WARM VINAIGRETTE

Thank you Annie Roberts, Executive Chef at Robert Mondavi Winery, for this elegant recipe.

1 cup pitted Kalamata olives
1 tablespoon coarsely chopped anchovies
1/4 cup capers
1 tablespoon Italian parsley, chopped
3 tablespoons chopped shallots, divided
1 tablespoon chopped garlic
3/4 cup olive oil

1 teaspoon lemon juice
Salt, to taste
Freshly ground black pepper, to taste
2 tablespoons white wine vinegar
2 tablespoons sherry vinegar
1 Chilean sea bass, cut crosswise
    in 4 portions

Make a tapenade, processing olives, anchovies, and capers in a food processor until well blended. Add parsley, 2 tablespoons chopped shallots, garlic, 1/4 cup olive oil, lemon juice, salt and pepper; blend again. Set aside. Prepare a vinaigrette in a small saucepan, mixing together the vinegars, 1/2 cup olive oil, 1 tablespoon shallots, salt and pepper. Set aside. In a steamer, steam fish over water for about 5 minutes, or microwave in a covered dish for 3 to 4 minutes. Place fish on serving plates. Drizzle with warmed vinaigrette and top with tapenade. Serve immediately.

Preparation Time: 30 minutes
Servings: 4

Robert Mondavi Fume Blanc

SOLE FILETS WITH ALMOND BUTTER

3 eggs, beaten
3 tablespoons freshly grated
    Parmesan cheese
1 1/2 tablespoons chopped parsley
1/2 teaspoon salt
1/4 teaspoon freshly ground pepper
1/2 cup flour

3 tablespoons extra virgin olive oil
2 1/2 pounds sole or other white fish
1/2 cup butter or margarine
1/2 cup sliced almonds
3 tablespoons lemon juice
2 tablespoons dry white wine
2 lemons, thinly sliced

In a pie plate, combine eggs, cheese, parsley, salt, and pepper. Spread flour evenly in another pie plate. Coat fish with the flour and dip into the egg mixture. In a large frying pan, heat oil and cook fish until lightly browned. Keep fish warm on a platter in a low heated oven.

In a small pan, melt butter and stir in almonds, cooking until nuts are just golden in color. Remove pan from heat and add lemon juice and wine, stirring to mix well. Spoon almond butter over the fish and garnish with lemon slices. Serve immediately.

Preparation Time: 45 minutes
Servings: 6 to 8

Byron Sauvignon Blanc

SOLE STUFFED WITH SHRIMP

1/4 cup unsalted butter
1/4 cup finely chopped shallots
6 sole filets, approximately
    4 to 5 ounces each
Salt and freshly ground white pepper,
    to taste

12 medium to large shrimp, peeled
    and cleaned, approximately 1/2 pound
1/2 cup white wine
1 cup heavy cream
2 teaspoons fresh lemon juice

Preheat oven to 425 degrees. In a small skillet, melt butter and saute shallots until soft. Spread half the shallots in a buttered 7 x 11-inch glass baking dish.

Season filets with salt and pepper. Spread each with 1 teaspoon of the remaining shallots on the skin side of the fish. The skin side is slightly darker in color. Place 2 shrimp, side by side and head to tail across each fillet. Roll the filets and place seam-side down over the shallots.

Pour the wine over fish rolls and cover with a sheet of buttered foil. Bake for 15 minutes. The fish should be nearly done, almost completely opaque. Turn off the oven. Carefully pour all of the cooking liquid into a large skillet and return the fish, covered, to the oven.

Boil the cooking liquid for about 5 minutes, until reduced to about 3 tablespoons. Mixture will be syrupy. Add cream and lemon juice and cook rapidly for 3 minutes, or until the sauce is thickened. Season to taste with salt and freshly ground white pepper.

Arrange fish on serving plates and top with sauce. Serve immediately.

Preparation Time: 30 minutes
Servings: 4

Byron Chardonnay Reserve

HALIBUT EN PAPILLOTE

2 pounds halibut, tilefish, or other
   meaty filets of fish
Juice of 1 lemon
1 large onion, finely chopped
1 clove garlic, finely chopped
Salt and freshly ground pepper
2 1/2 cups peeled and chopped
   fresh tomatoes

1/2 teaspoon crushed fennel seeds
1 tablespoon vegetable oil
2/3 cup finely chopped scallions,
   divided
6 thin lemon slices

Divide the fish into 6 equal portions and place in a dish with the lemon juice to marinate. In a saucepan over low heat, place the onion and garlic , cover, and cook until the onions have wilted and become translucent, about 10 minutes. Add salt, pepper, tomatoes, and fennel seeds; cook briefly over high heat.

Preheat oven to 375 degrees. Scatter half of the scallions among 6 squares of lightly oiled heavy-duty aluminum foil. Top each with a piece of fish, then divide the tomato mixture evenly over each. Scatter the remaining scallions over the top of each piece of fish and top with a lemon slice. Seal the foil loosely but securely. Bake approximately 20 minutes. Serve by placing the papillote on each plate, allowing guests to open packages themselves when ready to dine.

Preparation time: 30 minutes
Cooking time: 20 minutes
Servings: 6

Vichon Chevrignon

HALIBUT KEBOBS

2 pounds halibut
1/2 cup dry white wine
1/4 cup extra virgin olive oil
2 tablespoons lemon juice
1 tablespoon minced onion
1 clove garlic, crushed
1 teaspoon salt

1/2 teaspoon oregano, crushed
1/8 teaspoon black pepper
12 cherry tomatoes
1 large green bell pepper,
   seeded and cut into squares
6 mushrooms, cleaned and stemmed

Cut fish into chunks, discarding skin and bones. Combine wine, oil, lemon juice, onion, garlic, salt, oregano, and pepper. Pour mixture over halibut and marinate, covered, several hours or overnight in the refrigerator. Thread halibut, peppers, tomatoes, and mushrooms on skewers. Grill or broil, basting frequently with marinade, until the fish flakes, turning once or twice. Serve with a pasta or fresh fruit salad.

Preparation Time: 30 minutes
Cooking Time: 20 minutes or until done
Servings: 6

Robert Mondavi Fumé Blanc

HALIBUT IN CHARDONNAY CREAM SAUCE

1/2 cup butter, divided	Freshly ground pepper, to taste
2/3 cup flour, divided	2 medium yellow squash, diced
1/2 cup milk	2 zucchini squash, diced
1/4 cup Chardonnay wine	2 medium tomatoes, seeded and diced
1/2 cup minced fresh basil	4 large mushrooms, sliced
4 halibut steaks	4 pancakes, from a mix
Salt, to taste	1 cup quartered and finely sliced onion

In a saucepan, melt 1/4 cup butter; whisk in 1/3 cup flour; add milk and cook until smooth and thick, stirring constantly. Remove from heat; stir in wine and basil. Set aside.

Preheat oven to 350 degrees. Sprinkle both sides of fish with salt and pepper. Place in a buttered 13 x 9-inch glass baking dish. Steam squash and zucchini for 5 minutes in a vegetable steamer. Place steamed vegetables, tomato, and mushrooms on top of the halibut and sprinkle with salt and pepper. Pour half the chardonnay cream sauce over halibut and bake, uncovered, for 30 minutes

While the halibut is baking, set out pancakes. Dip slices of onion in 1/4 cup flour and fry in 1/4 cup butter until crisp. Set aside on paper towels to absorb any excess butter.

To serve, place one teaspoon of remaining chardonnay cream sauce on each plate; add one pancake on top of the sauce. Place a halibut steak on each pancake and equally divide the remaining sauce over the top of each serving. Garnish with the fried onions.

Preparation Time: 30 minutes   Robert Mondavi Chardonnay Reserve
Baking time: 30 minutes
Servings: 4

RED SNAPPER WITH CILANTRO

This is a great barbeque recipe for a summer party dish.

6 tablespoons extra virgin olive oil
1 medium onion, diced
3 jalapeno peppers,
  seeded and finely chopped
3 tablespoons chopped fresh basil
3/4 cup chopped fresh cilantro

1/4 cup lemon juice
2 tablespoons lemon zest
4 6 to 8-ounce red snapper filets
Salt and fresh ground black pepper,
  to taste

Heat oil and saute onion for 2 minutes, then add peppers, basil, cilantro, and lemon juice. Cook for 1 minute and remove from heat.

Place each fish filet on a piece of well-oiled foil and top with the cilantro mixture, adding lemon zest, salt and freshly ground black pepper. Seal the foil into leak-proof packets and grill over hot coals approximately 10 minutes. Remove from grill and serve on plates, allowing guest to open individual packets at the table.

Preparation Time: 30 minutes
Baking Time: 10 minutes
Servings: 4

Vichon Chevrignon

RED SNAPPER IN A SNAP

3 tablespoons butter
1 large onion, sliced
1 1/2 pounds red snapper filets
1/2 cup mayonnaise
1/4 cup Parmesan cheese
2 tablespoons lemon juice

1 teaspoon Worcestershire sauce
2 teaspoons paprika
1/2 teaspoon salt
Oregano, to taste
Parsley, to taste

Preheat oven to 350 degrees. Melt the butter in a 13 x 9-inch glass baking dish. Add sliced onion and top with red snapper. Combine mayonnaise, Parmesan cheese, lemon juice, Worcestershire sauce, paprika, and salt. Spread over snapper and sprinkle to taste with oregano and parsley. Bake approximately 35 to 40 minutes. Serve immediately.

Note: This quick sauce is good with any favorite fish filets.

Preparation Time: 10 minutes
Baking Time: 40 minutes
Servings: 4

Robert Mondavi Chardonnay

CROWN OF THE SEA CRAB SOUFFLE

3/4 to 1 pound crab meat
2 tablespoons finely chopped onion
4 tablespoons butter
2/3 cup flour
1 1/2 cups milk
1/2 teaspoon dry mustard

Salt and pepper to taste
4 eggs, separated
2 tablespoons lemon juice
2 tablespoons chopped parsley
Dill-wine sauce, recipe follows

Preheat oven to 350 degrees. Flake crab meat, removing any shell, and saute briefly with onions. Set aside. Melt butter in saucepan. Stir in flour and gradually add milk, continue to stir until smooth, about 15 to 20 minutes. Remove from heat. Add mustard, salt and pepper.

Beat egg yolks until light and fluffy. Add some of the sauce to the yolks, then combine with remaining sauce, continuing to stir. Add crabmeat mixture, lemon juice, and parsley. Beat egg whites until stiff and carefully fold into the crab mixture. Fill a 1 1/2-quart souffle casserole with mixture. Bake 40 minutes, or until souffle is firm in the center. Meanwhile prepare dill-wine sauce. Serve immediately.

Preparation Time: 30 minutes
Baking Time: 40 minutes
Servings: 6

DILL-WINE SAUCE

1/2 cup clam juice
1/4 cup unsalted butter, softened
2 egg yolks, slightly beaten
4 tablespoons heavy cream

1/2 cup white wine
1 teaspoon dill weed
Salt to taste

Heat clam juice and add butter. Combine egg yolks, cream, and wine and whisk into heated clam juice mixture. Add seasonings and continue to whisk over low heat until slightly thickened.

Note: Serve this sauce with seafood. Heavenly!

Preparation Time: 20 minutes
Yield: 1 1/2 cups

THE CENTER OF FASHION

It should come as no surprise that a fashion show at the Orange County Performing Arts Center is a show indeed. No simple ramp or demure, white-gloved commentator here! For its *Center of Fashion*, The Guilds of The Center present a glittering extravaganza complete with lavish musical numbers, high-stepping dancers, and striking stage sets. And the fashions? Showcasing dozens of Orange County's finest designers and retailers and more than a million dollars' worth of elegant apparel, this event has all the excitement of a New York opening.

After months of training and rehearsals, about 150 models—some professional, some drawn from The Guilds' 3,000-strong membership—take part in the spectacular production. Volunteer make-up artists and hair stylists work backstage to transform them into the breathtaking beauties in evening gowns who will light up the stage with their glamour and flair. Besides raising substantial funds for The Center, *The Center of Fashion* combines the chic of haute couture with the thrill of live theater.

**In a glittering procession of the latest fashions
from Paris, London, New York, and Los Angeles, The Center volunteers,
professional models, and Orange County's top fashion retailers unite to present
this unique fashion-theater extravaganza. Photograph underwritten by
SOUTH COAST PLAZA**

Guilds members are busy. They head symphony and PTA support groups; they volunteer in hospitals and art museums. They enjoy family activities, travel, cultural and sporting events, and spending time with friends. When they entertain, they prefer a warm, comfortable atmosphere. If a dinner party is formal, it is also relaxed. They often entertain outdoors on the patio or even on a picnic blanket before an outdoor concert, sporting event, or fireworks display. Their lives are too full to allow them time to prepare many seven-course extravaganzas, so they focus on simple, yet elegant dishes and beautiful presentation. Great flavor, sophisticated style, and ease of preparation: these are the elements sure to put a smile on the face of even the busiest hostess.

MEAT

Good friends, memorable food, and a view that goes forever—what better prelude to a night at the theater? Guests at this pre-theater party at a home in the Anaheim Hills have a spectacular view of the Santa Ana River Basin looking toward Yorba Linda. Beautiful crystal courtesy of Galleri Orrefors Kosta Boda.

BEEF MEDALLIONS
WITH LINGONBERRIES AND PORT SAUCE

3 shallots, finely chopped
1 cup finely chopped mushrooms
3 to 4 tablespoons olive oil, divided
2 cups beef stock
1/2 teaspoon dry mustard
2 tablespoons instant blending flour

1/3 cup port wine
Salt and pepper, to taste
1/2 cup lingonberries in sugar
6 beef medallions, cut approximately
   1-inch thick from tenderloin

Saute shallots and mushrooms in 2 tablespoons olive oil, adding more oil if necessary. Add stock and simmer. Stir in dry mustard, flour, wine, salt and pepper. When sauce has reduced by one-third, add the lingonberries. Place remaining olive oil in a skillet. When oil is hot, saute beef medallions, 2 to 5 minutes on each side. Place meat on a platter and top with sauce. Serve hot.

Preparation Time: 5 minutes
Cooking Time: 15 to 20 minutes
Servings: 6

Robert Mondavi Cabernet Sauvignon Reserve

FILET MIGNON WITH TARRAGON SAUCE

2 cups beef stock
1/4 cup olive oil
4 1 1/2-inch thick filet mignon steaks
Salt, to taste
1/4 cup cognac

2 tablespoons chopped fresh tarragon,
   or 1 tablespoon dried
1 cup heavy cream
4 slices hearty bread
Fresh tarragon, for garnish

Place stock in a saucepan and reduce by half over high heat. Meanwhile, season beef with salt. In a heavy skillet, heat olive oil over high heat. Add steaks and quickly brown on both sides. Add cognac and ignite with a match. When the flames die, reduce heat to medium. Add tarragon, reduced beef stock, and cream.

Cook the steaks until done, about 5 minutes for rare, or 8 minutes for medium. Remove steaks from sauce and set aside, keeping warm. Continue cooking the sauce until slightly thickened. Trim bread to fit the steaks and toast on each side under broiler. Place a slice of toast on each plate. Top with a steak and some of the sauce. Garnish with fresh tarragon.

Preparation Time: 10 minutes
Cooking Time: 25 minutes
Servings: 4

Robert Mondavi Cabernet Sauvignon Reserve

STEAK IN GREEN PEPPERCORN-HORSERADISH SAUCE

1 cup chicken stock
1 cup beef stock
2 tablespoons olive oil
4 steak filets, cut 1 1/2-inches thick
Salt and pepper, to taste
1 tablespoon butter
2 tablespoons chopped shallots

1 tablespoon crushed dry
  green peppercorns
1/2 cup dry red wine vinegar
2 tablespoons cognac
2 cups whipping cream
2 1/2 tablespoons fresh grated horseradish
  or 2 tablespoons prepared horseradish

Boil chicken and beef stocks in a heavy saucepan until liquid is reduced to 1/2 cup, about 15 minutes. This can be done ahead. Heat oil in a heavy skillet over medium high heat. Season beef with salt and pepper, add beef to skillet. Reduce heat to medium; brown the meat and cook approximately 5 minutes per side for medium rare. Remove beef from skillet and keep warm.

Pour off oil; add butter to skillet, stirring over medium heat until melted. Add shallots and crushed green peppercorns. Cook until shallots are golden brown. Increase heat to high; add vinegar and cognac. Boil until liquid is reduced to 1/4 cup, about 5 minutes. Add reduced stock and cream. Boil until sauce is a thick consistency, stirring occasionally. Mix grated horseradish into sauce; season with salt and spoon over steaks.

Preparation Time: 40 minutes
Cooking Time: 10 minutes
Servings: 4

Vichon Cabernet Sauvignon, Stag's Leap District

PACIFIC RIM SIRLOIN

1 2 to 3-pound beef sirloin steak,
  2-inches thick
1 cup dry sherry
1/2 cup soy sauce
4 tablespoons brown sugar

1 teaspoon ground ginger
1 clove garlic
4 tablespoons water
Watercress or parsley, for garnish

Place beef in a large plastic bag. Combine sherry, soy sauce, brown sugar, ginger, garlic, and water; pour marinade into bag and close tightly. Let stand two hours at room temperature or overnight in the refrigerator. Turn bag occasionally.

Preheat oven to 425 degrees. When ready to cook, place meat on a broiler pan. Bake for 45 to 50 minutes, basting occasionally with the marinade. Heat the remaining marinade, or make another batch to serve on the side. Slice the meat and arrange on a platter. Spoon some of the sauce over the meat. Garnish with watercress or parsley, if desired.

Note: Marinated steak can be grilled on the barbecue with great results!

Preparation Time: 10 minutes
Marinating Time: 2 hours
Cooking Time: 45 to 50 minutes
Servings: 4 to 5

Vichon Cabernet Sauvignon

ORIENTAL BEEF STIR-FRY

1 1/2 pounds round steak,
  cut in thin strips
8 tablespoons soy sauce
2 large cloves garlic, finely minced
1/4 teaspoon pepper
2 tablespoons cornstarch

1 small green bell pepper,
  cut into strips
1 medium tomato, chopped
2 tablespoons peanut oil
3 cups steamed rice

Place meat strips in a bowl and add soy sauce, garlic, and pepper. Marinate for several hours or overnight in the refrigerator. When ready to prepare, stir in the cornstarch. Parboil green pepper and drain. In a heavy skillet or wok, heat peanut oil over high heat. Add meat and cook rapidly, tossing for about 5 minutes. Lower heat, and add pepper strips and tomato. Cook, tossing until the vegetables are heated through, approximately 5 minutes. Serve over steamed rice.

Preparation Time: 15 minutes
Marinating Time: 3 hours or overnight
Cooking Time: 10 to 12 minutes
Servings: 4

Byron Pinot Noir

BOEUF BOURGUIGNON

Boeuf Bourguignon, the king of all stews, is from the Burgundy region of France, where some of the best French cooking was born.

6 slices of bacon, diced
2 1/2 pounds lean stewing beef,
   cut into 1 1/2-inch cubes
1/4 cup brandy
1 teaspoon flour
1 teaspoon salt
1/2 teaspoon black pepper
1/2 teaspoon dried thyme
1 1/2 cups dry red wine

1 tablespoon butter
1 large onion, chopped
2 medium carrots, cut into pieces
3 cloves garlic, pressed
Bouquet garni, see note
1 16-ounce can beef broth, approximate
1 tablespoon tomato paste
1 pound sliced mushrooms
1 cup fresh pearl onions

In a heavy skillet, cook the bacon until crisp. Remove with a slotted spoon and drain. In the same skillet, brown the stewing meat thoroughly in small batches.

Heat brandy in the microwave. Pour over the meat, then flame by lighting the brandy with a match. When flame dies down, stir flour into meat. Season with salt, pepper, and thyme. Transfer to a Dutch oven and add red wine and bacon.

Heat butter with the remaining fat in skillet and brown the chopped onions. Add the onions, carrots, garlic, bouquet garni, beef broth, and tomato paste to the meat. Simmer, covered, over lowest heat on stove until very tender. If you prefer, cook in a preheated 350 degree oven for 2 hours.

Add the sliced mushrooms and pearl onions. Cook another 30 minutes. Remove bouquet garni before serving.

Note: This bouquet garni is 4 whole cloves, 6 peppercorns, parsley sprigs, 1 stalk celery, and 2 bay leaves tightly tied in a piece of cheesecloth.

Preparation Time: 45 minutes
Cooking Time: 2 1/2 hours
Servings: 6 to 8

Robert Mondavi Pinot Noir Reserve

BEEF AND ZUCCHINI MOUSSAKA

This is a California version of the Greek Moussaka, substituting ground beef for ground lamb and zucchini for eggplant.

4 tablespoons olive oil, divided
2 pounds zucchini, sliced 1/4-inch thick
2 pounds ground beef
1 cup chopped onion
2 tablespoons tomato paste
2 tomatoes, peeled and chopped
1/4 cup chopped parsley
1/2 cup red wine
1 teaspoon oregano
1 clove garlic, minced

1/4 teaspoon cinnamon
6 tablespoons butter
6 tablespoons flour
3 cups milk
Salt and pepper to taste
Dash nutmeg
4 egg yolks
1/4 pound grated Swiss or Gruyere cheese
4 tablespoons Parmesan cheese

In a frying pan, heat 2 tablespoons olive oil. Brown zucchini; remove from pan and set aside. Heat remaining olive oil; saute meat and onion until meat is browned. Add tomato paste, tomatoes, parsley, wine, oregano, garlic, and cinnamon.

In a saucepan, melt butter; add flour and stir until blended. Mixture should bubble for a minute. Add the milk and continue cooking until thickened. Add salt, pepper, and nutmeg. Beat egg yolks and add slowly to the sauce, stirring constantly, and cook for 3 more minutes. Remove from heat.

Preheat oven to 350 degrees. Grease an ovenproof casserole and layer ingredients, beginning with 1/3 of the zucchini, then 1/2 the meat and 1/2 the Swiss cheese. Repeat layers, finishing with the zucchini. Cover with the sauce and sprinkle with Parmesan cheese. Bake for one hour. Serve hot.

Preparation Time: 30 minutes
Baking Time: 1 hour
Servings: 6

Robert Mondavi Cabernet Sauvignon

MEXICAN LASAGNA

1 1/2 pounds ground beef	1/4 teaspoon pepper
1 medium onion	1/4 cup vegetable oil
1 clove garlic, minced	8 corn tortillas, cut in half
1 16-ounce can tomatoes	8 ounces ricotta cheese
1 10-ounce can red chili sauce	1 egg
1 11-ounce can whole kernel corn	1/2 pound Jack cheese, thickly sliced
1 3.8-ounce can chopped ripe olives	3 to 4 ounces tortilla chips, crumbled
1 teaspoon salt	1 cup grated Cheddar cheese

Brown meat, onion, and garlic in a large skillet. Combine tomatoes, chili sauce, corn, olives, and salt and pepper. Bring to a boil, reduce heat, and simmer about 2 minutes, stirring occasionally.

In a small skillet, heat oil and add tortillas, one at a time, cooking to soften. Drain on paper towels. In a small bowl, combine the ricotta and egg. Preheat oven to 350 degrees.

In a 13 x 9-inch baking dish, layer ingredients, using 1/3 of the meat mixture, 1/2 the cheese slices, all the ricotta and egg, and 1/2 the tortillas. Continue layering 1/3 meat, remaining cheese and tortillas, and topping with the remaining meat. Add crumbled tortilla chips and grated cheese. Bake until lasagne becomes bubbly, about 20 minutes. Let set briefly before serving.

Preparation Time: 30 minutes   Robert Mondavi Woodbridge Zinfandel
Baking Time: 20 minutes
Servings: 6 to 8

CALIFORNIA CHILI

2 tablespoons vegetable oil
3 pounds boneless beef round or chuck,
   cut into 1/2 to 1-inch cubes
3 cloves garlic, minced
3/4 cup chopped yellow onions
4 to 6 tablespoons chili powder
1 tablespoon ground cumin
1 tablespoon dried oregano

3 tablespoons flour
4 cups beef broth, divided
Salt and pepper to taste
2 15-ounce cans pinto beans,
   rinsed and drained
Sour cream, for garnish
Chopped green onion, for garnish
Fresh lime wedges, for garnish

In a large sauce pan or Dutch oven, heat oil; add beef, stirring frequently until meat changes color, but does not brown, about 10 minutes. Lower heat; add garlic and onions, and continue cooking another 2 to 3 minutes. Add the chili powder, cumin, oregano, and flour. Stir to evenly coat the meat.

Add 3 cups of broth, stirring to blend. Season with salt and pepper. Bring to a boil and reduce heat. Simmer, partially covered, for 2 to 2 1/2 hours. Stir occasionally and, if needed, add more broth. Cook until meat is almost falling apart.

Cool; refrigerate overnight. When ready to serve, add beans and reheat, adding more beef broth if necessary. Serve in bowls with a dollop of sour cream, a sprinkling of green onions, and a lime wedge to garnish.

Note: For a variation, replace the beef with boneless pork, or half beef and half pork.

Preparation Time: 30 minutes
Chilling Time: Overnight
Cooking Time: 3 hours
Servings: 8

Robert Mondavi Woodbridge Zinfandel

SILVERADO CANYON CHILI

2 tablespoons olive oil
4 pounds coarsely ground beef
1 large onion, chopped
2 cloves garlic, minced
2 teaspoons oregano
2 teaspoons ground cumin
2 tablespoons hot Mexican
   chili powder

2 16-ounce cans tomatoes,
   including liquid
2 cups hot water
1 teaspoon salt
2 tablespoons chopped cilantro,
   optional
1 cup grated Monterey Jack cheese
   optional

In a heavy pot, heat the olive oil. When hot, add the meat, and cook until it loses its pink color. Add the onions, garlic, and cook until onion is translucent. Add remaining ingredients. Bring to a boil; then simmer covered for at least 1 hour. Skim off any grease. Adjust seasonings. Pass cilantro and cheese to top chili, if desired.

Preparation Time: 20 minutes
Cooking Time: 1 hour
Servings: 8

Robert Mondavi Woodbridge Cabernet Sauvignon

TERIYAKI MEATSTICKS

1 1/2 pounds flank steak
Bamboo skewers, soaked in water
1/4 cup soy sauce
1 teaspoon sesame oil

3 tablespoons salad oil
1 teaspoon brown sugar
2 cloves garlic, crushed

Slice flank steak diagonally across the grain. Slices should be about 1/8-inch thick.

In a large plastic container with lid, combine soy sauce, sesame oil, salad oil, brown sugar, and garlic . Add steak strips. Cover and shake well to coat all the meat. Marinate for at least 1 hour. Weave the strips of beef onto bamboo skewers and barbecue for about one minute on each side.

Note: These make wonderful appetizers, sliced into smaller pieces. This marinade can be used for steak or fish.

Preparation Time: 20 minutes
Marinating Time: 1 hour or more
Cooking Time: 2 or 3 minutes
Servings: 6

Robert Mondavi Merlot

ROAST VEAL WITH ORANGE SAUCE

2 teaspoons orange zest	2 tablespoons butter
1/2 teaspoon lemon zest	1/2 cup dry white wine
1 teaspoon Dijon mustard	1/4 cup Grand Marnier
1 teaspoon dry chicken bouillon	1/2 cup fresh orange juice
3 pounds boned and rolled veal shoulder or leg	1 tablespoon corn starch
1/2 teaspoon salt	1/2 cup fresh orange juice
1 tablespoon flour	1/4 cup heavy cream
	2 oranges, sliced, for garnish

Preheat oven to 350 degrees. Mix together orange and lemon zest, mustard, and chicken bouillon. Spread over veal to coat. Let stand at room temperature 1 to 2 hours. Gently remove coating from meat and pat dry with paper towels. Sprinkle veal lightly with salt and flour. In a skillet over medium-high heat, melt butter and quickly brown roast on all sides.

Place veal in a shallow baking pan and roast 15 minutes. Remove from oven; add white wine, Grand Marnier, and orange juice. Return to oven and continue roasting 1 hour. Baste with pan juices several times. Transfer veal to a carving platter and let rest, keeping warm. Combine cornstarch with orange juice and blend until smooth. Pour into hot roasting pan, stirring constantly and scraping up browned bits from the bottom. Bring the mixture to a boil over direct heat. Reduce heat to low and add whipping cream, stirring to make thin sauce.

To serve, thinly slice veal and arrange in an overlapping pattern in the center of a serving platter. Garnish with orange slices around the meat. Spoon some orange sauce over the meat.

Preparation Time: 1 hour   Robert Mondavi Chardonnay
Cooking Time: 1 hour 30 minutes
Servings: 6 to 8

OSSOBUCO ALLA MILANESE

6 veal shanks, about 3 pounds
1/2 cup flour
Salt and pepper, to taste
1/4 cup olive oil
1 onion, thinly sliced
2 carrots, thinly sliced
1 celery stalk, thinly sliced
1 teaspoon rosemary
1/2 teaspoon thyme

1 cup dry white wine
2 or 3 tomatoes, peeled, seeded,
  and chopped
1 cup chicken stock
1 clove garlic, minced
1/4 cup chopped parsley
1 tablespoon lemon zest
Additional chopped parsley,
  for garnish

Dredge all sides of veal shanks with flour, salt, and pepper. Heat oil in a heavy casserole or Dutch oven. Brown the veal shanks on all sides, adding a little more oil, if necessary. Remove from the pan and keep warm.

Briefly, saute onion, carrots, and celery. Add the veal to the pan and sprinkle with rosemary and thyme. Stir in the wine. When the wine is reduced to about 1/2 in volume, add tomatoes and stock. Cover casserole and reduce heat. Simmer 1 1/2 to 2 hours or until the meat is tender enough to almost fall off the bone. Season with more salt and pepper, if necessary.

Add the garlic, parsley, and lemon zest. Continue to cook for another 10 minutes. At serving time, arrange on serving platter or on individual plates. Garnish with additional parsley.

Preparation Time: 30 minutes
Cooking Time: 2 hours
Servings: 4 to 6

Robert Mondavi Pinot Noir Reserve

PAUPIETTES OF VEAL WITH ASPARAGUS

8 to 12 asparagus spears
4 thin veal scallops, about 3/4 pound
1/2 cup grated Swiss cheese
2 tablespoons olive oil or butter
1/2 cup chicken broth
3 tablespoons flour

1/2 cup milk
Cold water, as needed
1/2 teaspoon dried tarragon
2 tablespoons chopped chives
1 tablespoon lemon juice

Slightly saute or steam asparagus. They will cook more during the preparation of this dish. Pound veal scallops to even thickness, less than 1/4 inch thick; place grated cheese and 3 asparagus spears on each scallop. Roll up and secure with wooden toothpicks.

In a skillet, heat olive oil and brown veal rolls on all sides. Add broth and simmer, covered, about 10 minutes. Remove veal rolls to a platter and keep warm. Remove any melted cheese from the skillet. Add the flour to the pan and simmer. Add milk. Add water, if necessary for more liquid. Stir until smooth. Add tarragon, chives, and lemon juice, stirring until mixture thickens. Serve sauce over veal rolls.

Preparation Time: 30 minutes
Cooking Time: 25 minutes
Servings: 4

Robert Mondavi Chardonnay Reserve

DOLMAS

2 pounds ground lamb or beef
2 eggs, beaten
2 cups raw rice
1 8-ounce can tomato sauce
3 tablespoons chopped parsley
1/4 cup sliced green onion
1 tablespoon chopped mint, optional
Salt and pepper, to taste

1 8-ounce jar grape leaves, drained
1/2 bunch parsley sprigs
2 tablespoons butter
3 cloves garlic, minced
1 28-ounce can whole tomatoes,
   including liquid
1/2 cup water

Combine meat, eggs, rice, tomato sauce, parsley, onion, mint, salt and pepper. Roll into meatballs and wrap in grape leaves. Place parsley sprigs at the bottom of a Dutch oven. Layer rolled grape leaves on top. Dot with butter and garlic. Pour tomatoes and water on top. Cook on low heat for 30 minutes, being careful not to let liquid evaporate. Add water, if necessary. These can be made ahead and reheated.

Preparation Time: 1 hour
Cooking Time: 30 minutes
Servings: 12 to 15

Vichon Cabernet Sauvignon

GRILLED BUTTERFLIED LEG OF LAMB

1 cup Pinot Noir, or a dry red wine
1/2 cup soy sauce, preferably low salt
1/4 cup extra virgin olive oil
5 large cloves garlic, minced
2 tablespoons fresh rosemary
   leaves or 1 tablespoon
   dried rosemary leaves

1/2 cup fresh mint leaves,
   coarsely chopped
2 tablespoons fresh oregano leaves,
   or 1 tablespoon dried oregano leaves
1 tablespoon black pepper
1 leg of lamb, about 4 to 5 pounds,
   butterflied, flat and untied

In a bowl, combine the wine, soy sauce, oil, garlic, rosemary, mint leaves, oregano, and black pepper; mix well. Place lamb in a glass baking dish or a large plastic bag and add the marinade. Cover and place in the refrigerator for 8 hours or overnight, turning lamb occasionally.

When ready to grill, remove meat from marinade. Grill, brushing with reserved marinade. When cooked, about 20 to 30 minutes, slice and place on platter for serving.

Preparation Time: 10 minutes
Marinating Time: 8 hours or overnight
Cooking Time: 20 to 30 minutes
Servings: 8

Byron Pinot Noir Reserve

LAMB CHOPS WITH MINT PESTO

1 clove garlic
1/2 cup firmly packed mint leaves
1/3 cup walnuts
1/2 teaspoon salt

1/4 teaspoon black pepper
1/4 to 1/3 cup olive oil
6 loin, or rib lamb chops
Salt and freshly ground pepper, to taste

To make the mint pesto, place garlic, mint, walnuts, salt, and pepper in a food processor and pulse until minced. With processor running, add oil very slowly. Set aside. Pesto can be made ahead and refrigerated up to a week.

Sprinkle the chops with salt and pepper. Place on a broiler pan and broil on high temperature, or grill on barbecue to desired doneness, about 4 minutes on each side. Serve with a dollop of mint pesto.

Preparation Time: 20 minutes
Cooking Time: 8 minutes
Mint Pesto Yield: 1 1/4 cups
Servings: 6

Robert Mondavi Cabernet Sauvignon Reserve

LAMB SHANKS IN BARBECUE SAUCE

This is an easy and economical lamb recipe!

2 tablespoons vegetable oil
4 lamb shanks
1 cup sliced onion
2 teaspoons salt
2 teaspoons dry mustard

1/4 cup brown sugar
2 tablespoons Worcestershire sauce
1/2 cup vinegar
1 cup ketchup
1 cup water

Heat oil in heavy Dutch oven. Add lamb shanks and quickly brown on all sides. Add sliced onion and reduce heat. In a bowl, stir together remaining ingredients. Pour over lamb shanks and onion. Cover pan and simmer gently over low heat until meat is very tender, approximately 2 hours.

Note: For best results, prepare the day before serving, refrigerate overnight, skim off any fat, and then reheat before serving.

Preparation Time: 15 minutes
Cooking Time: 2 hours
Servings: 4

Robert Mondavi Pinot Noir Reserve

CASSOULET

This Cassoulet is a hearty, garlicky bean stew with meats and sausages. Serve with a green salad, crusty bread, and red wine.

1 pound great northern beans, washed
2 quarts water
1 tablespoon salt
Bouquet garni, see note
4 cloves garlic, mashed
3 carrots, quartered
1 onion studded with 4 or 5 whole cloves
3 slices bacon, diced
2 tablespoons cooking oil
1 1/2 pounds lean boneless pork, cubed

1 pound boneless lamb, cubed
1 onion, chopped
1/2 cup chopped shallots
1 cup thinly sliced celery
2 cups tomato juice
1 cup dry white wine
1 pound Polish sausage, sliced
Freshly ground pepper, to taste
1 14-ounce can chicken broth, optional
1/2 cup chopped fresh parsley

In a large pot, combine beans, water, and salt. Soak, following package directions. When beans are ready, add bouquet garni, garlic, carrots, clove-studded onion, and bacon. Bring to a boil. Reduce heat and simmer, covered, for 1 hour, skimming the fat off the surface as needed. Remove and discard bouquet garni and onion.

Heat oil in a skillet and brown pork and lamb on all sides. Transfer meat to bean mixture. In the same skillet, saute chopped onions, shallots, and celery until soft. Add tomato juice and wine. Simmer for 5 minutes. Add to bean mixture along with sausage. Simmer, covered, over low heat for another hour, or until meat and beans are tender. Stir occasionally. If necessary, add broth to prevent scorching. Skim off excess fat.

Preheat oven to 350 degrees. Transfer bean mixture to a large 4 to 5-quart casserole. Add pepper. Bake, covered, for 45 minutes, adding more broth, if needed. Adjust seasonings. Serve hot, sprinkled with parsley.

Note: This bouquet garni is sprigs of fresh parsley, 2 stalks celery, 2 bay leaves, and sprigs of thyme tightly tied in a piece of cheesecloth.

Preparation Time: 1/2 hour, plus bean-soaking time
Cooking Time: 3 hours
Servings: 12 to 16

Robert Mondavi Cabernet Sauvignon

PORK CARNITAS WITH PEACH SALSA

3 pounds pork shoulder or pork
   sirloin roast
2 tablespoons olive oil
1 10 3/4-ounce can beef broth
2 ribs celery, diced
1 green bell pepper, seeded and diced
1 yellow onion, diced
1 Jalapeno pepper, seeded and diced
Salt to taste

Ground pepper, to taste
1/2 teaspoon ground cumin
1 teaspoon chili powder
1 tablespoon fresh lime juice
8 to 10 tortillas
Sour cream
Jack or Cheddar cheese
Peach Salsa, recipe follows

In a 3-quart Dutch oven, quickly brown all sides of the pork in olive oil over high heat. Deglaze the pan with broth. Add celery, peppers, onions, and jalapeno pepper. Simmer 2 hours. Remove pork, reserving 1/2 of the broth and shred with a fork. Place pork in a frying pan and add reserved broth. Season to taste with salt, pepper, cumin, and chili powder. Over high heat, reduce the broth in half and slightly brown the meat. Sprinkle with lime juice. Serve carnitas on warm tortillas with sour cream, Jack or Cheddar cheese, and Peach Salsa.

Preparation Time: 20 minutes
Cooking Time: 2 hours
Servings: 6

Robert Mondavi Chenin Blanc

PEACH SALSA

3 medium peaches, peeled and
   finely diced
1 tablespoon fresh lime juice
   or lemon juice
2 medium ripe tomatoes,
   seeded and diced
1 tablespoon finely chopped
   jalapeno pepper

4 green onion tops, chopped
2 tablespoons coarsely
   chopped cilantro
6 tablespoons virgin olive oil
1 tablespoon honey
3 tablespoons sherry vinegar
Salt, to taste

In a bowl, toss peaches with lime juice. Add tomatoes, jalapeno pepper, onion tops, and cilantro. Toss to combine. In a separate bowl, whisk together oil, honey, and vinegar. Sprinkle with salt. Add to peach mixture and toss.

Note: This salsa is wonderful on grilled seafood. You can use frozen peaches or papayas.

Preparation Time: 10 to 15 minutes
Yield: 3 cups

CROWN ROAST OF PORK

The crown roast of pork is dramatic for a perfect dining treat.

1 crown roast of pork, allowing 2 ribs per serving
Mandarin wild rice or curried apricot rice, see index
Pan gravy, optional

Preheat oven to 450 degrees. Wipe roast with a cloth; protect bone ends by covering with aluminum foil. Place roast in preheated oven and immediately reduce heat to 350 degrees. Allow 30 minutes per pound roasting time, removing roast 45 minutes before it is done and fill the center with rice. Cover the stuffing only with foil; return the roast to the oven and complete the cooking, removing the foil the last 15 minutes. Serve with pan gravy if you wish.

Note: An apricot or apple stuffing may be substituted; just remove an hour before cooking is done to add the stuffing.

Preparation Time: 20 minutes   Robert Mondavi Pinot Noir
Roasting Time: 40 minutes per pound
Servings: Allow 2 ribs per person

PORK WITH VEGETABLES IN RUM SAUCE

4 rib or loin pork chops   **1/2 teaspoon salt**
1 tablespoon vegetable oil   **1/4 teaspoon pepper**
2 cups julienned carrots   **1 1/2 cups vegetable or beef broth**
4 green onions, sliced   **1/4 cup light rum**
1 9-ounce package frozen artichoke hearts,   **2 tablespoons cornstarch**
   thawed and cut into pieces   **2 tablespoons chopped Italian parsley**

In a large skillet, brown chops well in oil. Remove chops and drain on paper towels. Saute carrots and green onions in pan drippings. Add artichoke hearts and saute 2 minutes. Add salt, pepper, and broth. Stir until well blended. Return chops to skillet. Bring to a boil and lower heat. Cover and simmer 20 minutes, or until chops are tender. Remove chops to serving platter and keep warm.

Combine rum and cornstarch until smooth. Stir into skillet. Cook for 5 minutes, stirring often. Spoon sauce over the chops and garnish with parsley.

Preparation Time: 15 minutes
Cooking Time: 40 minutes
Servings: 4

ROAST PORK EN CROUTE WITH MUSTARD SAUCE

A spectacular entree and ideal for a special occasion.

1 3-pound boneless pork loin roast	**1 sheet puff pastry**
Salt and pepper, to taste	**1 egg, slightly beaten**
1/4 cup Dijon mustard	**Mustard sauce, recipe follows**
1 1/2 tablespoons fresh chopped herbs	

Preheat oven to 325 degrees. Sprinkle the roast with salt and pepper and spread mustard over the entire surface. Place in a roasting pan; press herbs into the mustard. Roast until meat thermometer registers 175 degrees, or about 15 minutes per pound. Let the roast cool.

Reset oven heat to 425 degrees. Roll out the puff pastry. Wrap pastry around the cooled roast. Brush the pastry with the beaten egg, making sure all edges are sealed. Make a few 1-inch slashes in the dough to let the steam escape. Bake for 20 minutes, or until pastry is golden. Let rest for 10 minutes. Carve into thick slices. Serve immediately with mustard sauce.

Note: Garden fresh herbs such as rosemary, thyme, marjoram, or savory, or a combination of several herbs, may be used in preparing this elegant roast.

Preparation Time: 40 minutes   Robert Mondavi Cabernet Sauvignon Reserve
Cooking Time: 65 minutes
Servings: 6 to 8

MUSTARD SAUCE

2 egg yolks	**3/4 cup vegetable oil**
2 tablespoons Dijon mustard	**1 tablespoon chopped shallots**
1 1/2 teaspoons dry mustard	**3 tablespoons heavy cream**
1 teaspoon salt	**1 tablespoon sour cream**
Dash cayenne pepper	**2 tablespoons beef broth**
2 teaspoons tarragon vinegar	

Put the egg yolks, mustards, salt, and cayenne pepper in a food processor or blender. Blend until very thick. Blend in the vinegar. Slowly add the oil until the sauce thickens. Mix in the remaining ingredients.

Preparation Time: 5 to 10 minutes
Yield: 1 cup

COLD BRAISED CITRUS PORK

1 cup fresh orange juice	1 teaspoon ground ginger
1/2 cup fresh lemon juice	2 bay leaves
2 teaspoons dried marjoram, crumbled	3 1/2 pounds boneless pork tenderloins
1 teaspoon cumin seed	Salt and freshly ground pepper
1 cup sherry	2 tablespoons butter
1/2 cup olive oil	2 tablespoons red currant jelly
2 teaspoons grated lemon zest	2 teaspoons Dijon mustard

Combine orange juice, lemon juice, marjoram, cumin seed, sherry, olive oil, lemon zest, ginger, and bay leaves in a large plastic bag. Add pork and marinate 2 to 3 hours in the refrigerator, turning frequently.

Preheat oven to 325 degrees. Remove pork from bag, reserving marinade; sprinkle with salt and pepper. In Dutch oven, or heavy roasting pan, melt butter over medium heat; add pork and brown on all sides, about 20 minutes. Pour reserved marinade over pork. Cover and bake, basting often, until thermometer inserted in thickest part of meat registers 165 to 170 degrees, about 1 hour.

Remove pork from cooking liquid and cool to room temperature. Wrap pork tightly and refrigerate up to 2 days. Strain cooking liquid and refrigerate.

Just before serving, discard fat from the surface of cooking liquid and bring to simmer over medium heat. Stir in currant jelly and mustard. Remove from heat. Slice chilled pork and arrange on platter. Pour warm sauce over and serve.

Preparation Time: 15 minutes
Marinating Time: 2 to 3 hours
Baking Time: 1 hour, 20 minutes
Servings: 6

Robert Mondavi Pinot Noir

227

CLASSICAL MUSIC UNDER THE STARS

Part of the charm of Orange County living is that almost everything can be done outdoors. We dine on the patio, we drive cars with the tops down, and most of our sports and hobbies are pursued outdoors.

On warm summer nights, even our music moves outside. We pack our picnic baskets and head for outdoor amphitheaters and concerts in the park, where the music is set off by the balmy evening air, starlight, and soft sea breezes.

One of the highlights of an Orange County summer is hearing Pacific Symphony Orchestra performing outdoors at Irvine Meadows. On nights like these, surrounded by good friends and stirring music, reveling in the irresistible summer twilight, one wonders how anyone could live anywhere else.

The Center is home for Pacific Symphony during The Center season, where they bring the magic of great music, classical and pops as well as family series to Orange County audiences.

It wouldn't be the Fourth of July without the *1812 Overture* and fireworks, and Pacific Symphony Orchestra doesn't disappoint! Concertgoers enjoy rousing music as fireworks explode overhead in the annual outdoor spectacular at Irvine Meadows. Photograph was underwritten by the ORANGE COUNTY REGISTER

DESSERTS

The best part of every meal? We think so!
This photo of a poolside dessert buffet
in the Back Bay of Newport Beach is underwritten by
PAT AND ALAN RYPINSKI

CHOCOLATE GANACHE

6 large eggs
1 cup sugar
2/3 cup flour
1/3 cup unsweetened cocoa powder
3/4 teaspoon salt
2 teaspoons vanilla, divided
6 tablespoons unsalted butter, melted,
   and cooled to lukewarm

1 12-ounce jar seedless raspberry jam
1 box raspberries, optional
6 ounces semi-sweet chocolate,
   finely chopped
3/4 cup whipping cream
1 tablespoon light corn syrup
1 tablespoon raspberry liqueur
Sliced almonds, toasted, for garnish

Preheat oven to 350 degrees. Butter a 9-inch round cake pan and line with wax paper cut to fit. In a metal bowl, whisk together eggs and sugar. Set the bowl over a pan of simmering water; stir until mixture is warm and sugar is dissolved. Remove bowl from water. With a mixer at high speed, beat mixture for 10 to 15 minutes or until tripled in volume and cooled to room temperature. Sift together flour, cocoa, and salt. Fold flour mixture into egg mixture, 1/3 cup at a time, until blended. Combine 1 1/2 teaspoons vanilla and butter. Fold egg mixture into butter. Gently pour batter into prepared pan, leveling batter on top of pan. Bake 20 to 25 minutes. Cool cake in pan to room temperature; cover with plastic wrap and refrigerate for 1 hour.

Remove cake from refrigerator and run a knife around edge of pan to loosen. Remove cake from pan, remove wax paper , and place right side up on a cake round. Slice the cake in half horizontally. Spread the bottom half with a thin layer of raspberry jam. Cover the jam with fresh raspberries. Spread more jam over raspberries to barely cover. Place other half of cake on top, cut side up. Smooth sides, removing any extra jam. Cover with plastic wrap and refrigerate 30 minutes.

Put chopped chocolate in a medium bowl. Set aside. In a small saucepan over medium heat, combine cream and corn syrup, stirring constantly until mixture comes to a boil. Pour hot cream over chocolate; let stand for 30 seconds to melt chocolate and gently whisk until smooth. Stir in liqueur and 1 teaspoon vanilla.

Remove cake from refrigerator and place on wire rack over wax paper. Pour warm chocolate glaze over cake, coating it evenly. Refrigerate cake for 10 minutes to set glaze. Drippings may be used to pipe a decorative trim on cake. Gently press toasted almonds against bottom edge of cake. Store under a glass dome up to three days at room temperature.

Preparation Time: 1 hour
Baking Time: 25 minutes
Chilling Time: 1 hour 40 minutes
Servings: 10

Robert Mondavi Cabernet Sauvignon Reserve

TIRAMISU

This recipe brings rave reviews!

6 egg yolks
1 1/4 cups sugar
1 1/4 cups mascarpone cheese
1 1/2 cups whipping cream

1/2 cup rum
1/2 cup cold strong coffee
2 7-ounce packages Italian ladyfingers
Unsweetened cocoa

Cover a cookie sheet or platter with foil, making a 7 x 13-inch rectangle. In a large bowl, cream yolks and sugar until smooth. Add mascarpone and mix on low speed 2 minutes. Whip cream until soft peaks form. Fold into cheese mixture.

In a small bowl, combine rum and coffee. Quickly dip or brush each ladyfinger with coffee mixture and arrange in a single layer on foil. Cover with half of cheese mixture. Repeat layers with 15 more ladyfingers dipped in coffee mixture and remaining cheese mixture. Sift chocolate evenly over top. Cut remaining ladyfingers in half, arrange vertically around edge of cake, rounded ends pointing up. Refrigerate at least 4 hours. Cut into squares to serve.

Note: Best if made a day ahead.

Preparation Time: 30 minutes
Chilling Time: 4 hours
Servings: 8 to 10

TORTA d'ARANCI

This is a traditional Italian dessert.

2 medium oranges
1 cup water
6 eggs

1 cup finely ground almonds
1 cup sugar
Powdered sugar, optional

In a saucepan, simmer whole oranges with peel in 1 cup water for 2 hours. Add more water if needed. Cool. Preheat oven to 350 degrees. In food processor, blend oranges, eggs, almonds, and sugar. Pour into an 8-inch springform pan. Bake 1 hour. Cool. Remove from pan. Dust with fine powdered sugar. Garnish with whipped cream.

Preparation Time: 2 hours 15 minutes
Baking Time: 1 hour
Servngs: 8

CHOCOLATE ANGEL CAKE

This cake is a simple, elegant, light dessert.

2/3 cup sifted cake flour
1/3 cup unsweetened cocoa powder
1 1/2 cups sugar, divided
12 large egg whites

1 1/2 teaspoons vanilla
1 1/2 teaspoons cream of tartar
1/2 teaspoon salt

Preheat oven to 375 degrees. Sift flour, cocoa, and 3/4 cup sugar together three times. Set aside. In a large mixing bowl, beat egg whites at low speed until foamy, about 5 minutes. Add vanilla, cream of tartar, and salt. Gradually increase mixing speed while adding 3/4 cup sugar, a tablespoon at a time. After sugar is added, continue beating until stiff peaks form. Sift 1/3 of the dry mixture over whites; fold in gently with a rubber spatula. Repeat process 2 more times until blended.

Gently spoon batter into an ungreased 10-inch tube pan. Run a knife through batter to remove air pockets. Bake 35 to 40 minutes until top springs back when lightly touched. Immediately invert cake onto a funnel or bottle to cool. Loosen sides of cake from pan; remove cake. Serve with fresh fruit. This cake may be frozen.

Preparation Time: 40 minutes
Baking Time: 40 minutes
Servings: 12

NUTCRACKER SWEET CAKE

Easy and delicious!

1 German chocolate cake mix
1 14-ounce can sweetened
  condensed milk
1 12-ounce jar caramel sauce

1 13 1/2-ounce container frozen
  non-dairy whipped topping, thawed
8 chocolate-covered toffee candy bars, frozen

Preheat oven to 350 degrees. Prepare cake mix according to package directions and bake in a 13 x 9-inch pan for 30 to 35 minutes. Cool. Poke holes in cake with end of wooden spoon about 1 inch apart. Pour condensed milk in holes. Spread caramel sauce over cake. Frost with thawed whipped topping. Crumble candy bars and sprinkle on top. Refrigerate overnight.

Preparation Time: 30 minutes
Baking Time: 30 to 35 minutes
Chilling Time: Overnight
Servings: 15

CHOCOLATE IRISH CREAM CAKE

1 18 1/4-ounce package yellow cake mix
1 4-ounce package instant
   chocolate pudding mix
3/4 cup vegetable oil
1/4 cup water
1/4 cup vodka

1/4 cup Irish cream liqueur
4 eggs
Irish custard sauce, optional,
   recipe follows
Strawberries, for garnish, optional

Preheat oven to 350 degrees. Grease and flour a 10-inch bundt pan. In a mixing bowl, combine cake mix, pudding mix, oil, water, vodka, liqueur, and eggs. Beat until smooth. Pour batter into prepared bundt pan. Bake 40 to 50 minutes or until a wooden pick comes out clean. Invert cake to cool. Remove from pan. Dust with powdered sugar. Cake may be served plain or with Irish Custard sauce. Garnish with strawberries.

Preparation Time: 15 minutes
Baking Time: 50 minutes
Servings: 12

IRISH CUSTARD SAUCE

6 large egg yolks
1/3 cup sugar
1/3 cup Irish whiskey

In a medium-sized metal bowl, whisk egg yolks, sugar, and whiskey. Set bowl over saucepan of simmering water and whisk until mixture is foamy, triples in volume, and holds its shape in a spoon, about 6 minutes. Remove pan from water. Cool.

Preparation Time: 15 minutes
Yield: 2 1/2 cups

CHOCOLATE PECAN CAKE

Rich, but worth every bite!

2 cups pecans, divided	1 cup unsweetened cocoa
1 1/2 cup butter, divided	6 eggs
12 ounces semisweet chocolate, divided	1 1/2 teaspoons vanilla
1 1/2 cups sugar	1/4 cup bourbon

Preheat oven to 350 degrees. Spread 2 cups pecans on baking sheet and toast in oven about 10 minutes. Cool. Butter one 9-inch round cake pan and line with parchment paper cut to fit. Melt 1 cup butter and 8 ounces chocolate in top of double boiler over simmering water. Stir until very smooth. Cool.

Combine sugar, cocoa powder, and eggs, stirring until well mixed. Add melted chocolate, stirring well. Coarsely chop 1 1/2 cups pecans and add to chocolate mixture. Stir in vanilla and bourbon.

Pour batter into prepared pan. Place pan inside larger pan and fill with hot water to level of about 1 inch of outer pan. Bake until cake is firm to touch, about 45 minutes. Cake surface may crack slightly. Cool cake on wire rack, then remove from pan, leaving parchment paper attached. Wrap cake in plastic wrap and refrigerate overnight.

The next day, melt 4 ounces chocolate and butter in top of a double boiler over simmering water. Stir until completely smooth. Cool 5 minutes. Remove cake from refrigerator and place upside down on wire rack with sheet of waxed paper underneath to catch drips. Peel off parchment. Drizzle spoonfuls of glaze along sides of cake. When completely covered, spoon remaining glaze on top of cake and smooth with spatula. Cover sides of cake with 1/2 cup pecans, pressing gently against glaze. Refrigerate cake until 1/2 hour before serving.

Preparation Time: 1 hour
Baking Time: 45 minutes
Chilling Time: Overnight
Servings: 14

ALMOND CAKE WITH RASPBERRY PUREE

3/4 cup plus 2 tablespoons sugar, divided
1/2 cup unsalted butter, room temperature
8 ounces almond paste
3 eggs
1 tablespoon Triple Sec
1/4 teaspoon almond extract

1/4 cup all-purpose flour
1/3 teaspoon baking powder
Powdered sugar
1 12-ounce package frozen raspberries,
   thawed

Preheat oven to 350 degrees. Generously butter and flour an 8-inch round cake pan. Line with parchment paper cut to fit; butter and flour. In a medium mixing bowl, combine 3/4 cup sugar, butter, and almond paste; blend well. Beat in eggs, Triple Sec, and almond extract. Add flour and baking powder, beating until just mixed. Pour batter into prepared pan. Bake 30 to 35 minutes or until cake springs back when touched. Cool in pan 5 minutes. Invert on cake rack and remove pan. Cool at least 2 hours.

Puree raspberries in blender. Strain to remove seeds. Add 2 tablespoons sugar and mix well. Cover and chill several hours or overnight. To serve, spoon raspberry puree on individual plates. Dust cake with powdered sugar; cut into wedges and place on plates.

Preparation Time: 30 minutes
Chilling Time: 2 hours
Baking Time: 30 to 35 minutes
Servings: 8

Robert Mondavi Moscato d'Oro

ALMOND POUND CAKE

2 cups sugar
1 cup butter
5 large eggs

2 cups all-purpose flour
1 1/4 teaspoons almond extract

Preheat oven to 350 degrees. Grease a 9-inch tube springform pan. Cream sugar and butter; add eggs, one at a time, beating well after each addition. Gradually add flour, beating on low speed just until blended. Stir in almond extract. Pour batter into prepared pan. Bake 60 minutes, or until a toothpick inserted near the center comes out clean. Cool on wire rack for 10 minutes. Remove from pan. Cool thoroughly. Serve with fresh fruit.

Preparation Time: 30 minutes
Baking Time: 1 hour
Servings: 16 to 24

Robert Mondavi Moscato d'Oro

DECADENT FUDGE FROSTING

2 ounces semi-sweet chocolate
2 cups sugar
1/4 cup light corn syrup
1 cup milk

4 tablespoons butter
1 teaspoon vanilla
1 cup chopped pecans
Cake of choice

In a heavy skillet, melt chocolate over very low heat. Add sugar, syrup, and milk; mix well. Bring mixture to a rolling boil and cook, stirring until it begins to form threads as it is dropped from a spoon, or 230 F. on candy thermometer.

Remove skillet from heat immediately and cool slightly. Add butter and vanilla; beat with whisk until thick enough to spread. Stir in nuts and cool thoroughly. Frost a 2-layer cake, or a large single-layer cake.

Preparation Time: 20 minutes
Yield: Frosting for 1 cake

ORANGES CARAMEL

8 naval oranges
2 large lemons
3 cups water

1 1/3 cups sugar
1 cup plus 2 1/2 tablespoons dry white wine
2 1/2 tablespoons Grand Marnier

Remove colored part of the peel of the oranges and lemons with a vegetable peeler, cutting from top to bottom of fruit to obtain 1/2 x 3-inch strips. Slice strips into very long, thin julienne pieces. Trim top and bases of oranges, trimming away all pith. Place oranges on a serving platter or on individual plates.

In a medium saucepan, bring water to a boil. Add peel; boil 5 minutes. Drain. Transfer to a heavy non-aluminum 2-quart saucepan. Add sugar and 1 cup wine. Place over medium-low heat and cook until sugar dissolves, swirling pan occasionally. Increase heat to high and boil until syrup becomes a medium caramel color. Remove from heat, stir in Grand Marnier and 2 1/2 tablespoons wine. With a slotted spoon, remove and reserve peel; pour syrup over oranges. Using fork, mound peels on top of oranges and around serving plates. Serve at room temperature.

Preparation Time: 30 minutes
Servings: 8

FRUIT PIZZETTA

1 cup butter, softened
2 cups powdered sugar, divided
1/3 cup plus 1/2 cup sugar
1 egg
1 1/2 teaspoons vanilla, divided
2 1/2 cups flour
2 1/2 teaspoons baking soda
2 1/2 teaspoons cream of tartar

2 8-ounce packages cream cheese,
 softened
4 cups sliced fresh fruit, see note
1 cup orange juice
1/4 cup lemon juice
4 teaspoons cornstarch
Mint leaves, for garnish

Preheat oven to 325 degrees. Lightly grease two 12-inch pizza pans. In a large mixing bowl, beat butter, 1 cup powdered sugar, and 1/3 cup sugar until light and fluffy. Add egg and 1/2 teaspoon vanilla, beating well. Combine flour, baking soda, and cream of tartar; add to butter mixture and blend thoroughly. Divide dough in half. Pat dough onto prepared pizza pans. Bake 12 to 15 minutes. Cool.

Combine cream cheese, remaining powdered sugar, and vanilla. Beat until well blended. Spread mixture over cooled crust. Arrange sliced fruit over the cream cheese mixture, completely covering the crust.

In a small saucepan, combine 1/2 cup sugar, orange juice, lemon juice, and cornstarch. Cook over medium heat, stirring until mixture is thick. Cool. Pour over fruit. To serve, slice into wedges. Garnish with mint leaves.

Note: Possible fruit choices for this fun dessert pizza could be peaches, nectarines, bananas, kiwi, apples, grapes, and berries.

Preparation Time: 1 hour 15 minutes
Servings: 16

Robert Mondavi Moscato d'Oro

FRUIT GRATIN WITH ZABAGLIONE

5 cups sliced fresh fruit	2 tablespoons fruity wine, champagne
3 large eggs, beaten	2 tablespoons powdered sugar
6 tablespoons sugar	2 tablespoons sliced almonds

Divide fruit equally among 4 to 6 shallow ovenproof bowls about 5 inches wide. In top of double boiler over simmering water, blend eggs, sugar, and wine. Beat rapidly with whisk until egg mixture holds a slight peak when whisk is lifted and volume triples, about 3 to 5 minutes. Pour hot mixture over fruit. Dust with powdered sugar and sprinkle with almonds. Place bowls on a rack 4 inches below heat source and broil until topping is a rich golden brown, about 1 minute. Watch carefully to avoid scorching. Serve immediately.

Note: Lemon-lime beverage can be substituted for the champagne.

Preparation Time: 30 minutes   Robert Mondavi Moscato d'Oro
Servings: 4 to 6

CHILLED LEMON SOUFFLE

2 envelopes unflavored gelatin	2 cups sugar, divided
1/2 cup cold water	2 teaspoons grated lemon peel
8 eggs, separated	2 cups whipping cream
1 cup lemon juice	Fresh berries and lemon zest, for garnish
1 teaspoon salt	

Prepare 1 1/2 quart souffle dish with collar; measure foil to go around top edge of souffle dish with a 1-inch overlap; fold in thirds lengthwise. Extend collar 2 inches above top of dish; fasten with tape or string.

In a small bowl, sprinkle gelatin over cold water. Set aside. In a double boiler, combine egg yolks, lemon juice, salt, and 1 cup sugar. Place over boiling water and cook until slightly thickened, stirring constantly. Stir in gelatin and lemon peel. Pour into a large bowl to cool.

In a mixing bowl, beat egg whites until soft peaks form. Gradually add 1 cup sugar; beat until stiff peaks form. Whip cream until firm. Fold whipped cream and egg whites into lemon-creme mixture. Pour gently into souffle dish. Refrigerate at least 3 hours. Garnish with fresh berries and lemon zest.

Preparation Time: 1 hour   Robert Mondavi Moscato d'Oro
Chilling Time: 3 hours or more
Servings: 10 to 12

ALMOND MERINGUES WITH SUMMER BERRIES

1/3 cup finely ground blanched almonds
1 cup plus 1 tablespoon powdered
  sugar, divided
2 tablespoons flour
3 egg whites
2 tablespoons sugar

2 tablespoons unsalted butter,
  melted and cooled
1 1/2 pounds strawberries, sliced, divided
Juice of 1/2 lemon
1/2 cup whipping cream
Mint leaves, for garnish

Preheat oven to 325 degrees. Butter and flour a baking sheet. Mix almonds, 1/2 cup powdered sugar, and flour. Set aside. In a mixing bowl, beat egg whites until soft peaks form; add sugar and continue beating until stiff peaks form. Gently fold the almond mixture into egg whites. Add cooled, melted butter. Blend. Spoon the batter into eight 4-inch rounds on baking sheet. Bake 15 minutes. Cool on rack. Store in an airtight container.

To make coulis, puree 3/4 pound strawberries in a blender or food processor until smooth. Strain through a fine mesh strainer. Add 1/2 cup powdered sugar and lemon juice. Chill the coulis for 2 hours or overnight.

In a bowl, beat whipping cream until soft peaks form. Add 1 tablespoon powdered sugar; blend and refrigerate. To serve, place a meringue round in center of each plate; cover with a layer of whipped cream, a layer of sliced strawberries, another layer of whipped cream, top with another meringue round. Drizzle strawberry coulis on the plate around the meringues. Garnish with mint leaves. Serve immediately.

Preparation Time: 1 hour
Chilling Time: 2 hours
Baking Time: 15 minutes
Servings: 4

STRAWBERRIES CASSIS

1 12-ounce package frozen
  raspberries, thawed
2 tablespoons powdered sugar

4 ounces Creme de Cassis
2 pints strawberries, cleaned

Puree raspberries until smooth. Strain puree to remove seeds. Add sugar and cassis. Cover and chill. When ready to serve, arrange strawberries in long-stemmed glasses. Spoon raspberry sauce over strawberries.

Preparation Time: 15 minutes
Servings: 4 to 6

PAVLOVA

This melt-in-your-mouth dessert is said to have been created in honor of the great Russian ballerina, Anna Matveyevna Pavlova.

Cornstarch
6 egg whites, room temperature
Pinch of salt
1 1/2 cups sugar
1 1/2 teaspoons baking powder
1 1/2 teaspoons vanilla

1 1/2 teaspoons vinegar
1 cup whipping cream
3 tablespoons powdered sugar
3 cups peeled and sliced kiwi,
    sliced strawberries, or passion fruit

Preheat oven to 300 degrees. Lightly butter a cookie sheet; line with foil and butter foil. Sprinkle lightly with cornstarch. Mark an 8-inch circle on foil.

In a large mixing bowl, beat egg whites with salt at high speed until soft peaks form. Add sugar, 1 tablespoon at a time, beating after each addition for 1 minute. Continue beating until stiff peaks form. Fold in baking powder, vanilla, and vinegar. Spread mixture on cookie sheet within marked circle, spooning batter higher on the edges to form a hollow.

Reduce oven to 200 degrees. Bake 1 1/2 to 2 hours until dry. Remove from oven. Cool 10 minutes. Quickly, invert onto a large plate; gently remove foil and turn right side up. It may crack a little. Cool completely. Just before serving, whip cream and add powdered sugar. Fill center of shell with fresh fruit. Spoon whipped cream on top. Garnish with additional fruit.

Preparation Time: 40 minutes
Baking Time: 2 hours
Servings: 8 to 10

BRILLIANT BAKED PEARS

1/2 cup grenadine syrup
1/2 cup water
1/4 cup lemon juice

6 Anjou pears
Mint leaves, for garnish

Preheat oven to 325 degrees. In a bowl, combine grenadine, water, and lemon juice. Peel pears, core from the bottom, and trim so pears will stand straight. Arrange in an 8 x 8-inch baking dish. Pour grenadine mixture over pears and bake for 30 minutes, basting frequently.

Cool pears in syrup, basting often to even color. Serve at room temperature or slightly chilled. Garnish plates with mint leaves to compliment the red pears.

Preparation Time: 15 minutes
Baking Time: 30 minutes
Servings: 6

Robert Mondavi Moscato d'Oro

PEARS WITH BUTTERSCOTCH SAUCE

5 ripe firm Bartlett pears
3 tablespoons lemon juice, divided
3/4 cup unsalted butter
3/4 cup sugar, divided

2 tablespoons water
1 tablespoon apricot brandy
Vanilla or coffee ice cream

Peel and core pears. Cut each pear into 6 wedges. Place in a bowl and toss with 2 tablespoons lemon juice.

In a large skillet, melt butter over moderate heat. Add pears and cook for 2 minutes, shaking skillet. Sprinkle pears with 1/4 cup sugar and cook until sugar is dissolved and pears are tender, again shaking skillet to prevent burning. Transfer pears to a bowl with a slotted spoon. Set aside.

To make the sauce, add 1/2 cup sugar to the skillet, stirring occasionally until it begins to turn a golden-caramel color. Remove skillet from heat and stir in water, 1 tablespoon lemon juice, and apricot brandy. The sauce will appear separated. Return pears to the skillet and cook over moderately low heat, stirring gently until the sauce is blended. Divide the pears with sauce among 6 plates and serve with ice cream.

Preparation Time: 30 minutes
Servings: 6

Robert Mondavi Sauvignon Blanc Botrytis

POACHED PEARS WITH CARAMEL CREAM

1 cup light brown sugar
8 cups water
1/2 cup lemon juice
1/2 large cinnamon stick

2 whole cloves
6 ripe firm Bosc or Anjou pears
Caramel cream sauce, recipe follows

In a 5-quart saucepan over medium heat, cook sugar and water until sugar is dissolved. Add lemon juice, cinnamon, and cloves; simmer, covered, for 5 minutes. Meanwhile, pare pears, retaining stems, and core from bottom with a small knife, being careful to keep pear intact. Add pears to simmering liquid. Poach uncovered until tender but still firm, about 15 to 25 minutes. Spoon syrup over pears occasionally. Remove from heat; gently transfer pears to a large bowl. Ladle some cooking syrup over pears. Cover and refrigerate for several hours or overnight.

To serve, remove pears from liquid and drain. Place in serving dishes with caramel cream sauce.

Preparation Time: 35 to 45 minutes
Chilling Time: 2 hours or overnight
Servings: 6

CARAMEL CREAM SAUCE

3 tablespoons butter
1 1/2 cups light brown sugar
1/2 cup light corn syrup

1/2 cup heavy cream
1/2 teaspoon vanilla

In a saucepan over medium heat, melt the butter. Stir in sugar and syrup. Bring to a boil until sugar melts, stirring constantly. Gradually add cream and bring to a boil, stirring constantly. Remove from heat. Add vanilla. Cool.

Preparation Time: 20 to 30 minutes
Servings: 6

LEMON TART

2/3 cup freshly squeezed lemon juice
2/3 cup sugar
3 tablespoons whipping cream

5 large eggs
1 9-inch baked tart shell, recipe follows
Whipped cream and berries, for garnish

Preheat oven to 375 degrees. In a mixing bowl, whisk together lemon juice, sugar, and cream, until well blended. Whisk in eggs, one at a time, blending well after each. Pour lemon mixture into baked tart shell. Bake in oven for 20 to 25 minutes or until firm. Place on rack to cool. Garnish with whipped cream and berries.

Preparation Time: 40 minutes
Servings: 8

Robert Mondavi Moscato d'Oro

FRESH BERRY TART

3 cups fresh blueberries, or
   strawberries, rinsed and drained
1 9-inch baked tart shell, recipe follows

1/2 cup currant jelly or apricot jam
3 tablespoons berry-flavored liqueur or water
Mint, for garnish

Arrange berries in a 9-inch baked tart shell. Melt jelly and liqueur over medium heat until jelly melts. Spoon evenly over berries. Chill until jelly sets, about 30 minutes. Garnish with mint. Best if served within several hours.

Preparation Time: 15 minutes
Servings: 8

Robert Mondavi Moscato d'Oro

TART PASTRY

1 1/2 cups flour
2 tablespoons sugar
1/4 teaspoon salt

1/2 cup unsalted butter, cold, cut in small bits
2 large egg yolks
1/4 cup ice water

In a large mixing bowl, mix flour, sugar, and salt. Cut butter into flour until mixture resembles coarse meal. Mix egg yolks and ice water in a small bowl; stir a little at a time into flour mixture until dough sticks together. Turn out onto floured surface and knead briefly. Form a thick disk; wrap in plastic wrap. Refrigerate 1 hour. Press dough into a 10-inch tart pan, extending dough 1/4 inch above rim. Trim top to make neat edge. Refrigerate until ready to use. To bake crust, preheat oven to 375 degrees. Line tart shell with foil filled with pie weights or dried beans. Bake 20 minutes; remove foil and weights, bake another 5 minutes or until light brown. Cool.

Preparation Time: 30 minutes
Chilling Time: 1 hour
Baking Time: 25 minutes
Yield: 1 tart pastry

APPLE TART

9 tablespoons unsalted butter, divided
1 cup flour
6 tablespoons sugar, divided
4 tablespoons cold water, divided

4 Golden Delicious apples
1 tablespoon Calvados,
  or apricot brandy
3 tablespoons apricot jam

In a food processor, combine 6 tablespoons unsalted butter, flour, and 2 tablespoons sugar. Process until mixture resembles coarse meal. With the machine running, pour 3 tablespoons cold water through the feed tube to form dough. Wrap dough in plastic wrap and refrigerate at least 1 hour.

Roll out dough into a 10 1/2-inch circle on a lightly floured surface. Line a 9-inch tart pan with a removable bottom with the dough; trim and crimp the edges. Put crust in freezer while making filling.

Preheat oven to 375 degrees. Peel apples, cut in half from top to bottom, core and place each half apple flat side on a cutting board. Cut into thin slices without separating slices. Maintain the shape of the apple halves as best you can.

Remove tart shell from the freezer. Arrange apples in tart by fanning each half. Beginning at the outer edge, place fanned apples in a circular spiral, ending with the last one in the center. Apples will appear very crowded. Sprinkle 4 tablespoons sugar evenly over the apple slices and dot with 3 tablespoons butter, cut into very small pieces. Sprinkle with brandy.

Bake until light golden brown, about 45 minutes. While the tart is baking, heat jam and 1 tablespoon water until jam is melted. Brush the glaze evenly over the baked warm tart. Serve tart warm or at room temperature.

Preparation Time: 45 minutes
Chilling Time: 1 hour
Baking Time: 45 minutes
Servings: 8

Robert Mondavi Sauvignon Blanc Botrytis

RASPBERRY COBBLER

2 tablespoons cornstarch
1/4 cup cold water
1 to 1 1/2 cups sugar, divided
1 tablespoon lemon juice
5 cups raspberries, fresh or frozen
1 cup flour

1 teaspoon baking powder
1/2 teaspoon salt
6 tablespoons butter, cut into bits
1/4 cup boiling water
Vanilla ice cream, optional

Preheat oven to 400 degrees. Stir together cornstarch and cold water until the cornstarch is dissolved. Add 1/2 to 1 cup sugar, depending on tartness of the berries, lemon juice, and berries. Stir until blended; place in an 11 x 7-inch baking dish. Place in oven and bring to a boil. In a mixing bowl, combine flour with 1/2 cup sugar, baking powder, and salt. Cut in butter until mixture resembles coarse meal. Add boiling water and stir to form dough. Drop spoonfuls of dough on top of boiling raspberry mixture. Continue baking, 20 to 25 minutes until lightly browned. Serve with ice cream.

Preparation Time: 20 minutes
Baking Time: 40 minutes
Servings: 6 to 8

Robert Mondavi Moscato d'Oro

ANTICIPATION PEACH PIE

Serve this pie when peaches are unavailable in the market.

2 1/2 pounds peaches
1/2 teaspoon ascorbic acid
1 quart water
3/4 cup sugar

2 tablespoons tapioca
1 tablespoon lemon juice
Dash of salt
Pastry for double crust pie

Line an 8-inch pie pan with foil, letting foil extend 6 inches beyond rim. Scald, peel, and slice peaches to measure 4 cups. Dissolve acid in water. Add peaches and drain. Combine peaches with sugar, tapioca, lemon juice, and salt. Place filling in the foil-lined pan. Fold foil over loosely; freeze until firm. Cover tightly with additional foil; remove from pan and return to freezer. Peaches may be stored 6 months.

When ready to bake, preheat oven to 425 degrees. Prepare pastry for double crust pie. Place in 9-inch pie pan. Remove foil from filling and place in pastry-lined pan. <u>Do</u> <u>not</u> <u>thaw</u>. Add top crust. Seal and flute edges. Cut slits in top crust. Bake for 1 hour.

Prepartion Time: 40 minutes
Baking Time: 1 hour
Servings: 8

Robert Mondavi Sauvignon Blanc Botrytis

PEACH COBBLER

3 cups sliced peaches
1 tablespoon lemon juice
3/4 cup sugar
1 cup flour, sifted

1/2 teaspoon salt
1 egg, beaten
2 tablespoons butter, melted
Ice cream or creme fraiche

Preheat oven to 375 degrees. Place peaches in an ungreased 8 x 8-inch baking dish. Sprinkle with lemon juice. Mix sugar, flour, and salt. Add egg to dry ingredients. Toss with fork until crumbly. Sprinkle over peaches. Drizzle melted butter over flour mixture. Bake for 35 minutes or until lightly browned. Serve warm or at room temperature with ice cream or creme fraiche.

Preparation Time: 10 minutes
Baking Time: 35 minutes
Servings: 6 to 8

Robert Mondavi Johannisberg Riesling Botrytis

MACADAMIA NUT PIE

1 1/2 cups flour, sifted
3/4 teaspoon salt, divided
9 tablespoons shortening
1/4 cup ice water
1 envelope unflavored gelatin
1/4 cup cold water

4 eggs, separated
1 cup sugar, divided
1 cup milk
1/4 cup macadamia nuts, chopped
1/4 teaspoon vanilla
Whipped cream, optional

Preheat oven to 400 degrees. In a mixing bowl, combine flour and 1/2 teaspoon salt. Cut in shortening until mixture resembles meal. Add ice water and toss well. Form into a ball and knead with palm of hand for a few seconds; dust lightly with flour. Wrap in waxed paper and chill 1 hour. Roll to 1/8-inch thickness and fit into a 9-inch pie pan. Prick bottom with a fork. Bake for 12 minutes or until lightly browned. Cool.

Dissolve gelatin in cold water. In a medium saucepan, combine egg yolks, 1/2 cup sugar, milk, and 1/4 teaspoon salt. Cook over moderate heat, stirring until thickened and spoon is coated. Do not boil. Remove from heat; stir in softened gelatin. Cool. Beat egg whites until foamy. Gradually add 1/2 cup sugar; beat until stiff peaks form. Carefully fold egg whites into egg yolk mixture. Fold in macadamia nuts and vanilla. Spoon filling into pie shell and chill. Garnish with additional macadamia nuts. Serve with whipped cream, if desired.

Preparation Time: 1 hour
Chilling Time: 1 hour
Baking Time: 12 minutes
Servings: 8

Robert Mondavi Sauvignon Blanc Botrytis

RIBBON PUMPKIN PIE

Expect raves!

1 9-inch pie shell, baked
1/3 cup butter
1/3 cup brown sugar, packed
1/2 cup pecans, chopped
1 envelope unflavored gelatin
1/4 cup cold water
3 eggs, separated

1/3 cup plus 1/4 cup sugar, divided
1 1/4 cups canned pumpkin
1/2 cup sour cream
1/2 teaspoon salt
1 1/2 teaspoons pumpkin pie spice
1 tablespoon chopped candied ginger
1 cup whipping cream, divided

Preheat oven to 425 degrees. In a saucepan, combine butter and brown sugar. Cook over medium heat and stir until sugar melts and bubbles vigorously. Remove from heat; stir in pecans. Spread praline mixture over bottom of pie shell. Bake for 5 minutes or until bubbly. Remove from oven; cool thoroughly.

Soften gelatin in cold water. In a mixing bowl, beat egg yolks with 1/3 cup sugar until light in color. In a saucepan, combine egg mixture, pumpkin, sour cream, salt, pumpkin pie spice, and ginger. Cook and stir over medium heat until mixture comes to a boil. Reduce heat; simmer 2 minutes, stirring constantly. Remove from heat; add gelatin; stir until dissolved. Cool.

In large mixing bowl, beat egg whites until frothy. Gradually add 1/4 cup sugar; continue beating until stiff peaks form. Fold whites into pumpkin mixture. Spoon half of mixture over praline filling in pie shell. Chill until almost set. Whip cream. Spread one-half of cream over pumpkin filling. Top with remaining pumpkin mixture. Chill until set. Garnish with remaining whipped cream. Keep refrigerated.

Preparation Time: 1 1/2 hours
Chilling Time: 2 hours
Servings: 8 to 10

SUNSHINE LEMON MERINGUE PIE

An All-American pie!

1 9-inch baked pie shell
5 eggs, divided
1 cup plus 6 tablespoons sugar

1/4 cup margarine
Juice of 2 lemons

Preheat oven to 350 degrees. Separate eggs, reserving 3 egg whites for meringue. In double boiler, combine yolks, 2 egg whites, 1 cup sugar, margarine, and lemon juice over simmering water. Stirring constantly with a whisk, cook until thickened, approximately 15 minutes. Pour into baked pie shell. Set aside.

To prepare the meringue, beat 3 egg whites until foamy and continue beating while gradually adding 6 tablespoons of sugar. Beat until stiff peaks form. Spread over lemon filling, sealing edges to pie crust to prevent shrinkage during baking. Bake 15 minutes until light brown. Set aside to cool. Refrigerate until serving time.

Preparation Time: 30 minutes
Baking Time: 25 minutes
Servings: 6 to 8

Robert Mondavi Moscato d'Oro

FUDGE PIE

A wonderful crustless pie!

1/2 cup butter
2 ounces unsweetened chocolate
1 cup sugar
1/4 cup flour

1/4 teaspoon salt
2 eggs, beaten
1 teaspoon vanilla
Vanilla ice cream

Preheat oven to 350 degrees. Butter a 9-inch pie pan. In a small pan, melt butter and chocolate. Add sugar. Stir in flour, salt, beaten eggs, and vanilla. Pour into pie pan. Bake for 30 minutes. Serve immediately with vanilla ice cream.

Preparation Time: 15 minutes
Baking Time: 30 minutes
Servings: 6 to 8

MELON MOUSSE IN PHYLLO CUPS

1 small melon, peeled, seeded,
  and cut in chunks
1/4 cup lime juice
1/4 cup sugar
1 envelope unflavored gelatin

1/4 cup cold water
1/4 cup whipping cream
Phyllo cups, recipe follows
Melon balls and assorted fruit

In a blender or food processor, puree melon. Blend in lime juice and sugar. Remove and set aside 1 cup of puree. Add gelatin to cold water; dissolve over hot water. Stir into remaining puree mixture. Fold in whipping cream. Chill until set.

When ready to serve, spoon reserved puree onto bottom of serving dishes. Place phyllo cups over puree; spoon mousse into cups and top with melon balls and fruit.

Preparation Time: 30 minutes
Servings: 6

PHYLLO CUPS

4 sheets phyllo dough, thawed
1/3 cup butter, melted
6 teaspoons dry white bread crumbs

1 teaspoon sugar
1 teaspoon cinnamon
Filling of choice

Preheat oven to 350 degrees. Prepare twelve 1/2-cup muffin tins, using two 12-cup tins and buttering every other cup. Brush one phyllo sheet with butter and sprinkle with 2 teaspoons dry bread crumbs. Mix sugar and cinnamon. Sprinkle 1/3 mixture over crumbs; top with second phyllo sheet. Repeat procedure with second and third phyllo sheets. Top with fourth sheet, brushed with butter.

Cut twelve 4-inch squares from phyllo. Put one square in each buttered cup, pressing pastry down in center and around edges to mold to cup; pastry edges should stick up. Bake until just golden brown and crisp, about 10 minutes. Remove from tins and cool completely. Cups may be prepared 2 days ahead. Store in airtight container.

Note: These cups filled with ice cream, fresh fruits, puddings, sorbets, melon mousse, and yogurt make a nice presentation.

Preparation Time: 30 minutes
Baking Time: 10 minutes
Yield: 12 cups

CREME CARAMEL

1 1/2 cups sugar, divided
1 quart milk
6 eggs plus 4 egg yolks
Dash of salt

2 teaspoons vanilla
Berries, whipped cream, mint leaves,
    or orange zest for garnish, optional

In a heavy frying pan over medium heat, carmelize 1 cup sugar, stirring constantly, until light golden brown. Pour into a 1 1/2-quart souffle dish; cool.

Preheat oven to 325 degrees. In a medium saucepan, scald milk; do not boil. In a large bowl, beat eggs, 1/2 cup sugar, salt, and vanilla with a whisk. Gradually add scalded milk to egg mixture while stirring constantly.

Pour over carmelized sugar in souffle dish, and set in pan of hot water in the oven; water level should be about halfway up the sides of the souffle dish. Bake 1 hour, or until knife inserted in the middle comes out clean. Remove from oven; remove dish from pan of water; allow to cool on rack. Refrigerate overnight.

Before serving, run a knife around sides of souffle dish to loosen. Place dish in two inches of warm water to soften caramel. Invert on large rimmed platter. Serve plain or garnish with berries, whipped cream, mint leaves, or orange zest.

Preparation Time: 30 minutes
Baking Time: 1 hour
Chilling Time: Overnight
Yield: 10 to 12 servings

Robert Mondavi Moscato de'Oro

CREME BRULEE WITH RASPBERRIES

10 eggs, separated
3/4 cup sugar, divided
3/4 cup milk
2 1/4 cups whipping cream

2 teaspoons vanilla
1 box raspberries, cleaned
1/4 cup brown sugar, packed

Preheat oven to 350 degrees. In a large mixing bowl, mix egg yolks and 1/2 cup sugar until combined and sugar has dissolved. Add milk, whipping cream, and vanilla; mix well. Gently fold in raspberries.

Pour mixture into six 5-inch or ten 3-inch ramekins, filling 3/4 full. Place ramekins in a baking pan; add hot water to pan and bake 30 to 40 minutes or until knife inserted near center comes out clean. Remove ramekins from hot water and set aside to cool.

Before serving, combine remaining 1/4 cup sugar and brown sugar. Sprinkle sugar over top of each serving and broil for 5 minutes to brown, being careful not to scorch the creme brulee.

Preparation Time: 25 minutes
Baking Time: 40 minutes
Servings: 6 to 10

Robert Mondavi Johannisberg Riesling Botrytis

RUSSIAN CREAM AND STRAWBERRIES

3/4 cup sugar
1 envelope unflavored gelatin
1/2 cup water
1 cup whipping cream

1 1/2 cups sour cream
1 teaspoon vanilla
1 pint strawberries, cleaned and sliced

In saucepan, combine sugar, gelatin, and water. Let stand 5 minutes. Over medium heat, bring to boil, stirring constantly with a whisk. Remove from heat. Continue stirring and add whipping cream; mix until well blended.

In a large bowl, combine sour cream and vanilla. Gradually pour hot mixture into sour cream, beating constantly. Pour into a 4-cup mold or 4 individual serving dishes. Chill. To serve, arrange sliced strawberries on top.

Preparation Time: 20 minutes
Chilling Time: 2 hours
Servings: 4

OAK CANYON APPLE CRISP

6 large McIntosh apples
1/4 cup water
1/2 teaspoon cinnamon
1 cup sugar, divided

3/4 cup flour
6 tablespoons butter or margarine
Vanilla ice cream

Preheat oven to 375 degrees. Peel, core, and slice apples into a deep 1 1/2-quart baking dish. Add water. Combine cinnamon with 1/2 cup sugar and sprinkle over apples. Combine 1/2 cup sugar with flour; work in butter with pastry blender until mixture resembles coarse meal. Sprinkle over apples; pat smooth with spoon. Bake for 40 minutes or until apples are tender and crust is crisp and lightly browned. Serve warm or chilled with vanilla ice cream.

Preparation Time: 20 minutes
Baking Time: 40 minutes
Servings: 6 to 8

Robert Mondavi Moscato d'Oro

OLD-FASHIONED RICE PUDDING

1 cup boiling water
1/2 cup long grain rice
1/2 teaspoon salt
1 quart milk
1/4 cup butter

2 eggs, beaten
1/2 cup sugar
1 teaspoon vanilla
1/2 cup golden or dark raisins
Cinnamon, or nutmeg, for garnish

Combine water, rice, and salt in a medium saucepan. Bring to a boil and cook 7 minutes. Add milk and butter. Bring to a boil again and reduce heat to low; simmer, covered, for 1 1/4 hours, stirring occasionally. In a small bowl, combine eggs, sugar, and vanilla. Gradually add 1/2 cup of hot rice mixture into egg mixture, and continue stirring. Slowly add egg mixture into rice mixture, stirring constantly. Remove from heat; add raisins. Place rice in a serving dish or individual custard cups; sprinkle with cinnamon or nutmeg. Chill 2 hours.

Preparation Time: 10 minutes
Cooking Time: 1 1/2 hours
Chilling Time: 2 hours
Servings: 8

Robert Mondavi Johannisberg Riesling Botrytis

CALIFORNIA-LITE BREAD PUDDING

3 1/2 cups nonfat milk
3/4 cup sugar
3/4 cup frozen egg substitute
1/2 cup raisins
2 tablespoons vanilla
1 teaspoon imitation butter flavoring

1 teaspoon ground cinnamon
9 slices French bread, cut
   into 3/4 inch cubes
2 tablespoons margarine, melted
Vegetable cooking spray
Rum sauce, recipe follows

In a large bowl, combine milk, sugar, egg substitute, raisins, vanilla, butter flavoring, and cinnamon. Stir to blend liquid ingredients. Add bread, toss gently. Let mixture stand 1 hour.

Preheat oven to 350 degrees. Add margarine to mixture and toss gently. Prepare a 9 x 13-inch baking dish by coating with cooking spray. Spoon bread mixture into baking dish and bake 45 minutes, or until pudding is set. Serve warm or at room temperature with sauce.

Preparation Time: 1 hour, 15 minutes
Baking Time: 45 minutes
Servings: 6 to 8

RUM SAUCE

1/2 cup unsweetened apple juice
1/4 cup sugar
1/4 cup rum
2 tablespoons margarine

1/8 teaspoon ground cinnamon
2/3 cup water
2 1/2 teaspoons cornstarch

In a small saucepan, combine juice, sugar, rum, margarine, and cinnamon. Cook over medium heat, stirring frequently until sugar dissolves. Combine water and cornstarch; stir well, and add to juice mixture. Bring to boil; cook 1 minute, stirring constantly. Serve warm.

Note: If desired, substitute 1 tablespoon imitation rum extract and 3 tablespoons water for rum.

Preparation Time: 10 minutes
Yield: 1 1/3 cups

STRAWBERRY DIABLO SAUCE

A surprise treat with ice cream!

4 tablespoons sugar
3/4 cup orange juice
1 lemon
4 cups thickly sliced strawberries

4 to 6 peppercorns, crushed
Powdered sugar, for garnish
Vanilla ice cream
Whipped cream, for garnish

In a heavy pan, heat sugar until light brown and caramelized. Remove from heat; cool a little. Stir in orange juice and juice of 1 lemon. Add strawberries and bring to a boil. Reduce heat to medium-low and simmer for 15 minutes or until liquid is reduced in half. Do not stir. Sprinkle peppercorns over berries while simmering. Cool and refrigerate. On plates dusted with powdered sugar, serve sauce over vanilla ice cream. Garnish with a dollop of whipped cream.

Note: The sauce may be frozen.

Preparation Time: 45 minutes
Servings: 4

DRESS REHEARSAL CHOCOLATE SAUCE

A fast and easy recipe to keep on hand!

9 ounces imported semi-sweet chocolate
1 cup whipping cream, heated
1/8 teaspoon almond extract, optional

Melt chocolate in double boiler over simmering water. Slowly add heated whipping cream; stirring constantly. Add almond extract. Remove from heat. Cool and serve over ice cream, fruit, or cake.

Note: If made ahead, store in refrigerator. Heat in microwave oven and serve.

Preparation Time: 15 minutes
Servings: 4 to 6
Yield: 1 1/2 cups

ORANGE-GINGER GLACE

1 quart vanilla ice cream or frozen yogurt
1 tablespoon grated orange peel
2 tablespoons minced ginger or
   preserved ginger, grated
7 coconut macaroons, crushed

4 tablespoons countreau,
   or triple sec liqueur
Orange twists, for garnish
Chocolate curls, for garnish

Soften ice cream. Add orange peel, ginger, and macaroons. Stir until blended. Freeze.
To serve; remove from freezer and thaw enough to easily spoon into 4 chilled stemmed
glasses. Pour one tablespoon liqueur over ice cream in each glass. Garnish with orange
twists and chocolate curls.

Preparation Time: 15 minutes
Freezing Time: 1 hour
Servings: 4

CHOCOLATE-COFFEE ICE CREAM PIE

Great for a large crowd and always enjoyed!

3 1/2 cups walnuts, chopped
1/2 cup flour
1/4 cup brown sugar
1/2 cup butter, melted
1 quart chocolate ice cream
1 quart vanilla ice cream

3 tablespoons hot fudge sauce
1 quart coffee ice cream
1 cup whipping cream
2 tablespoons powdered sugar
1/2 teaspoon vanilla
1/2 cup pecans, coarsely chopped

Preheat oven to 325 degrees. Combine walnuts, flour, brown sugar, and butter. Press
firmly over bottom of a 9-inch springform pan. Bake 25 minutes. Set aside to cool.
Freeze. Over crust, spread 1 quart chocolate ice cream, reserving 1/2 cup and freeze until
set. Top with a 3/4-inch layer vanilla ice cream. Combine reserved chocolate ice cream
with hot fudge sauce to make a thin syrup. Lightly swirl syrup into vanilla layer. Freeze
until set. Top with 3/4-inch layer coffee ice cream. Put in freezer. Whip cream and add
powdered sugar and vanilla, whipping until cream is stiff. Spread on top of coffee ice
cream. Sprinkle the top with nuts. Freeze until 15 minutes before serving.

Preparation Time: 2 hours
Baking Time: 2 hours
Servings: 12

ICE CREAM SUNDAE SQUARES

1/2 7-ounce box plain vanilla
   wafers, divided
1/2 cup butter
3 ounces semi-sweet chocolate
3 eggs

1 cup salted nuts, coarsely chopped
2 cups powdered sugar
1 quart vanilla ice cream
1 quart chocolate ice cream

Crumble vanilla wafers, reserving 1/2 cup, and press on bottom of a 13 x 9-inch pan. Melt butter and chocolate in double boiler over simmering water. Cool. Add slightly beaten eggs. Stir in nuts and powdered sugar. Spread mixture evenly over vanilla wafers. Freeze.

Soften vanilla ice cream and spread over frozen chocolate mixture. Freeze until firm. Soften chocolate ice cream and spread over vanilla ice cream. Sprinkle a few wafer crumbs over top. Return to freezer until ready to serve. To serve, cut into squares.

Preparation Time: 2 hour
Servings: 12

MONKEY BARS

A bar even grown-ups love!

1 cup margarine, divided
6 ounces semi-sweet chocolate, divided
1 1/2 cups graham cracker crumbs
1 cup flaked coconut
1/2 cup unsalted peanuts, chopped

2 8-ounce packages cream cheese,
   room temperature
1 cup sugar
1 teaspoon vanilla

Microwave 3/4 cup margarine and 2 ounces chocolate on high 1 to 2 minutes, or until melted, stirring every 30 seconds. Stir in cracker crumbs, coconut, and peanuts. Press into bottom of a 9 x 13-inch baking dish. Chill 30 minutes. Combine cream cheese, sugar, and vanilla until well blended. Spread over crust. Chill 30 minutes.

Microwave remaining margarine and chocolate on high 1 to 2 minutes, or until melted, stirring every 30 seconds. Spread over cream cheese layer. Chill. Cut into squares.

Preparation Time: 15 minutes
Chilling Time: 1 hour 15 minutes
Yield: 4 dozen

APPLAUSE CHEESECAKE

1 12-ounce package pecan
  shortbread cookies
1 cup pecans, coarsely chopped
1/2 cup brown sugar, packed
1 tablespoon Grand Marnier, for crust
1 6-ounce package English toffee bits
3 8-ounce packages cream cheese,
  room temperature
1 cup sugar
3 eggs, room temperature

1 tablespoon vanilla
1/2 cup whipping cream,
  room temperature
1 tablespoon flour
8 ounces semi-sweet chocolate bits
1/4 cup sour cream
1 1/4 cups broken pecan pieces,
  may be toasted
1/2 cup caramel flavored topping
1 ounce Grand Marnier

In a food processor, blend cookies, pecans, and brown sugar until fine. Add 1 tablespoon Grand Marnier and mix until blended Press into bottom and up the sides of a 9 1/2-inch springform pan. Sprinkle the toffee bits over the crumb crust. Chill while preparing filling.

Preheat oven to 325 degrees. In a medium bowl, beat cream cheese with sugar until smooth and creamy. Add eggs, one at a time, beating after each addition. Add vanilla, whipping cream, and flour; beat for 5 minutes. Pour into crust. Bake for 1 hour and 15 minutes. Cool.

Melt chocolate bits. Cool. Blend chocolate with sour cream and spread mixture over top of cheesecake. Sprinkle pecans over chocolate.

Combine caramel flavored topping and Grand Marnier; heat slightly. Drizzle sauce over nuts. Chill at least 6 hours.

Preparation Time: 1 hour
Baking Time: 1 hour 15 minutes
Chilling Time: 6 hours or longer
Servings: 16

CAST PARTY CHEESECAKE

Best if made a day before serving.

1 1/2 cups finely ground zwieback	1 1/2 teaspoons lemon juice
1/2 cup butter, melted	1/2 teaspoon salt
3/4 cup plus 8 tablespoons sugar, divided	Cinnamon
6 tablespoons ground, unblanched almonds	1 1/2 cups sour cream
	1/2 teaspoon vanilla
3 eggs	Dash of salt
18 ounces cream cheese, softened	

Preheat oven to 350 degrees. Butter a 9-inch springform pan. Combine zwieback crumbs with melted butter. Add 6 tablespoons sugar and ground almonds. Press crumb mixture against bottom and 1 1/2 inches up the sides of prepared springform pan. Bake 15 minutes. Let cool and chill in refrigerator.

Reset oven to 375 degrees. Beat eggs; blend with softened cream cheese, 3/4 cup sugar, lemon juice, and 1/2 teaspoon salt. Pour filling into prepared shell. Bake for 20 minutes. Turn off heat; open oven door and let cheesecake cool in oven. Remove from oven and dust surface lightly with cinnamon.

Reset oven to 425 degrees. To make topping, combine sour cream, 2 tablespoons sugar, vanilla, and a dash of salt. Pour over cheesecake. Bake for 5 minutes. Turn off oven; allow cheesecake to cool in oven. Refrigerate.

Preparation Time: 30 minutes
Baking Time: 40 minutes
Servings: 12 to 16

BOYSENBERRY CHEESECAKE

Thanks to Knott's Berry Farm for donating this recipe. Knott's began in Orange County as a small roadside stand selling berry pies.

1 1/2 cups graham cracker crumbs
1/4 cup sugar
5 tablespoons butter or
   margarine, melted
3 8-ounce packages cream
   cheese, softened
1/2 tablespoon grated lemon peel
1 teaspoon vanilla

1 cup sugar
2 tablespoons all purpose flour
1/2 tablespoon salt
4 eggs
3/4 cup whippng cream
1 16-ounce jar Knott's Berry Farm
   Boysenberry Preserves

Preheat oven to 350 degrees. Mix cracker crumbs, sugar, and butter and pat firmly into bottom and half up the sides of a 9-inch springform pan. Bake 20 minutes. Set aside to cool 15 minutes.

Beat cream cheese until creamy; add lemon peel and vanilla, mixing well to blend. In a separate bowl, combine sugar, flour, and salt; add gradually to the cream cheese mixture. Add eggs, one at a time, beating after each addition just until blended. Stir in whipping cream. Add 2 tablespoons of preserves to remaining 1/2 cup of filling and slowly drizzle back and forth across top of cheesecake. Using a blunt knife, gently weave through batter of cheesecake to make a ribbon pattern. Bake 65 to 70 minutes. Remove from the oven and let cool 30 minutes. Loosen sides with spatula. Cool 2 or 3 hours longer. Stir remaining preserves and spread evenly over cheesecake. Refrigerate overnight, if desired.

Preparation Time: 1 hour
Baking Time: Divided: 20 minutes; 65 to 70 minutes
Chilling Time: 2 1/2 to 3 1/2 hours
Servings: 12

Robert Mondavi Moscato d'Oro

TOFFEE CHEESECAKE WITH CARAMEL SAUCE

1 1/2 cups graham cracker crumbs
6 tablespoons unsalted butter, melted
1/4 cup dark brown sugar, packed
2 pounds cream cheese,
   room temperature

1 1/2 cups sugar
5 large eggs, room temperature
2 1/2 teaspoons vanilla
2 teaspoons lemon juice
Caramel cream sauce, see page 244

Preheat oven to 350 degrees. Lightly butter a springform pan. In a small bowl, combine crumbs, unsalted butter and dark brown sugar . Press mixture over bottom and 1 inch up sides of pan. Refrigerate crust.

Beat cream cheese in a large bowl until fluffy. Add sugar and beat until smooth. Beat in eggs, one at a time. Mix in vanilla and lemon juice. Pour filling into prepared crust. Bake about 1 hour 15 minutes or until cake rises 1/2 inch over rim and center moves only slightly when pan is shaken. Cool on rack. Cake will fall as it cools, sinking in center. Cover and refrigerate until well chilled, at least 6 hours. Can be made a day ahead. Meanwhile make Caramel cream sauce.

Before serving, pour caramel sauce over center of cheesecake or serve on the side of plate with the cheesecake when serving individual servings.

Note: Prepared caramel topping may be substituted.

Preparation Time: 1 hour
Chilling Time: 6 hours
Baking Time: 1 hour 15 minutes
Servings: 12 to 16

CON GUSTO CHEESECAKE

1 8-ounce package cream cheese
1 3-ounce package cream cheese
1/4 cup sugar
1 egg
1 1/2 tablespoons whipping cream

1 8-ounce chocolate bar with hazelnuts
1 1/2 tablespoons hazelnut liqueur
Powdered sugar
Strawberries, for garnish

Preheat oven to 350 degrees. Butter an 8-inch round cake pan. Line bottom with waxed paper and butter. In a mixing bowl, beat cream cheese with sugar until well mixed. Add egg and cream; beat until blended.

Coarsely chop chocolate; place in double boiler over simmering water to melt. Stir melted chocolate and liqueur into cream cheese mixture. Pour batter into prepared pan. Set cake pan in a larger pan and place in oven. Add boiling water to larger pan until it is about 2/3 up sides of cake pan. Bake until cake is set in center when pan is gently shaken, about 50 minutes. Remove from oven; let stand until cool; cover and chill at least one hour. Remove from pan. Dust top with powdered sugar. Garnish with strawberries.

Preparation Time: 20 minutes
Baking Time: 50 minutes
Chilling Time: 1 hour
Servings: 8

PUMPKIN CHEESECAKE

1 1/4 cups graham cracker crumbs
1 teaspoon ground cinnamon
2 1/4 cups sugar, divided
1/4 cup butter, melted
2 pounds cream cheese
3 eggs

1 cup whipping cream
2 1-pound cans pumpkin
1 tablespoon plus 2 teaspoons
   vanilla, divided
1 tablespoon pumpkin pie spices
2 cups sour cream

Butter a 10-inch springform pan. To make crust, combine crumbs, cinnamon, 1/4 cup sugar, and melted butter. Press onto bottom of pan. Set aside. Preheat oven to 300 degrees. Blend cream cheese with 1 1/2 cups sugar until smooth. Add eggs, 1 at a time, beating until blended. Add whipping cream, pumpkin, 2 teaspoons vanilla, and spices, blending thoroughly. Pour filling into graham cracker crust. Bake 1 1/2 hours or until cake sets. Remove and let cool 10 minutes before adding topping. To make topping: blend sour cream, 1/2 cup sugar, and 1 tablespoon vanilla until smooth. Pour over cooled cheesecake. Chill thoroughly before removing from pan. Store in refrigerator.

Preparation Time: 30 minutes
Baking Time: 1 1/2 hours
Servings: 12 to 16

PRALINE COOKIE CUPS

This is a cookie recipe that makes beautiful praline cups. Thank you to Ed Mitchell, chef of the Center Club, for sharing this dessert recipe.

1/2 cup butter	**1 cup flour**
1 1/4 cups brown sugar	**Ice cream of choice**
1/2 cup light corn syrup	**Fresh fruit of choice**
1 1/4 cups almonds, finely chopped	

Preheat oven to 325 degrees. Butter a large cookie sheet. In a saucepan, mix butter, sugar, and corn syrup; bring to a boil. Boil 2 minutes. Remove from heat. Combine almonds and flour; stir into hot mixture, mixing well. For each cookie, place 1 tablespoon batter on cookie sheet, spacing 4 inches apart. With fingers press each one to flatten. Bake 5 to 10 minutes until golden brown. Remove from oven and let rest until cool enough to touch. With a metal spatula, lift cookies gently and place over an inverted 9-ounce plastic glass to form a shaped cup. Cool completely. Do not remove cookie from the glass until cold or the cookie cup will loose its shape. Store in an airtight container. Serve with ice cream and fresh fruit.

Preparation Time: 1 hour, 15 minutes
Yield: 12 cups

THREE-CORNERED COOKIE CUPS

5 tablespoons unsalted butter, softened	**4 egg whites**
1/2 cup sugar	**1/2 cup plus 2 tablespoons flour**
1/8 teaspoon salt	**1/2 teaspoon cornstarch**
1 teaspoon vanilla	**Filling of choice**

Preheat oven to 350 degrees. Set out inverted glass custard cups. Generously butter and flour 2 heavy baking sheets. Mark two 5-inch circles on each sheet.

Cream butter, sugar, salt, and vanilla until light and fluffy. Add egg whites slowly. Mixture will look slightly curdled. Fold in flour and cornstarch and mix until smooth. Place a rounded tablespoon of batter in the center of each circle and spread to fill circle. Bake 5 to 7 minutes or until lightly browned on the edges.

Quickly remove cookie from cookie sheet with spatula and drape over inverted custard cups, shaping cookie to make a 3-cornered cup. Repeat with remaining batter. Cool thoroughly before removing and storing in an airtight container.

Cups may be filled with fresh fruit, ice cream, or yogurt and topped with a flavored sauce.

Preparation Time: 40 minutes
Yield: 18 cups

RASPBERRY FUDGE BROWNIES

1/2 cup butter, softened
1 cup sugar
3 eggs
1 12-ounce jar raspberry jam,
  divided

18 chocolate wafer cookies,
  finely ground
1/2 cup flour
1 cup chocolate chips
1 cup chopped walnuts

Preheat oven to 350 degrees. Grease a 7 x 11-inch baking dish. In a large bowl, cream butter and sugar until fluffy. Add eggs and 1/2 cup jam, and beat until smooth. Add cookie crumbs and flour. Mix well. Pour batter into baking dish and sprinkle with chocolate chips. Bake for 35 to 40 minutes.

In a small saucepan, melt remaining jam over low heat, stirring constantly. Add walnuts; pour over brownies. Cool completely. To serve, cut into squares.

Preparation Time: 20 minutes
Baking Time: 35 to 40 minutes
Yield: 24

STAGE DOOR APPLE SQUARES

2 cups flour
2 cups brown sugar, lightly packed
1/2 cup margarine
1 cup chopped nuts
1 teaspoon cinnamon
1 teaspoon soda
1/2 teaspoon salt

1 cup sour cream
1 teaspoon vanilla
1 egg
2 cups peeled, finely chopped apples
Ice cream, optional
Caramel sauce, optional

Preheat oven to 350 degrees. Combine flour, sugar, and margarine in food processor. Blend until crumbly. Stir in nuts. Press 2 3/4 cups crumb mixture into an ungreased 13 x 9-inch baking dish. To remaining mixture, add cinnamon, soda, salt, sour cream, vanilla, and egg. Blend well. Stir in apples. Spread mixture evenly over crumb layer in baking dish. Bake 25 minutes or until lightly browned. Serve with ice cream and caramel sauce.

Preparation Time: 15 minutes
Baking Time: 25 minutes
Servings: 12 to 15

SUNBURST COOKIES

2 cups butter
1 cup sugar
3 cups flour
1 teaspoon vanilla

2 cups crushed potato chips
1/2 cup chopped pecans
Powdered sugar, sifted

In mixing bowl, cream butter and sugar until fluffy. Add flour and vanilla; mix well. Add crushed potato chips and pecans; mix until blended. Chill at least one hour.

Preheat oven to 325 degrees. For small cookies, shape dough into dime-size balls. Place on ungreased cookie sheet. Flatten slightly with a fork. Bake 13 to 15 minutes, or until cookies are light in color with only a hint of brown on the edges. Remove from cookie sheets to wire racks to cool. Sprinkle cookies with sifted powdered sugar. Store in an air-tight container. Cookies may be frozen.

Preparation Time: 15 minutes
Chilling Time: 1 hour
Baking Time: 1 hour 30 minutes
Yield: 6 dozen

ORANGE TEA SQUARES

1 cup flour plus 2 tablespoons flour,
    divided
1/2 cup plus 3 tablespoons softened
    butter or margarine, divided
1 3/4 cups sifted powdered sugar,
    divided
1 cup coconut
1 1/2 cups brown sugar

1 1/2 cups chopped walnuts, divided
1/2 teaspoon vanilla
1/4 teaspoon baking powder
1/4 teaspoon salt
2 eggs, beaten
2 tablespoons orange juice
1 teaspoon grated orange rind,
    optional

Preheat oven to 325 degrees. Lightly grease the bottom of a 13 x 9-inch baking pan. Blend 1 cup flour, 1/2 cup butter, and 1/4 cup powdered sugar until mixture begins to stick together; press evenly onto bottom of prepared pan. Bake 15 minutes.

In large bowl, combine coconut, brown sugar, 1 cup walnuts, 2 tablespoons flour, vanilla, baking powder, and salt. Add eggs. Blend. Pour over baked crust. Return to oven; bake 20 minutes. Cool.

Combine 1 1/2 cups powdered sugar, 3 tablespoons softened butter, and orange juice. Spread evenly over cooled filling. Top with 1/2 cup chopped walnuts and grated orange rind. Cut into squares.

Preparation Time: 45 minutes
Baking Time: 35 minutes
Yield: 2 to 3 dozen

HEAVENLY DESSERT MORSELS

1 1/2 cups butter
1 cup light brown sugar, packed
12 ounces chocolate chips

1/2 cup chopped walnuts or pecans
1/4 package buttery rectangular
   crackers

Preheat oven to 350 degrees. Line a 13 x 9-inch baking dish with foil; butter the foil. Cover bottom of baking dish with a layer of crackers, salt side up. In a small saucepan over medium heat, melt butter and sugar. Bring to a boil. Boil for 3 minutes, stirring constantly. Pour mixture over crackers. Sprinkle chocolate chips over butter mixture. Bake 1 to 2 minutes to soften chocolate chips. Gently smooth chocolate over top. Sprinkle with nuts. Chill. Cut into bite-size pieces.

Preparation Time: 20 minutes
Servings: 30 to 35 small pieces

PECAN SWEETS

1 cup margarine, softened
1 cup sugar
1/2 teaspoon baking soda

1 1/2 cups flour, sifted
1 1/2 teaspoons white distilled vinegar
54 pecan halves

Preheat oven to 300 degrees. Combine margarine, sugar, and soda in food processor. Add flour and vinegar. Mix well. Drop by teaspoon 2 inches apart on an ungreased cookie sheet. Gently place pecan half on top of each cookie. Bake 20 to 25 minutes. Let cool 5 minutes. Place cookies on wire rack. Store in airtight container.

Preparation Time: 15 minutes
Baking Time: 1 hour
Yield: 4 1/2 dozen

PECAN BARS

1 2/3 cups butter, divided
2/3 cup powdered sugar
2 cups flour
1/2 cup honey

3 tablespoons cream
1/2 cup dark brown sugar
3 cups whole pecans

Preheat oven to 350 degrees. In food processor, combine 1 cup butter, powdered sugar, and flour. With on-and-off motion, mix until crumbly. Pat into the bottom of ungreased 13 x 9-inch pan. Bake until light brown, 20 to 25 minutes. Crust may crack. Combine 2/3 cup butter, honey, cream, and brown sugar in medium saucepan. Heat until sugar dissolves. Remove from heat. Add pecans, stirring until well coated. Spread on top of crust. Bake 20 minutes. Cool completely before cutting into small bars.

Preparation Time: 20 minutes
Baking Time: 40 to 50 minutes
Yield: 30 bars

TRIPLE CHOCOLATE COOKIES

1/4 cup all-purpose flour
1/4 cup unsweetened cocoa
1 1/2 teaspoons ground cinnamon
1/4 teaspoon baking powder
Pinch of salt
6 tablespoons unsalted butter,
  room temperature

7 tablespoons sugar
2 large eggs
8 ounces semi-sweet chocolate, melted
1 cup milk chocolate chips
1 cup chopped walnuts, toasted
40 walnut halves
Semi-sweet chocolate, melted, optional

Preheat oven to 350 degrees. Butter large cookie sheets. In bowl, combine flour, cocoa, cinnamon, baking powder, and salt. Set aside. In a mixing bowl, cream butter, sugar, and eggs; beat well. Stir in melted semi-sweet chocolate. Add dry ingredients and blend well. Add chocolate chips and chopped walnuts.

Drop dough by tablespoons onto prepared sheets, spacing 2 inches apart. Press walnut half onto each cookie. Bake about 11 minutes, until cookies look dry and cracked but feel soft when lightly pressed. Cool on cookie sheet for 5 minutes. Transfer to racks and cool completely. If desired, dip fork tines into melted chocolate and drizzle over cookies in zigzag pattern. When chocolate has set, store in airtight container or freeze.

Preparation Time: 1 1/2 hours
Yield: 3 dozen

WHITE CHOCOLATE OATMEAL COOKIES

1 cup margarine or butter, at
  room temperature
1 1/2 cups sugar
2 teaspoons baking soda

1 large egg
1 cup flour
2 cups rolled oats
6 ounces white chocolate chips

Preheat oven to 350 degrees. In large bowl, beat butter, sugar, and baking soda until creamy; beat in egg. Gradually add flour and oats, blending thoroughly. Stir in chips. On buttered cookie sheet, drop 2 tablespoons of dough, spacing 4 inches apart. Bake until light brown, 10 to 12 minutes. Cool on pan until firm; then, transfer to wire racks to cool. Store in airtight container or freeze for longer storage.

Note: These are large and lacy cookies. They can be topped with ice cream and caramel sauce.

Preparation Time: 20 minutes
Baking Time: 1 hour 15 minutes
Yield: 24 to 30

WALNUT CHEESECAKE COOKIES

1/2 cup butter or margarine, softened
1 3-ounce package cream cheese,
  softened
1 large egg, separated
1 teaspoon vanilla

1 teaspoon grated lemon peel
1 cup sifted powdered sugar
1 cup sifted all-purpose flour
2 cups finely chopped walnuts
Apricot or cherry jam

Cream together butter, cream cheese, egg yolk, vanilla and lemon peel until well blended. Gradually mix in powdered sugar and flour to make a stiff dough. Chill dough for at least 1 hour for easier handling.

Preheat oven to 325 degrees. Shape chilled dough into 1-inch balls Beat egg white until foamy. Dip balls one at a time into the egg white, allowing excess to drip off, then roll in finely chopped walnuts. Arrange about 2 inches apart on ungreased cookie sheets and make a depression in the center of each. Bake for about 15 minutes until cookies just begin to brown on the bottom. Half way through the cooking time, poke each cookie to make the depression more pronounced. Remove from pan and cool. Before serving, fill each center with 1/2 teaspoon of jam.

Preparation Time: 45 minutes
Chilling Time: 1 hour
Yield: 30 cookies

"THE FIRE BIRD"

Soaring through The Center's red granite facade, "The Fire Bird" casts shimmering patterns of silver, red, and gold on the mirrored surfaces of the grand staircase. Reaching 60 feet high and 120 feet across, Richard Lippold's dazzling metal sculpture spans the interior and exterior of the Grand Portal, the distinctive 12-story arch that graces the entrance to the Orange County Performing Arts Center.

With its vibrant color and remarkable feeling of movement, "The Fire Bird" lives up to its name. From the staircases, from the balconies, from both inside and outside The Center, this vast, delicate, sparkling bird appears to fly right through the building. Captivating and constantly changing with the shifting patterns of sunlight or moonlight, "The Fire Bird" seems a radiant testimony to the eternal spirit of the arts.

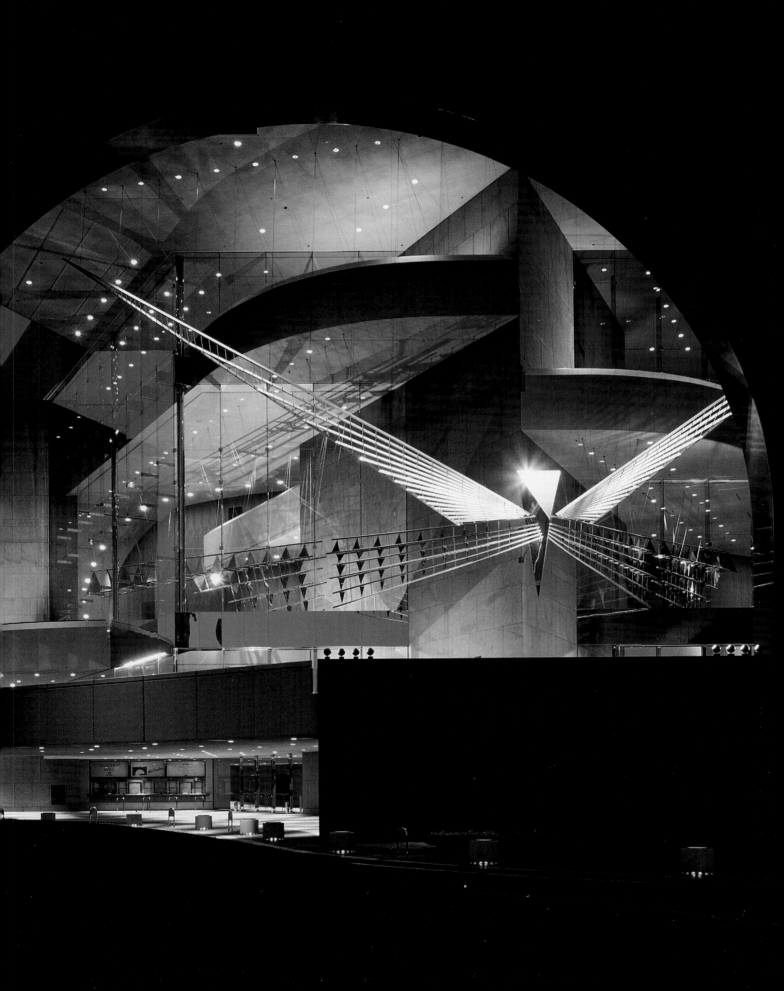

The Sterling Performances Committee would like to thank the following people:

Christine Adamson	Susan M. Carter	Sally Fenton	Rosemary Hauser
Marian Alexander	Laura Cate	Pat Fintor	Carol Hayden
Marilyn Anania	Fifi Chao	Mary Fitzgerald	Robert Hayden
Ruth Anderson	Trudy Chartham	Maria Fiore	Dione Hayes
Betty Andrews	Faith Cherney	Kathy Fischbeck	Irene Hayek
Fran Arnold	Jane Cheroske	Jeanne Fleming	Carol Heim
Victoria Avey-Gertner	Norma Clayton	Marilyn Foreman	Phyllis Helland
Cindy Baker	Connie Coble	Gail Forney	Jennifer Herley
Phyllis Baker	Jan Collier	Betty Forrest	LeAnn Herley
Virginia Baker	Laura Condrey	Lillian Foucault	Karen M. Hex
Sally Barden	Donna Connally	Loretta Freund	Carole Hicks
Kris Barry	Diana Conner	Thelma Friedel	Patty Hillier
Marjorie Barth	Jean Cook	Dorothy Frieden	Mae Hillman
Chris Beaver	Lynn Davies Cook	Marietta Fryer	Joyce Hintz
Sue Bechtel	Ellen Cooley	Mary Fryer	Mary Jo Hitchner
Dorothy Benford	Annie Cordrey	Karen Fullerton	Joan Hobin
Barbara Benson	Gloria Cormier	Patty Fullmer	Shirley Hoesterey
Marcia Bergh	Brenda Corwin	Jan Gale	Ed Hookway
Lee Berres	Cathy Couture	Pamela Gallegos	Ellie Hotmann
Bill Biel	Judy Couture	Jana Brown Galt	Ann Howard
Jane Biel	Priscilla Couture	Marilyn Galt	Barbie Hoyt
Shawna Biel	Sherri Couture	Patsy Gamble	Jackie Hubbard
Corinne P. Black	Ann Crisham	Pat Gandsey	Linda Hughes
Ginnie Black	Stephanie Crisp	Patti Garrity	Brian Humphreys
Carolyn Blakesley	Lynn Crowell	Diane Gaynor-McCue	Bob Huntington
Joanne Blanchard	Vesta Curry	Peggy Gazse	Dorothy Hurford
Marty Blixt	Debbie Curtis	Dahlia Geldin	Suzanne Hurlbut
Barbara Block	Gail Daniels	Mona Gennawey	Dorothy Hurley
Kathie Bobenrieth	Carol Davies	Madeline Giambastiani	Patrick Hurley
Elaine Boehmer	Deloma Davis	Johanne Gibson	Nancy Illo
Connie Bonomo	Sally Davis-Peterson	Sara G. Gioeli	Gail Ivey
JoAnn Bowell	Sally deBrun	Joan Gleiss	Sharon Jackson
Betty Braun	Barbara DeMott	Brittney Glenn	Rilda Jamieson
Diana Brewster	Betty Donnell	Lynn Glenn	Diane Janssen
Sara Brodie	Marjorie Doty	Emily Glover	Valerie Jessen
Ann Brown	Madelyn Dudenhefer	Ellen Goodwin	Kasia S. Johnson
Karen Brown	Michele Elekes	E. C. Grace	Mary Ann Kandel
Norma Jean Brown	Myrna Elliott	Sue Green	Colleen Kane
Mary Bryant	Lorena Elston	Jeanne Griffin	Peggy Kansteiner
Becky Buis	Lorraine Allison Engle	Priscilla Groot	Janice Keeler
Birthe Burnett	Jane Erdmann	Genevieve Gulizia	Barbara Kehke
Carlton Burnett	Carmen Etemad-Amini	Jocelyn Gutierrez	Nancy Kelly
Claire Burt	Jean Evans	Ginny Hale	Rosemarie Kenna
Mary Busche	Dottie Evertz	Shirley Halperin	Lis Kenyon
Eva Callahan	Deborah Fabricant	Leonor Hammond	Monica Keogh
Sally Campbell	Georgene Fairbanks	Virginia Harchol	Connie Ketron
Nancy Canfield	Trudy Farrington	Diana Hardy	Sharon Kinney
JoAnn Carr	Erika Faust	Fran Hardy	Barbara Kirkwood
Hope Carroll	Cerise Tadwin Feeley	Vaili Harris	Barbara Kneeshaw
Helen Carter	Pat Felbinger	Addie Hatch	Dianne Kniffing

Joey Knudson
Ruth Ann Kubis
Rose Kuhn
Mary Kunz
Pam La Fata
Pat Landwehr
Shirley Lashmett
Stephanie Laylon
Gale Layman
Barbara Lebovitz
Jeanne Lewand
Connie Lewis
Harriet Lewis
Diane Lister
Marilyn Ludwig
Nancy E. Luster
Carolyn Mabie
Barbara Mahler
Mary Ann Malamut
Coco Malchow
Sheila Mann
Barbara Marceau
Carolyn Marshall
Don Martens
Jan Martens
Linda Martin
Mary Mastroni
Joann Matos
Delores Maxson
Shirley McBurney
Gail McCall
Marilyn McCloskey
Maggie McDonald
Mary Ann McGaughey
Suzie McGinty
Elouise McLaughlin
Carol McMillan
Carol Ann McPhail
Brenda Meharg
Sharon Messick
Mimi Michael
Cheryl Moore
Juanita Moore
Ruth Motley
Maggie Murdy
Lo Ann Murray
Linda Mushet
Janet Nash
Eloise Neely
Gussie Nelson
Mike Nielsen
Ann Niven

Bear Noecker
Gina Norberte
Carolyn Noring
Sue O'Brien
Jackie O'Hara
JoDee Olson
Mike Olson
Tess Osborne
Virginia Owen
JoAnn Palmer
Marian Parsons
Annette Pate
Pat Patel
Ann Paulson
JoAnn Peels
Barbara Penrose
Enid Perrin
Virginia Perryman
Fiona Petersen
Patricia Pfleiderer
Gilda Pinedo
Patti Pitaccio
Nancy Plows
Marti Poivre
Bunny Poolos
Stephanie Pores
Jan Powell
Pat Prickett
JoAnn Puls
Marcia Kay Radeley
Cynthia Rainey
Sharlene Rauch
Mary Raymond
Sharon Redeiss
Elsie Reed
Pat Reheuser
Beverly Rikel
Cynthia Roberts
Patty Rowley Robertson
Diana Roby
Patricia Ann Rock
Mrs. Edward Roemer
Lyla Rogers
Kathy Rolfes
Linda Ronnow
Sunny Rosen
Corinne Rostoker
Rene Rowell
Millie Rutledge
Roma Ryan
Pat Rypinski
Gail Sahler

Jerry Saldarini
Bonnie Sanborn
Beverly Sandelman
Maria Sanz
Marty Schmid
Nola Schneer
Diane Arena Schultz
Jean Schumacher
Joan I. Scott
Joan J. Scott
Jane Sears
Lois Seed
Mary Jo Segretto
Connie Selin
Priscilla Selman
Patricia Sharp
Annette Sherwood
Marlene Short
Mary Lou Shunsky
Arlene Simmons
Jo Anne Simon
Esau Smith
Joan Irvine Smith
Mary Smith
Nancy Smith
Nancy Snyder
Terry Sonev
Barbara Sorenson
Babs Soros
Terry Ann Sovey
Georgia Spooner
Deloris St. John
Diane C. Stadlinger
Chire Stark
Linda Stenstrom
Donna Stephanson
Lori Stephanson
Michael Stephanson
Wendy Stephens
Eileen Stevens
Jean Stern
Patty Still
Joan Stoddard
Carole Stone
Susie Stone
Susan Strader
Margie Stratton-Myers
Patricia Sturges
Catheryn Swartz
Millicent Swenson
Patricia Sytnyk
Shirley Tedrick

Allison Terrell
Amy Terrell
Ann Marie Terrell
Jacquelyn Terrell
Janet Terrell
Lisa Terrell
Patti Thinger
Marie Thomas
Carol Thompson
Sue Thompson
Shari Tischler
Susan Tomasello
Alice Trainor
Marian Turpin
Nana Tustin
Sally Ulene
Janet Umberham
Margaret Upp
Ginni Valley
Harriet Van de Water
Lorrie Vergara
Bonnie von Hurwitz
Charlanne Wachtel
Ann Walker
Daphne Walker
Bonnie Walsh
Jackie Washburn
Laurine Wayman
Bea Webb
Ann Webster
Cynthia Weitz
Teddy Wells
Carol Westeren
Kitty Westover
Bonne Wheeler
Connie Wheeler
Elsie White
Sharon White
Mary Wicke
Haroldene Wiens
Robert Wiens
Kathleen Wilker
Faye Wilkinson
Doris Winters
Sistie Winton
Robbie Wolff
Angie Wood
Ciel Woodman
Dorris Wright
Regina Yang
Helen Howell Yates
Ginny Ziegler

CENTER INFORMATION AND SUPPORT
Board of Directors of The Center
Tom Tomlinson
Richard Bryant, Kathryn Lauer, and Rick Johnson

SPECIAL RECIPE CONTRIBUTORS

Alfred Boll
  Disneyland
Alan Greeley
  Golden Truffle
Zov Karamardian
  Zov's Bistro
The Chefs of
  Knott's Berry Farm
Hans Loeschl
  The Westin South Coast Plaza

John McLaughlin
  JW's at the Anaheim Marriott Hotel
Ed Mitchell
  Center Club
Annie Roberts
  Robert Mondavi Winery
Sarah Scott
  Robert Mondavi Wine and Food Center
Ulf Strandberg
  Gustaf Anders Restaurant

CENTER PHOTOGRAPHS
Listed in Order of Appearance

Mike Sasso
Chas McGrath
Kathi Kent Volzke
Prasad and Valeri
Kathi Kent Volzke
Kathi Kent Volzke
No Credit
Joan Marcus
Bob Ware
Chas McGrath

Center Exterior
Segerstrom Hall
The Kirov Ballet
Opera Pacific
Imagination Celebration
Triathlon
OCPS/Chicago Symphony Orchestra
Les Misérables
The Center of Fashion
"The Fire Bird"

TABLE SETTING PROPS FOR LIFESTYLE PHOTOS
Bullock's South Coast Plaza Home Store

MARKETING SUPPORT

Bristol Farms - Cook 'N' Things
Forrest W. Pond Jewelers

Calsonic Miura Graphics, Inc.
Trader Joe's Company

279